Modern Scala Projects

Leverage the power of Scala for building data-driven and high-performant projects

Ilango Gurusamy

BIRMINGHAM - MUMBAI

Modern Scala Projects

Commissioning Editor: Richa Tripathi
Acquisition Editor: Sandeep Mishra
Content Development Editor: Priyanka Sawant
Technical Editor: Gaurav Gala
Copy Editor: Safis Editing
Project Coordinator: Vaidehi Sawant
Proofreader: Safis Editing
Indexer: Mariammal Chettiyar
Graphics: Jason Monteiro
Production Coordinator: Aparna Bhagat

First published: July 2018

Production reference: 1280718

Published by Packt Publishing Ltd.
Livery Place
35 Livery Street
Birmingham
B3 2PB, UK.

ISBN 978-1-78862-411-4

www.packtpub.com

`mapt.io`

Mapt is an online digital library that gives you full access to over 5,000 books and videos, as well as industry leading tools to help you plan your personal development and advance your career. For more information, please visit our website.

Why subscribe?

- Spend less time learning and more time coding with practical eBooks and Videos from over 4,000 industry professionals

- Improve your learning with Skill Plans built especially for you

- Get a free eBook or video every month

- Mapt is fully searchable

- Copy and paste, print, and bookmark content

PacktPub.com

Did you know that Packt offers eBook versions of every book published, with PDF and ePub files available? You can upgrade to the eBook version at `www.PacktPub.com` and as a print book customer, you are entitled to a discount on the eBook copy. Get in touch with us at `service@packtpub.com` for more details.

At `www.PacktPub.com`, you can also read a collection of free technical articles, sign up for a range of free newsletters, and receive exclusive discounts and offers on Packt books and eBooks.

Contributors

About the author

Ilango Gurusamy holds an MS degree in computer science from California State University. He has lead Java projects at Northrop Grumman, AT&T, and such. He moved into Scala and Functional Programming. His current interests are IoT, navigational applications, and all things Scala related. A strategic thinker, speaker, and writer, he also loves yoga, skydiving, cars, dogs, and fishing. You can know more about his achievements in his blog, titled scalanirvana. His LinkedIn user name is ilangogurusamy.

About the reviewer

Adithya Selvaprithiviraj is a Scala developer in the Innovation Centre Network at SAP Labs. Currently, he is involved in the development of a modern typesafe framework to ease enterprise application development in the SAP landscape. Previously, Adithya was part of several machine learning projects. You can find out more about his achievements in his blog, titled adithyaselv.

Packt is searching for authors like you

If you're interested in becoming an author for Packt, please visit `authors.packtpub.com` and apply today. We have worked with thousands of developers and tech professionals, just like you, to help them share their insight with the global tech community. You can make a general application, apply for a specific hot topic that we are recruiting an author for, or submit your own idea.

Table of Contents

Preface

Scala, along with the Spark Framework, forms a rich and powerful data processing ecosystem. This book is a journey into the depths of this ecosystem. The machine learning (ML) projects presented in this book enable you to create practical, robust, data analytics solutions, with an emphasis on automating data workflows with the Spark ML pipeline API. This book showcases, or carefully cherry-picks from, Scala's functional libraries and other constructs to help readers roll out their own scalable data processing frameworks. The projects in this book enable data practitioners across all industries to gain insights into data that will help organizations to obtain a strategic and competitive advantage. *Modern Scala Projects* focuses on the application of supervisory learning ML techniques that classify data and make predictions. You'll begin with working on a project to predict a class of flower by implementing a simple machine learning model. Next, you'll create a cancer diagnosis classification pipeline, followed by projects delving into stock price prediction, spam filtering, fraud detection, and a recommendation engine.

By the end of this book, you will be able to build efficient data science projects that fulfill your software requirements.

Who this book is for

This book is for Scala developers who would like to gain some hands-on experience with some interesting real-world projects. Prior programming experience with Scala is necessary.

What this book covers

Chapter 1, *Predict the Class of a Flower from the Iris Dataset*, focuses on building a machine learning model leveraging a time-tested statistical method based on regression. The chapter draws the reader into data processing, all the way to training and testing a relatively simple machine learning model.

Chapter 2, *Build a Breast Cancer Prognosis Pipeline with the Power of Spark and Scala*, taps into a publicly available breast cancer dataset. It evaluates various feature selection algorithms, transforms data, and builds a classification model.

Chapter 3, *Stock Price Predictions*, says that stock price prediction can be an impossible task. In this chapter, we take a new approach. Accordingly, we build and train a neural network model with training data to solve the apparently intractable problem of stock price prediction. A data pipeline, with Spark at its core, distributes training of the model across multiple machines in a cluster. A real-life dataset is fed into the pipeline. Training data goes through preprocessing and normalization steps before a model is trained to fit the data. We may also provide a means to visualize the results of our prediction and evaluate our model after training.

Chapter 4, *Building a Spam Classification Pipeline*, informs the reader that the overarching learning objective of this chapter is to implement a spam filtering data analysis pipeline. We will rely on the Spark ML library's machine learning APIs and its supporting libraries to build a spam classification pipeline.

Chapter 5, *Build a Fraud Detection System*, applies machine learning techniques and algorithms to build a practical ML pipeline that helps find questionable charges on consumers' credit cards. The data is drawn from a publicly accessible Consumer Complaints Database. The chapter demonstrates the tools contained in Spark ML for building, evaluating, and tuning a pipeline. Feature extraction is one function served by Spark ML that is covered here.

Chapter 6, *Build Flights Performance Prediction Model*, makes us able to leverage flight departure and arrival data to predict for the user if their flight is delayed or canceled. Here, we will build a decisions trees-based model to derive useful predictors, such as what time of the day is best to have a seat on a flight, with a minimum chance of delay.

Chapter 7, *Building a Recommendation Engine*, draws the reader into the implementation of a scalable recommendations engine. The collaborative-filtering approach is laid out as the reader walks through a phased recommendations-generating process based on users' past preferences.

To get the most out of this book

Prior knowledge of Scala is assumed. Knowledge of basic concepts like Spark ML will be an add-on.

Download the example code files

You can download the example code files for this book from your account at
`www.packtpub.com`. If you purchased this book elsewhere, you can visit
`www.packtpub.com/support` and register to have the files emailed directly to you.

You can download the code files by following these steps:

1. Log in or register at `www.packtpub.com`.
2. Select the **SUPPORT** tab.
3. Click on **Code Downloads & Errata**.
4. Enter the name of the book in the **Search** box and follow the onscreen instructions.

Once the file is downloaded, please make sure that you unzip or extract the folder using the latest version of:

- WinRAR/7-Zip for Windows
- Zipeg/iZip/UnRarX for Mac
- 7-Zip/PeaZip for Linux

The code bundle for the book is also hosted on GitHub at `https://github.com/PacktPublishing/Modern-Scala-Projects`. In case there's an update to the code, it will be updated on the existing GitHub repository.

We also have other code bundles from our rich catalog of books and videos available at `https://github.com/PacktPublishing/`. Check them out!

Download the color images

We also provide a PDF file that has color images of the screenshots/diagrams used in this book. You can download it here: `https://www.packtpub.com/sites/default/files/downloads/ModernScalaProjects_ColorImages.pdf`

Conventions used

There are a number of text conventions used throughout this book.

`CodeInText`: Indicates code words in text, database table names, folder names, filenames, file extensions, pathnames, dummy URLs, user input, and Twitter handles. Here is an example: "A variable representing the age of a girl called `Huan` (`Age_Huan`)."

A block of code is set as follows:

```
val dataFrame = spark.createDataFrame(result5).toDF(featureVector,
speciesLabel)
```

When we wish to draw your attention to a particular part of a code block, the relevant lines or items are set in bold:

```
sc.getConf.getAll
res4: Array[(String, String)] =
Array((spark.repl.class.outputDir,C:\Users\Ilango\AppData\Local\Temp\spark-
10e24781-9aa8-495c-a8cc-afe121f8252a\repl-c8ccc3f3-62ee-46c7-a1f8-
d458019fa05f), (spark.app.name,Spark shell),
(spark.sql.catalogImplementation,hive), (spark.driver.port,58009),
(spark.debug.maxToStringFields,150),
```

Any command-line input or output is written as follows:

```
scala> val dataSetPath =
"C:\\Users\\Ilango\\Documents\\Packt\\DevProjects\\Chapter2\\"
```

Bold: Indicates a new term, an important word, or words that you see onscreen. For example, words in menus or dialog boxes appear in the text like this. Here is an example: "Select **System info** from the **Administration** panel."

 Warnings or important notes appear like this.

 Tips and tricks appear like this.

Get in touch

Feedback from our readers is always welcome.

General feedback: Email feedback@packtpub.com and mention the book title in the subject of your message. If you have questions about any aspect of this book, please email us at questions@packtpub.com.

Errata: Although we have taken every care to ensure the accuracy of our content, mistakes do happen. If you have found a mistake in this book, we would be grateful if you would report this to us. Please visit www.packtpub.com/submit-errata, selecting your book, clicking on the Errata Submission Form link, and entering the details.

Piracy: If you come across any illegal copies of our works in any form on the Internet, we would be grateful if you would provide us with the location address or website name. Please contact us at copyright@packtpub.com with a link to the material.

If you are interested in becoming an author: If there is a topic that you have expertise in and you are interested in either writing or contributing to a book, please visit authors.packtpub.com.

Reviews

Please leave a review. Once you have read and used this book, why not leave a review on the site that you purchased it from? Potential readers can then see and use your unbiased opinion to make purchase decisions, we at Packt can understand what you think about our products, and our authors can see your feedback on their book. Thank you!

For more information about Packt, please visit packtpub.com.

1

Predict the Class of a Flower from the Iris Dataset

This chapter kicks off a **machine learning** (**ML**) initiative in Scala and Spark. Speaking of Spark, its **Machine Learning Library** (**MLlib**) living under the `spark.ml` package and accessible via its MLlib `DataFrame`-based API will help us develop scalable data analysis applications. The MLlib `DataFrame`-based API, also known as Spark ML, provides powerful learning algorithms and pipeline building tools for data analysis. Needless to say, we will, starting this chapter, leverage MLlib's classification algorithms.

The Spark ecosystem, also boasting of APIs to R, Python, and Java in addition to Scala, empowers our readers, be they beginner, or seasoned data professionals, to make sense of and extract analytics from various datasets.

Speaking of datasets, the Iris dataset is the simplest, yet the most famous data analysis task in the ML space. This chapter builds a solution to the data analysis classification task that the Iris dataset represents.

Here is the dataset we will refer to:

- UCI Machine Learning Repository: Iris Data Set
- Accessed July 13, 2018
- Website URL: `https://archive.ics.uci.edu/ml/datasets/Iris`

The overarching learning objective of this chapter is to implement a Scala solution to the so-called **multivariate** classification task represented by the Iris dataset.

The following list is a section-wise breakdown of individual learning outcomes:

- A multivariate classification problem
- Project overview—problem formulation
- Getting started with Spark
- Implementing a multiclass classification pipeline

The following section offers the reader an in-depth perspective on the Iris dataset classification problem.

A multivariate classification problem

The most famous dataset in data science history is Sir Ronald Aylmer Fisher's classical Iris flower dataset, also known as Anderson's dataset. It was introduced in 1936, as a study in understanding multivariate (or multiclass) classification. What then is multivariate?

Understanding multivariate

The term multivariate can bear two meanings:

- In terms of an adjective, multivariate means having or involving one or more variables.
- In terms of a noun, multivariate may represent a mathematical vector whose individual elements are variate. Each individual element in this vector is a measurable quantity or variable.

Both meanings mentioned have a common denominator variable. Conducting a multivariate analysis of an experimental unit involves at least one measurable quantity or variable. A classic example of such an analysis is the Iris dataset, having one or more (outcome) variables per observation.

In this subsection, we understood multivariate in terms of variables. In the next subsection, we briefly touch upon different kinds of variables, one of them being categorical variables.

Different kinds of variables

In general, variables are of two types:

- **Quantitative variable**: It is a variable representing a measurement that is quantified by a numeric value. Some examples of quantitative variables are:
  - A variable representing the age of a girl called `Huan` (`Age_Huan`). In September of 2017, the variable representing her age contained the value 24. Next year, one year later, that variable would be the number 1 (arithmetically) added to her current age.
  - The variable representing the number of planets in the solar system (`Planet_Number`). Currently, pending the discovery of any new planets in the future, this variable contains the number 12. If scientists found a new celestial body tomorrow that they think qualifies to be a planet, the `Planet_Number` variable's new value would be bumped up from its current value of 12 to 13.
- **Categorical variable**: A variable that cannot be assigned a numerical measure in the natural order of things. For example, the status of an individual in the United States. It could be one of the following values: a citizen, permanent resident, or a non-resident.

In the next subsection, we will describe categorical variables in some detail.

Categorical variables

We will draw upon the definition of a categorical variable from the previous subsection. Categorical variables distinguish themselves from quantitative variables in a fundamental way. As opposed to a quantitative variable that represents a measure of a something in numerical terms, a categorical variable represents a grouping name or a category name, which can take one of the finite numbers of possible categories. For example, the species of an Iris flower is a categorical variable and the value it takes could be one value from a finite set of categorical values: Iris-setosa, Iris-virginica, and Iris-versicolor.

It may be useful to draw on other examples of categorical variables; these are listed here as follows:

- The blood group of an individual as in A+, A-, B+, B-, AB+, AB-, O+, or O-
- The county that an individual is a resident of given a finite list of counties in the state of Missouri
- The political affiliation of a United States citizen could take up categorical values in the form of Democrat, Republican, or Green Party
- In global warming studies, the type of a forest is a categorical variable that could take one of three values in the form of tropical, temperate, or taiga

The first item in the preceding list, the blood group of a person, is a categorical variable whose corresponding data (values) are categorized (classified) into eight groups (A, B, AB, or O with their positives or negatives). In a similar vein, the species of an Iris flower is a categorical variable whose data (values) are categorized (classified) into three species groups—Iris-setosa, Iris-versicolor, and Iris-virginica.

That said, a common data analysis task in ML is to index, or encode, current string representations of categorical values into a numeric form; doubles for example. Such indexing is a prelude to a prediction on the target or label, which we shall talk more about shortly.

In respect to the Iris flower dataset, its species variable data is subject to a classification (or categorization) task with the express purpose of being able to make a prediction on the species of an Iris flower. At this point, we want to examine the Iris dataset, its rows, row characteristics, and much more, which is the focus of the upcoming topic.

Fischer's Iris dataset

The Iris flower dataset comprises of a total of 150 rows, where each row represents one flower. Each row is also known as an **observation**. This 150 observation Iris dataset is made up of three kinds of observations related to three different Iris flower species. The following table is an illustration:

#	Observations related to flower species:	Number of observations
1	Iris-setosa	50
2	Iris-virginica	50
3	Iris-versicolor	50
	Total number of observations :---------------------------------- 150	

Iris dataset observation breakup table

Referring to the preceding table, it is clear that three flower species are represented in the Iris dataset. Each flower species in this dataset contributes equally to 50 observations apiece. Each observation holds four measurements. One measurement corresponds to one flower feature, where each flower feature corresponds to one of the following:

- **Sepal Length**
- **Sepal Width**
- **Petal Length**
- **Petal Width**

The features listed earlier are illustrated in the following table for clarity:

Feature Table	
Feature # 1	Sepal Length
Feature # 2	Sepal Width
Feature # 3	Petal Length
Feature # 4	Petal Width

Iris features

Okay, so three flower species are represented in the Iris dataset. Speaking of species, we will henceforth replace the term *species* with the term *classes* whenever there is the need to stick to an ML terminology context. That means #1-**Iris-setosa** from earlier refers to **Class # 1**, #2-**Iris-virginica** to **Class # 2**, and #3-**Iris-versicolor** to **Class # 3**.

We just listed three different Iris flower species that are represented in the Iris dataset. What do they look like? What do their features look like? These questions are answered in the following screenshot:

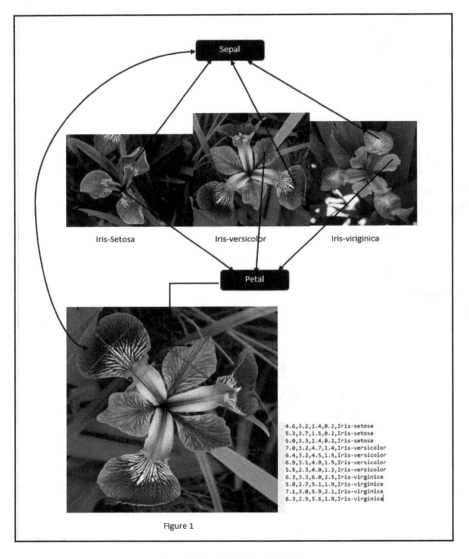

Figure 1

Representations of three species of Iris flower

That said, let's look at the **Sepal** and **Petal** portions of each class of Iris flower. The **Sepal** (the larger lower part) and **Petal** (the lower smaller part) dimensions are how each class of Iris flower bears a relationship to the other two classes of Iris flowers. In the next section, we will summarize our discussion and expand the scope of the discussion of the Iris dataset to a multiclass, multidimensional classification task.

The Iris dataset represents a multiclass, multidimensional classification task

In this section, we will restate the facts about the Iris dataset and describe it in the context of an ML classification task:

- The Iris dataset classification task is multiclass because a prediction of the class of a new incoming Iris flower from the wild can belong to any of three classes.
- Indeed, this chapter is all about attempting a species classification (inferring the target class of a new Iris flower) using sepal and petal dimensions as feature parameters.
- The Iris dataset classification is multidimensional because there are four features.
- There are 150 observations, where each observation is comprised of measurements on four features. These measurements are also known by the following terms:
  - Input attributes or instances
  - Predictor variables (X)
  - Input variables (X)

- Classification of an Iris flower picked in the wild is carried out by a model (the computed mapping function) that is given four flower feature measurements.
- The outcome of the Iris flower classification task is the identification of a (computed) predicted value for the response from the predictors by a process of learning (or fitting) a discrete number of targets or category labels (Y). The outcome or predicted value may mean the same as the following:
  - Categorical response variable: In a later section, we shall see that an indexer algorithm will transform all categorical values to numbers
  - Response or outcome variable (Y)

So far, we have claimed that the outcome (Y) of our multiclass classification task is dependent on inputs (X). Where will these inputs come from? This is answered in the next section.

The training dataset

An integral aspect of our data analysis or classification task we did not hitherto mention is the training dataset. A training dataset is our classification task's source of input data (X). We take advantage of this dataset to obtain a prediction on each target class, simply by deriving optimal perimeters or boundary conditions. We just redefined our classification process by adding in the extra detail of the training dataset. For a classification task, then we have X on one side and Y on the other, with an inferred mapping function in the middle. That brings us to the mapping or predictor function, which is the focus of the next section.

The mapping function

We have so far talked about an input variable (X) and an output variable (Y). The goal of any classification task, therefore, is to discover patterns and find a mapping (predictor) function that will take feature measurements (X) and map input over to the output (Y). That function is mathematically formulated as:

```
Y = f(x)
```

This mapping is how supervised learning works. A supervised learning algorithm is said to learn or discover this function. This will be the goal of the next section.

An algorithm and its mapping function

This section starts with a schematic depicting the components of the mapping function and an algorithm that learns the mapping function. The algorithm is learning the mapping function, as shown in the following diagram:

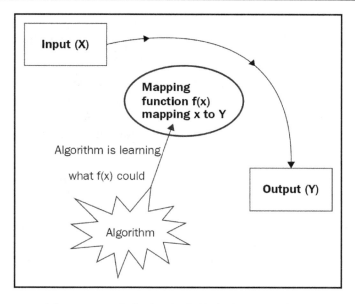

An input to output mapping function and an algorithm learning the mapping function

The goal of our classification process is to let the algorithm derive the best possible approximation of a mapping function by a learning (or fitting) process. When we find an Iris flower out in the wild and want to classify it, we use its input measurements as new input data that our algorithm's mapping function will accept in order to give us a predictor value (**Y**). In other words, given feature measurements of an Iris flower (the new data), the mapping function produced by a supervised learning algorithm (this will be a random forest) will classify the flower.

Two kinds of ML problems exist that supervised learning classification algorithms can solve. These are as follows:

- Classification tasks
- Regression tasks

In the following paragraph, we will talk about a mapping function with an example. We explain the role played by a "supervised learning classification task" in deducing the mapping function. The concept of a model is introduced.

Let's say we already knew that the (mapping) function `f(x)` for the Iris dataset classification task is exactly of the form `x + 1,` then there is there no need for us to find a new mapping function. If we recall, a mapping function is one that maps the relationship between flower features, such as sepal length and sepal width, on the species the flower belongs to? No.

Therefore, there is no preexisting function `x + 1` that clearly maps the relationship between flower features and the flower's species. What we need is a model that will model the aforementioned relationship as closely as possible. Data and its classification seldom tend to be straightforward. A supervised learning classification task starts life with no knowledge of what function `f(x)` is. A supervised learning classification process applies ML techniques and strategies in an iterative process of deduction to ultimately learn what `f(x)` is.

In our case, such an ML endeavor is a classification task, a task where the function or mapping function is referred to in statistical or ML terminology as a **model**.

In the next section, we will describe what supervised learning is and how it relates to the Iris dataset classification. Indeed, this apparently simplest of ML techniques finds wide applications in data analysis, especially in the business domain.

Supervised learning – how it relates to the Iris classification task

At the outset, the following is a list of salient aspects of supervised learning:

- The term **supervised** in supervised learning stems from the fact that the algorithm is learning or inferring what the mapping function is.
- A data analysis task, either classification or regression.
- It contains a process of learning or inferring a mapping function from a labeled training dataset.
- Our Iris training dataset has training examples or samples, where each example may be represented by an input feature vector consisting of four measurements.

- A supervised learning algorithm learns or infers or derives the best possible approximation of a mapping function by carrying out a data analysis on the training data. The mapping function is also known as a model in statistical or ML terminology.
- The algorithm provides our model with parameters that it learns from the training example set or training dataset in an iterative process, as follows:
  - Each iteration produces predicted class labels for new input instances from the wild
  - Each iteration of the learning process produces progressively better generalizations of what the output class label should be, and as in anything that has an end, the learning process for the algorithm also ends with a high degree of reasonable correctness on the prediction

- An ML classification process employing supervised learning has algorithm samples with correctly predetermined labels.
- The Iris dataset is a typical example of a supervised learning classification process. The term supervised arises from the fact that the algorithm at each step of an iterative learning process applies an appropriate correction on its previously generated model building process to generate its next best model.

In the next section, we will define a training dataset. In the next section, and in the remaining sections, we will use the Random Forest classification algorithm to run data analysis transformation tasks. One such task worth noting here is a process of transformation of string labels to an indexed label column represented by doubles.

Random Forest classification algorithm

In a preceding section, we noted the crucial role played by the input or training dataset. In this section, we reiterate the importance of this dataset. That said, the training dataset from an ML algorithm standpoint is one that the Random Forest algorithm takes advantage of to train or fit the model by generating the parameters it needs. These are parameters the model needs to come up with the next best-predicted value. In this chapter, we will put the Random Forest algorithm to work on training (and testing) Iris datasets. Indeed, the next paragraph starts with a discussion on Random Forest algorithms or simply Random Forests.

A Random Forest algorithm encompasses decision tree-based supervised learning methods. It can be viewed as a composite whole comprising a large number of decision trees. In ML terminology, a Random Forest is an ensemble resulting from a profusion of decision trees.

A decision tree, as the name implies, is a progressive decision-making process, made up of a root node followed by successive subtrees. The decision tree algorithm snakes its way up the tree, stopping at every node, starting with the root node, to pose a do-you-belong-to-a-certain-category question. Depending on whether the answer is a yes or a no, a decision is made to travel up a certain branch until the next node is encountered, where the algorithm repeats its interrogation. Of course, at each node, the answer received by the algorithm determines the next branch to be on. The final outcome is a predicted outcome on a leaf that terminates.

Speaking of trees, branches, and nodes, the dataset can be viewed as a tree made up of multiple subtrees. Each decision at a node of the dataset and the decision tree algorithm's choice of a certain branch is the result of an optimal composite of feature variables. Using a Random Forest algorithm, multiple decision trees are created. Each decision tree in this ensemble is the outcome of a randomized ordering of variables. That brings us to what random forests are—an ensemble of a multitude of decision trees.

It is to be noted that one decision tree by itself cannot work well for a smaller sample like the Iris dataset. This is where the Random Forest algorithm steps in. It brings together or aggregates all of the predictions from its forest of decision trees. All of the aggregated results from individual decision trees in this forest would form one ensemble, better known as a Random Forest.

We chose the Random Forest method to make our predictions for a good reason. The net prediction formed out of an ensemble of predictions is significantly more accurate.

In the next section, we will formulate our classification problem, and in the *Getting started with Spark* section that follows, implementation details for the project are given.

Project overview – problem formulation

The intent of this project is to develop an ML workflow or more accurately a pipeline. The goal is to solve the classification problem on the most famous dataset in data science history.

If we saw a flower out in the wild that we know belongs to one of three Iris species, we have a classification problem on our hands. If we made measurements (x) on the unknown flower, the task is to learn to recognize the species to which the flower (and its plant) belongs.

Categorical variables represent types of data which may be divided into groups. Examples of categorical variables are race, sex, age group, and educational level. While the latter two variables may also be considered in a numerical manner by using exact values for age and highest grade completed, it is often more informative to categorize such variables into a relatively small number of groups.

Analysis of categorical data generally involves the use of data tables. A two-way table presents categorical data by counting the number of observations that fall into each group for two variables, one divided into rows and the other divided into columns.

In a nutshell, the high-level formulation of the classification problem is given as follows:

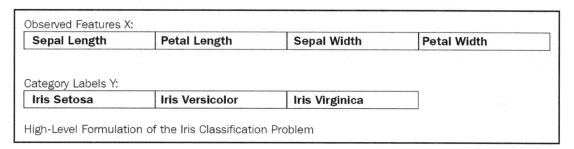

High-level formulation of the Iris supervised learning classification problem

 In the Iris dataset, each row contains categorical data (values) in the fifth column. Each such value is associated with a label (**Y**).

The formulation consists of the following:

- Observed features
- Category labels

Observed features are also known as **predictor variables**. Such variables have predetermined measured values. These are the inputs X. On the other hand, category labels denote possible output values that predicted variables can take.

The predictor variables are as follows:

- `sepal_length`: It represents sepal length, in centimeters, used as input
- `sepal_width`: It represents sepal width, in centimeters, used as input
- `petal_length`: It represents petal length, in centimeters, used as input

- `petal_width`: It represents petal width, in centimeters, used as input
- `setosa`: It represents Iris-setosa, true or false, used as target
- `versicolour`: It represents Iris-versicolour, true or false, used as target
- `virginica`: It represents Iris-virginica, true or false, used as target

Four outcome variables were measured from each sample; the length and the width of the sepals and petals.

The total build time of the project should be no more than a day in order to get everything working. For those new to the data science area, understanding the background theory, setting up the software, and getting to build the pipeline could take an extra day or two.

Getting started with Spark

The instructions are for Windows users. Note that to run Spark Version 2 and above, Java Version 8 and above, Scala Version 2.11, **Simple Build Tool** (**SBT**) version that is at least 0.13.8 is a prerequisite. The code for the Iris project depends on Spark 2.3.1, the latest distribution at the time of writing this chapter. This version was released on December 1, 2017. Implementations in subsequent chapters would likely be based on Spark 2.3.0, released February 28, 2017. Spark 2.3.0 is a major update version that comes with fixes to over 1,400 tickets.

The Spark 2.0 brought with it a raft of improvements. The introduction of the dataframe as the fundamental abstraction of data is one such improvement. Readers will find that the dataframe abstraction and its supporting APIs enhance their data science and analysis tasks, not to mention this powerful feature's improved performance over **Resilient Distributed Datasets** (**RDDs**). Support for RDDs is very much available in the latest Spark release as well.

Setting up prerequisite software

A note on hardware before jumping to prerequisites. The hardware infrastructure I use throughout in this chapter comprises of a 64-bit Windows Dell 8700 machine running Windows 10 with Intel(R) Core(TM) i7-4770 CPU @ 3.40 GHz and an installed memory of 32 GB.

In this subsection, we document three software prerequisites that must be in place before installing Spark.

At the time of this writing, my prerequisite software setup consisted of JDK 8, Scala 2.11.12, and SBT 0.13.8, respectively. The following list is a minimal, recommended setup (note that you are free to try a higher JDK 8 version and Scala 2.12.x).

Here is the required prerequisite list for this chapter:

- Java SE Development Kit 8
- Scala 2.11.12
- SBT 0.13.8 or above

If you are like me, dedicating an entire box with the sole ambition of evolving your own Spark big data ecosystem is not a bad idea. With that in mind, start with an appropriate machine (with ample space and at least 8 GB of memory), running your preferred OS, and install the preceding mentioned prerequisites listed in order. What about lower versions of the JDK, you may ask? Indeed, lower versions of the JDK are not compatible with Spark 2.3.1.

While I will not go into the JDK installation process here, here are a couple of notes. Download Java 8 (`http://www.oracle.com/technetwork/java/javase/downloads/jdk8-downloads-2133151.html`) and once the installer is done installing the `Java` folder, do not forget to set up two new system environment variables—the `JAVA_HOME` environment variable pointing to the root folder of your Java installation, and the `JAVA_HOME/bin` in your system path environment variable.

After setting the system `JAVA_HOME` environment, here is how to do a quick sanity check by listing the value of `JAVA_HOME` on the command line:

```
C:\Users\Ilango\Documents\Packt-Book-Writing-
Project\DevProjects\Chapter1>echo %JAVA_HOME%
C:\Program Files\Java\jdk1.8.0_102
```

Now what remains is to do another quick check to be certain you installed the JDK flawlessly. Issue the following commands on your command line or Terminal.

Note that this screen only represents the Windows command line:

```
C:\Users\Ilango\Documents\Packt\DevProjects\Chapter1>java -version
java version "1.8.0_131"
Java(TM) SE Runtime Environment (build 1.8.0_131-b11)
Java HotSpot(TM) 64-Bit Server VM (build 25.131-b11, mixed mode)

C:\Users\Ilango\Documents\Packt\DevProjects\Chapter1>javac -version
javac 1.8.0_102
```

At this point, if your sanity checks passed, the next step is to install Scala. The following brief steps outline that process. The Scala download page at `https://archive.ics.uci.edu/ml/datasets/iris` documents many ways to install Scala (for different OS environments). However, we only list three methods to install Scala.

 Before diving into the Scala installation, a quick note here. While the latest stable version of Scala is 2.12.4, I prefer a slightly older version, version 2.11.12, which is the version I will use in this chapter. You may download it at `http://scala-lang.org/download/2.11.12.html`. Whether you prefer version 2.12 or 2.11, the choice is yours to make, as long as the version is not anything below 2.11.x. The following installation methods listed will get you started down that path.

Scala can be installed through the following methods:

- **Install Scala**: Locate the section titled **Other ways to install Scala** at `http://scala-lang.org/download/` and download the Scala binaries from there. Then you can install Scala by following the instructions at `http://scala-lang.org/download/install.html`. Install SBT from `https://www.scala-sbt.org/download.html` and follow the setup instructions at `https://www.scala-sbt.org/1.0/docs/Setup.html`.
- **Scala in the IntelliJ IDE**: Instructions are given at `https://docs.scala-lang.org/getting-started-intellij-track/getting-started-with-scala-in-intellij.html`.
- **Scala in the IntelliJ IDE with SBT**: This is another handy way to play with Scala. Instructions are given at `https://docs.scala-lang.org/getting-started-intellij-track/getting-started-with-scala-in-intellij.html`.

 The acronym **SBT** that just appeared in the preceding list is short for **Simple Build Tool**. Indeed, you will run into references to SBT fairly often throughout this book.

Take up the item from the first method of the preceding list and work through the (mostly self-explanatory) instructions. Finally, if you forgot to set environment variables, do set up a brand new SCALA_HOME system environment variable (like JAVA_HOME), or simply update an existing SCALA_HOME. Naturally, the SCALA_HOME/bin entry is added to the path environment variable.

 You do not necessarily need Scala installed system-wide. The SBT environment gives us access to its own Scala environment anyway. However, having a system-wide Scala installation allows you to quickly implement Scala code rather than spinning up an entire SBT project.

Let us review what we have accomplished so far. We installed Scala by working through the first method Scala installation.

To confirm that we did install Scala, let's run a basic test:

```
C:\Users\Ilango\Documents\Packt\DevProjects\Chapter1>scala -version
Scala code runner version 2.11.12 -- Copyright 2002-2017, LAMP/EPFL
```

The preceding code listing confirms that our most basic Scala installation went off without a hitch. This paves the way for a system-wide SBT installation. Once again, it comes down to setting up the SBT_HOME system environment variable and setting $SBT_HOME/bin in the path. This is the most fundamental bridge to cross. Next, let's run a sanity check to verify that SBT is all set up. Open up a command-line window or Terminal. We installed SBT 0.13.17, as shown in the following code:

```
C:\Users\Ilango\Documents\Packt\DevProjects\Chapter1>sbt sbtVersion
Java HotSpot(TM) 64-Bit Server VM warning: ignoring option
MaxPermSize=256m; support was removed in 8.0
[info] Loading project definition from
C:\Users\Ilango\Documents\Packt\DevProjects\Chapter1\project
[info] Set current project to Chapter1 (in build
file:/C:/Users/Ilango/Documents/Packt/DevProjects/Chapter1/)
[info] 0.13.17
```

We are left with method two and method three. These are left as an exercise for the reader. Method three will let us take advantage of all the nice features that an IDE like IntelliJ has.

Shortly, the approach we will take in developing our pipeline involves taking an existing SBT project and importing it into IntelliJ, or we just create the SBT project in IntelliJ.

What's next? The Spark installation of course. Read all about it in the upcoming section.

Installing Spark in standalone deploy mode

In this section, we set up a Spark development environment in standalone deploy mode. To get started with Spark and start developing quickly, Spark's shell is the way to go.

 Spark supports Scala, Python, R, and Java with appropriate APIs.

The Spark binary download offers developers two components:

- The Spark's shell
- A standalone cluster

Once the binary is downloaded and extracted (instructions will follow), the Spark shell and standalone Scala application will let you spin up a standalone cluster in standalone cluster mode.

This cluster is self-contained and private because it is local to one machine. The Spark shell allows you to easily configure this standalone cluster. Not only does it give you quick access to an interactive Scala shell, but also lets you develop a Spark application that you can deploy into the cluster (lending it the name standalone deploy mode), right in the Scala shell.

In this mode, the cluster's driver node and worker nodes reside on the same machine, not to mention the fact that our Spark application will take up all the cores available on that machine by default. The important feature of this mode that makes all this possible is the interactive (Spark) Scala shell.

 Spark 2.3 is the latest version. It comes with over 1,400 fixes. A Spark 2.3 installation on Java 8 might be the first thing to do before we get started on our next project in Chapter 2, *Build a Breast Cancer Prognosis Pipeline with the Power of Spark and Scala.*

Without further ado, let's get started setting up Spark in standalone deploy mode. The following sequence of instructions are helpful:

1. System checks: First make sure you have at least 8 GB of memory, leaving at least 75% of this memory for Spark. Mine has 32 GB. Once the system checks pass, download the Spark 2.3.1 binary from here: `http://spark.apache.org/downloads.html`.

2. You will need a decompression utility capable of extracting the `.tar.gz` and `.gz` archives because Windows does not have native support for these archives. 7-Zip is a suitable program for this. You can obtain it from `http://7-zip.org/download.html`.

3. Choose the package type prebuilt for Apache Hadoop 2.7 and later and download `spark--2.2.1-bin-hadoop2.7.tgz`.

4. Extract the package to someplace convenient, which will become your Spark root folder. For example, my Spark root folder is: `C:\spark-2.2.1-bin-hadoop2.7`.

5. Now, set up the environment variable, `SPARK_HOME` pointing to the Spark root folder. We would also need a path entry in the `PATH` variable to point to `SPARK_HOME/bin`.

6. Next, set up the environment variable, `HADOOP_HOME`, to, say, `C:\Hadoop`, and create a new path entry for Spark by pointing it to the `bin` folder of the Spark home directory. Now, launch `spark-shell` like this:

```
spark-shell --master local[2]
```

What happens next might frustrate Windows users. If you are one of those users, you will run into the following error. The following screenshot is a representation of this problem:

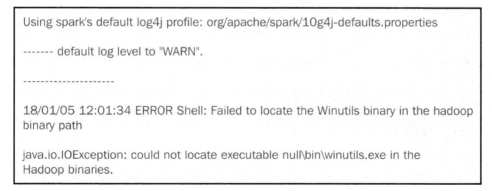

Using spark's default log4j profile: org/apache/spark/10g4j-defaults.properties

------- default log level to "WARN".

18/01/05 12:01:34 ERROR Shell: Failed to locate the Winutils binary in the hadoop binary path

java.io.IOException: could not locate executable null\bin\winutils.exe in the Hadoop binaries.

Error message on Windows

To get around this issue, you may proceed with the following steps:

1. Create a new folder as C:\tmp\hive.
2. Then get the missing WINUTILS.exe binary from here: https://github.com/steveloughran/winutils. Drop this into C\Hadoop\bin.

The preceding step 2 is necessary because the Spark download does not contain the WINUTILS.exe that is required to run Hadoop. That, then, is the source of the java.io.IOException.

With that knowledge, open up the Command Prompt window in administrator mode and execute the newly downloaded WINUTILS.EXE like this:

```
winutils.exe chmod -R 777 C:\tmp\hive
```

Next, issue the spark-shell command. This time around, Spark's interactive development environment launches normally, spinning up its own SparkContext instance sc and a SparkSession spark session, respectively. While the sc feature is a powerful entry point to the underlying local standalone cluster, spark is the main entry point to Spark's data processing APIs.

The following is the output from the spark-shell command. SparkContext is made available to you as sc and the Spark session is available to you as spark:

```
C:\Users\Ilango\Documents\Packt\DevProjects\Chapter1>spark-shell --master
local[2]
Spark context Web UI available at http://192.168.56.1:4040
Spark context available as 'sc' (master = local[2], app id =
local-1520484594646).
Spark session available as 'spark'.
Welcome to
      ____              __
     / __/__  ___ _____/ /__
    _\ \/ _ \/ _ `/ __/  '_/
   /___/ .__/\_,_/_/ /_/\_\   version 2.2.1
      /_/
Using Scala version 2.11.8 (Java HotSpot(TM) 64-Bit Server VM, Java
1.8.0_102)
Type in expressions to have them evaluated.
Type :help for more information.
scala>
```

The local[2] option in the spark-shell launch shown earlier lets us run Spark locally with 2 threads.

Before diving into the next topic in this section, it is a good idea to understand the following Spark shell development environment features that make development and data analysis possible:

- `SparkSession`
- `SparkBuilder`
- `SparkContext`
- `SparkConf`

The `SparkSession` API (https://spark.apache.org/docs/2.2.1/api/scala/index.html#org.apache.spark.sql.SparkSession) describes `SparkSession` as a programmatic access entry point to Spark's dataset and dataframe APIs, respectively.

What is `SparkBuilder`? The `SparkBuilder` companion object contains a `builder` method, which, when invoked, allows us to retrieve an existing `SparkSession` or even create one. We will now obtain our `SparkSession` instance in a two-step process, as follows:

1. Import the `SparkSession` class.
2. Invoke the `builder` method with `getOrCreate` on the resulting `builder`:

```scala
scala> import org.apache.spark.sql.SparkSession
import org.apache.spark.sql.SparkSession

scala> lazy val session: SparkSession =
SparkSession.builder().getOrCreate()
res7: org.apache.spark.sql.SparkSession =
org.apache.spark.sql.SparkSession@6f68756d
```

The `SparkContext` API (https://spark.apache.org/docs/2.2.1/api/scala/index.html#org.apache.spark.SparkContext) describes `SparkContext` as a first-line entry point for setting or configuring Spark cluster properties (RDDs, accumulators, broadcast variables, and much more) affecting the cluster's functionality. One way this configuration happens is by passing in a `SparkConf` instance as a `SparkContext` constructor parameter. One `SparkContext` exists per JVM instance.

In a sense, `SparkContext` is also how a Spark driver application connects to a cluster through, for example, Hadoop's Yarn **ResourceManager** (**RM**).

Let's inspect our Spark environment now. We will start by launching the Spark shell. That said, a typical Spark shell interactive environment screen has its own SparkSession available as `spark`, whose value we try to read off in the code block as follows:

```
scala> spark
res21: org.apache.spark.sql.SparkSession =
org.apache.spark.sql.SparkSession@6f68756d
```

 The Spark shell also boasts of its own `SparkContext` instance `sc`, which is associated with `SparkSession` spark. In the following code, `sc` returns `SparkContext`:

```
scala> sc
res5: org.apache.spark.SparkContext =
org.apache.spark.SparkContext@553ce348
```

`sc` can do more. In the following code, invoking the `version` method on `sc` gives us the version of Spark running in our cluster:

```
scala> sc.version
res2: String = 2.2.1
scala> spark
res3: org.apache.spark.sql.SparkSession =
org.apache.spark.sql.SparkSession@6f68756d
```

Since `sc` represents a connection to the Spark cluster, it holds a special object called `SparkConf`, holding cluster configuration properties in an `Array`. Invoking the `getConf` method on the `SparkContext` yields `SparkConf`, whose `getAll` method (shown as follows) yields an `Array` of cluster (or connection) properties, as shown in the following code:

```
scala> sc.getConf.getAll
res17: Array[(String, String)] = Array((spark.driver.port,51576),
(spark.debug.maxToStringFields,25), (spark.jars,""),
(spark.repl.class.outputDir,C:\Users\Ilango\AppData\Local\Temp\spark-47fee3
3b-4c60-49d0-93aa-3e3242bee7a3\repl-e5a1acbd-6eb9-4183-8c10-656ac22f71c2),
(spark.executor.id,driver), (spark.submit.deployMode,client),
(spark.driver.host,192.168.56.1), (spark.app.id,local-1520484594646),
(spark.master,local[2]), (spark.home,C:\spark-2.2.1-bin-hadoop2.7\bin\..))
```

There may be references to `sqlContext` and `sqlContext.implicits._` in the Spark shell. What is `sqlContext`? As of Spark 2 and the preceding versions, `sqlContext` is deprecated and `SparkSession.builder` is used instead to return a `SparkSession` instance, which we reiterate is the entry point to programming Spark with the dataset and dataframe API. Hence, we are going to ignore those `sqlContext` instances and focus on `SparkSession` instead.

Note that `spark.app.name` bears the default name `spark-shell`. Let's assign a different name to the `app-name` property as `Iris-Pipeline`. We do this by invoking the `setAppName` method and passing to it the new app name, as follows:

```
scala> sc.getConf.setAppName("Iris-Pipeline")
res22: org.apache.spark.SparkConf = org.apache.spark.SparkConf@e8ce5b1
```

To check if the configuration change took effect, let's invoke the `getAll` method again. The following output should reflect that change. It simply illustrates how `SparkContext` can be used to modify our cluster environment:

```
scala> sc.conf.getAll
res20: Array[(String, String)] = Array((spark.driver.port,51576),
(spark.app.name,Spark shell), (spark.sql.catalogImplementation,hive),
(spark.repl.class.uri,spark://192.168.56.1:51576/classes),
(spark.debug.maxToStringFields,150), (spark.jars,""),
(spark.repl.class.outputDir,C:\Users\Ilango\AppData\Local\Temp\spark-47fee3
3b-4c60-49d0-93aa-3e3242bee7a3\repl-e5a1acbd-6eb9-4183-8c10-656ac22f71c2),
(spark.executor.id,driver), (spark.submit.deployMode,client),
(spark.driver.host,192.168.56.1), (spark.app.id,local-1520484594646),
(spark.master,local[2]), (spark.home,C:\spark-2.2.1-bin-hadoop2.7\bin\..))
```

The `spark.app.name` property just had its value updated to the new name. Our goal in the next section is to use `spark-shell` to analyze data in an interactive fashion.

Developing a simple interactive data analysis utility

We will develop a simple Scala program in the Spark shell's interactive Scala shell. We will restate our goal, which is that we want to be able to analyze data interactively. That dataset—an external **comma-separated values (CSV)** file called `iris.csv`—resides in the same folder where `spark-shell` is launched from.

This program, which could just as well be written in a regular Scala **Read Eval Print Loop** (**REPL**) shell, reads a file, and prints out its contents, getting a data analysis task done. However, what is important here is that the Spark shell is flexible in that it also allows you to write Scala code that will allow you to easily connect your data with various Spark APIs and derive abstractions, such as dataframes or RDDs, in some useful way. More about DataFrame and Dataset to follow:

```
scala> object DataReader {
     |   def main(args: Array[String]): Unit = {
     |     val datasrc = Source.fromFile("iris.csv")
     |     try datasrc.getLines.foreach(println) finally datasrc.close()
     |   }
     | }
defined object DataReader

scala> DataReader.main("")
<console>:27: error: type mismatch;
 found    : String("")
 required: Array[String]
       DataReader.main("")
                       ^

scala> DataReader.main(Array(""))
java.io.FileNotFoundException: iris.csv (The system cannot find the file specified)
  at java.io.FileInputStream.open0(Native Method)
  at java.io.FileInputStream.open(FileInputStream.java:195)
  at java.io.FileInputStream.<init>(FileInputStream.java:138)
  at scala.io.Source$.fromFile(Source.scala:91)
  at scala.io.Source$.fromFile(Source.scala:76)
  at scala.io.Source$.fromFile(Source.scala:54)
  at DataReader$.main(<console>:26)
  ... 48 elided

scala> DataReader.main(Array(""))
sepal_length,sepal_width,petal_length,petal_width,species
5.1,3.5,1.4,0.2,setosa
4.9,3.0,1.4,0.2,setosa
4.7,3.2,1.3,0.2,setosa
4.6,3.1,1.5,0.2,setosa
5.0,3.6,1.4,0.2,setosa
5.4,3.9,1.7,0.4,setosa
```

Reading iris.csv with source

In the preceding program, nothing fancy is happening. We are trying to read a file called iris.csv using the Source class. We import the Source.scala file from the scala.io package and from there on, we create an object called DataReader and a main method inside it. Inside the main method, we invoke the fromFile method of the companion object Source. The fromFile method takes in a string representation of the dataset file path as an argument and returns a BufferedSource instance, which we assign to a val that we name datasrc. By the way, the API for Source can be found at https://www.scala-lang.org/api/current/scala/io/Source.html.

On the BufferedSource handle, we then invoke the getLines method that returns an iterator, which in turn invokes foreach that will print out all the lines in iris.csv minus the newline characters. We wrap all of this code in a try and a catch and a finally. The finally construct exists for a reason and that has to do with the fact that we need to close the BufferedSource instance datasrc after it is done working on the file.

Initially, we ran into a FileNotFoundException because the dataset file iris.csv was not found. The CSV file is then dropped in, the program is run, and the output is what we expect.

That wasn't so hard. In the next subsection, the goal is to read our iris.csv file and derive Dataset or DataFrame out of it.

Reading a data file and deriving DataFrame out of it

The Spark API for https://spark.apache.org/docs/2.2.1/api/scala/index.html#org.apache.spark.sql.Dataset has it that a DataFrame is Dataset[Row] and that Dataset contains a view called DataFrame. Falling back to the description of Dataset in the Spark documentation, we can redefine Dataset as a Spark abstraction of distributed collections holding data items. That said, Dataset[Row] contains rows. Row could be an abstraction representing a row from the raw file dataset.

We need to read the iris.csv file and transform it into DataFrame. That is the stated goal of this subsection and that is exactly what we shall accomplish very soon.

With all this in mind, lets get down to building DataFrame. We start by invoking the read method on spark, our SparkSession:

```
scala> val dfReader1 = spark.read
dfReader1: org.apache.spark.sql.DataFrameReader =
org.apache.spark.sql.DataFrameReader@66df362c
```

The read() invoke produced DataFrameReader dfReader1, which according to https://spark.apache.org/docs/2.2.1/api/scala/index.html#org.apache.spark.sql.DataFrameReader is an interface to load a dataset from external storage systems.

Next, we will inform Spark that our data is in CSV format. This is done by invoking the format method with a com.databricks.spark.csv argument that Spark recognizes:

```
scala> val dfReader2 = dfReader1.format("com.databricks.spark.csv")
dfReader2: org.apache.spark.sql.DataFrameReader =
org.apache.spark.sql.DataFrameReader@66df362c
```

The `format` method simply returned `DataFrameReader` again. The `iris.csv` file contains `header`. We could specify this as an input `option`:

```
scala> val dfReader3 = dfReader2.option("header", true)
dfReader3: org.apache.spark.sql.DataFrameReader =
org.apache.spark.sql.DataFrameReader@66df362c
```

That returned our same old `DataFrameReader`.

What we need next is a way to identify the schema for us. Invoking the `option` method again with a key `inferSchema` and a value of `true` lets Spark infer the schema automatically for us:

```
scala> val dfReader4 = dfReader3.option("inferSchema",true)
dfReader4: org.apache.spark.sql.DataFrameReader =
org.apache.spark.sql.DataFrameReader@66df362c
```

Let's `load` our input now:

```
scala> val dFrame = dfReader4.load("iris.csv")
dFrame: org.apache.spark.sql.DataFrame = [Id: int, SepalLengthCm: double
... 4 more fields]
```

`DataFrameReader` transformed our input CSV into `DataFrame`! This was exactly what we set out to do.

> `DataFrame` is simply an untyped view of `Dataset` as type `DataFrame`
> `= Dataset[Row]`.

With our `DataFrame` being a view on `Dataset[Row]`, all the methods on `Dataset` are available.

For now, we want to see what this dataset has in it. The raw file had 150 columns in it. Therefore, we want Spark to:

- Return the row count in our dataset
- Display the top 20 rows of our dataset

Next, we will invoke the `count` method. We want to reaffirm the number of rows contained in the dataset:

```
scala> dFrame.count
res1: Long = 150
```

We just invoked the count method on our DataFrame. That returned the number 150, which is right.

Next, we will bring together all of the code developed in this section into one line of code:

```
scala> val irisDataFrame =
spark.read.format("com.databricks.spark.csv").option("header",true).option(
"inferSchema", true).load("iris.csv").show
```

We just created DataFrame irisDataFrame. If you want to view the DataFrame, just invoke the show method on it. This will return the first 20 rows of the irisDataFrame DataFrame:

```
+---+------------+-----------+------------+-----------+-----------+
| Id|SepalLengthCm|SepalWidthCm|PetalLengthCm|PetalWidthCm|    Species|
+---+------------+-----------+------------+-----------+-----------+
|  1|         5.1|        3.5|         1.4|        0.2|Iris-setosa|
|  2|         4.9|        3.0|         1.4|        0.2|Iris-setosa|
|  3|         4.7|        3.2|         1.3|        0.2|Iris-setosa|
|  4|         4.6|        3.1|         1.5|        0.2|Iris-setosa|
|  5|         5.0|        3.6|         1.4|        0.2|Iris-setosa|
|  6|         5.4|        3.9|         1.7|        0.4|Iris-setosa|
|  7|         4.6|        3.4|         1.4|        0.3|Iris-setosa|
|  8|         5.0|        3.4|         1.5|        0.2|Iris-setosa|
|  9|         4.4|        2.9|         1.4|        0.2|Iris-setosa|
| 10|         4.9|        3.1|         1.5|        0.1|Iris-setosa|
| 11|         5.4|        3.7|         1.5|        0.2|Iris-setosa|
| 12|         4.8|        3.4|         1.6|        0.2|Iris-setosa|
| 13|         4.8|        3.0|         1.4|        0.1|Iris-setosa|
| 14|         4.3|        3.0|         1.1|        0.1|Iris-setosa|
| 15|         5.8|        4.0|         1.2|        0.2|Iris-setosa|
| 16|         5.7|        4.4|         1.5|        0.4|Iris-setosa|
| 17|         5.4|        3.9|         1.3|        0.4|Iris-setosa|
| 18|         5.1|        3.5|         1.4|        0.3|Iris-setosa|
| 19|         5.7|        3.8|         1.7|        0.3|Iris-setosa|
| 20|         5.1|        3.8|         1.5|        0.3|Iris-setosa|
+---+------------+-----------+------------+-----------+-----------+
only showing top 20 rows

irisDataFrame: Unit = ()
```

First 20 rows of the Iris dataset

At this point, type :quit or *Ctrl* + *D* to exit the Spark shell. This wraps up this section, but opens a segue to the next, where we take things to the next level. Instead of relying on spark-shell to develop a larger program, we will create our Iris prediction pipeline program in an SBT project. This is the focus of the next section.

Implementing the Iris pipeline

In this section, we will set forth what our pipeline implementation objectives are. We will document tangible results as we step through individual implementation steps.

Before we implement the Iris pipeline, we want to understand what a pipeline is from a conceptual and practical perspective. Therefore, we define a pipeline as a `DataFrame` processing workflow with multiple pipeline stages operating in a certain sequence.

A DataFrame is a Spark abstraction that provides an API. This API lets us work with collections of objects. At a high-level it represents a distributed collection holding rows of data, much like a relational database table. Each member of a row (for example, a Sepal-Width measurement) in this DataFrame falls under a named column called Sepal-Width.

Each stage in a pipeline is an algorithm that is either a `Transformer` or an `Estimator`. As a `DataFrame` or DataFrame(s) flow through the pipeline, two types of stages (algorithms) exist:

- `Transformer` stage: This involves a transformation action that transforms one `DataFrame` into another `DataFrame`
- `Estimator` stage: This involves a training action on a `DataFrame` that produces another `DataFrame`.

In summary, a pipeline is a single unit, requiring stages, but inclusive of parameters and DataFrame(s). The entire pipeline structure is listed as follows:

- `Transformer`
- `Estimator`
- `Parameters` (hyper or otherwise)
- `DataFrame`

This is where Spark comes in. Its MLlib library provides a set of pipeline APIs allowing developers to access multiple algorithms and facilitates their combining into a single pipeline of ordered stages, much like a sequence of choreographed motions in a ballet. In this chapter, we will use the random forest classifier.

We covered essential pipeline concepts. These are practicalities that will help us move into the section, where we will list implementation objectives.

Iris pipeline implementation objectives

Before listing the implementation objectives, we will lay out an architecture for our pipeline. Shown here under are two diagrams representing an ML workflow, a pipeline.

The following diagrams together help in understanding the different components of this project. That said, this pipeline involves training (fitting), transformation, and validation operations. More than one model is trained and the best model (or mapping function) is selected to give us an accurate approximation predicting the species of an Iris flower (based on measurements of those flowers):

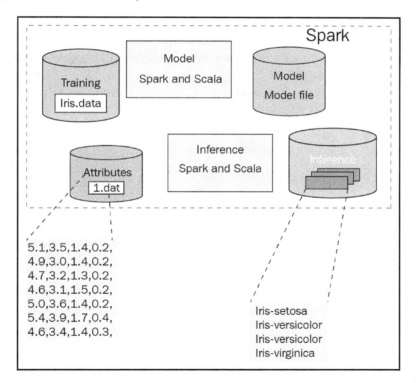

Project block diagram

A breakdown of the project block diagram is as follows:

- **Spark**, which represents the Spark cluster and its ecosystem
- **Training dataset**
- **Model**
- **Dataset attributes** or feature measurements
- An **inference** process, that produces a prediction column

The following diagram represents a more detailed description of the different phases in terms of the functions performed in each phase. Later we will come to visualize pipeline in terms of its constituent stages.

For now, the diagram depicts four stages, starting with a **data pre-processing** phase, which is considered separate from the numbered phases deliberately. Think of the pipeline as a two-step process:

1. A **data cleansing** phase, or **pre-processing** phase. An important phase that could include a subphase of **Exploratory Data Analysis (EDA)** (not explicitly depicted in the latter diagram).
2. A data analysis phase that begins with **Feature Extraction**, followed by **Model Fitting**, and **Model validation**, all the way to deployment of an Uber pipeline JAR into Spark:

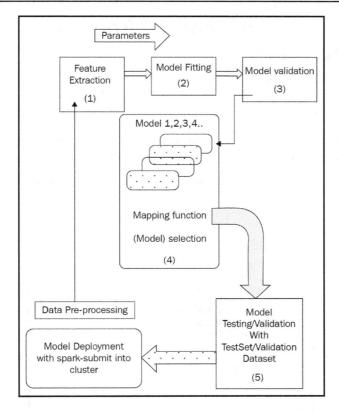

Pipeline diagram

Referring to the preceding diagram, the first implementation objective is to set up Spark inside an SBT project. An SBT project is a self-contained application, which we can run on the command line to predict Iris labels. In the SBT project, dependencies are specified in a `build.sbt` file and our application code will create its own `SparkSession` and `SparkContext`.

So that brings us to a listing of implementation objectives and these are as follows:

1. Get the Iris dataset from the UCI Machine Learning Repository
2. Conduct preliminary EDA in the Spark shell
3. Create a new Scala project in IntelliJ, and carry out all implementation steps, until the evaluation of the Random Forest classifier
4. Deploy the application to your local Spark cluster

Step 1 – getting the Iris dataset from the UCI Machine Learning Repository

Head over to the UCI Machine Learning Repository website at `https://archive.ics.uci.edu/ml/datasets/iris` and click on **Download: Data Folder**. Extract this folder someplace convenient and copy over `iris.csv` into the root of your project folder.

You may refer back to the project overview for an in-depth description of the Iris dataset. We depict the contents of the `iris.csv` file here, as follows:

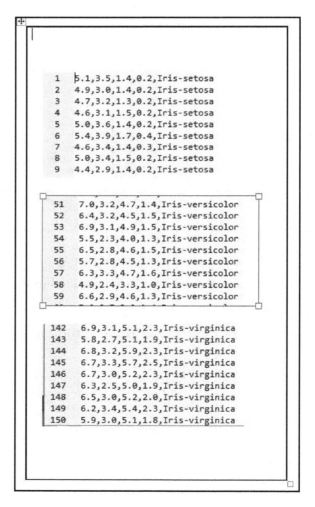

A snapshot of the Iris dataset with 150 sets

You may recall that the `iris.csv` file is a 150-row file, with comma-separated values.

Now that we have the dataset, the first step will be performing EDA on it. The Iris dataset is multivariate, meaning there is more than one (independent) variable, so we will carry out a basic multivariate EDA on it. But we need `DataFrame` to let us do that. How we create a dataframe as a prelude to EDA is the goal of the next section.

Step 2 – preliminary EDA

Before we get down to building the SBT pipeline project, we will conduct a preliminary EDA in `spark-shell`. The plan is to derive a dataframe out of the dataset and then calculate basic statistics on it.

We have three tasks at hand for `spark-shell`:

1. Fire up `spark-shell`
2. Load the `iris.csv` file and build `DataFrame`
3. Calculate the statistics

We will then port that code over to a Scala file inside our SBT project.

That said, let's get down to loading the `iris.csv` file (inputting the data source) before eventually building `DataFrame`.

Firing up Spark shell

Fire up the Spark Shell by issuing the following command on the command line.

```
spark-shell --master local[2]
```

In the next step, we start with the available Spark session 'spark'. 'spark' will be our entry point to programming with Spark. It also holds properties required to connect to our Spark (local) cluster. With this information, our next goal is to load the iris.csv file and produce a DataFrame

Loading the iris.csv file and building a DataFrame

The first step to loading the iris csv file is to invoke the `read` method on `spark`. The `read` method returns `DataFrameReader`, which can be used to read our dataset:

```
val dfReader1 = spark.read
dfReader1:
```

```
org.apache.spark.sql.DataFrameReader=org.apache.spark.sql.DataFrameReader@6
980d3b3
```

`dfReader1` is of type `org.apache.spark.sql.DataFrameReader`. Calling the `format` method on `dfReader1` with Spark's `com.databricks.spark.csv` CSV format-specifier string returns `DataFrameReader` again:

```
val dfReader2 = dfReader1.format("com.databricks.spark.csv")
dfReader2:
org.apache.spark.sql.DataFrameReader=org.apache.spark.sql.DataFrameReader@6
980d3b3
```

After all, `iris.csv` is a CSV file.

Needless to say, `dfReader1` and `dfReader2` are the same `DataFrameReader` instance.

At this point, `DataFrameReader` needs an input data source `option` in the form of a key-value pair. Invoke the `option` method with two arguments, a key `"header"` of type string and its value `true` of type Boolean:

```
val dfReader3 = dfReader2.option("header", true)
```

In the next step, we invoke the `option` method again with an argument `inferSchema` and a `true` value:

```
val dfReader4 = dfReader3.option("inferSchema", true)
```

What is `inferSchema` doing here? We are simply telling Spark to guess the schema of our input data source for us.

Up until now, we have been preparing `DataFrameReader` to load `iris.csv`. External data sources require a path for Spark to load the data for `DataFrameReader` to process and spit out `DataFrame`.

The time is now right to invoke the `load` method on `DataFrameReader` `dfReader4`. Pass into the `load` method the path to the Iris dataset file. In this case, the file is right under the root of the project folder:

```
val dFrame1 = dfReader4.load("iris.csv")
dFrame1: org.apache.spark.sql.DataFrame = [Id: int, SepalLengthCm: double
... 4 more fields]
```

That's it. We now have `DataFrame`!

Calculating statistics

Invoking the `describe` method on this `DataFrame` should cause Spark to perform a basic statistical analysis on each column of `DataFrame`:

```
dFrame1.describe("Id","SepalLengthCm","SepalWidthCm","PetalLengthCm","Petal
WidthCm","Species")
WARN Utils: Truncated the string representation of a plan since it was too
large. This behavior can be adjusted by setting
'spark.debug.maxToStringFields' in SparkEnv.conf.
res16: org.apache.spark.sql.DataFrame = [summary: string, Id: string ... 5
more fields]
```

Lets fix the `WARN.Utils` issue described in the preceding code block. The fix is to locate the file `spark-defaults-template.sh` under `SPARK_HOME/conf` and save it as `spark-defaults.sh`.

At the bottom of this file, add an entry for `spark.debug.maxToStringFields`. The following screenshot illustrates this:

```
# The ASF licenses this file to You under the Apache License, Version 2.0
# (the "License"); you may not use this file except in compliance with
# the License.  You may obtain a copy of the License at
#
#    http://www.apache.org/licenses/LICENSE-2.0
#
# Unless required by applicable law or agreed to in writing, software
# distributed under the License is distributed on an "AS IS" BASIS,
# WITHOUT WARRANTIES OR CONDITIONS OF ANY KIND, either express or implied.
# See the License for the specific language governing permissions and
# limitations under the License.
#


# Default system properties included when running spark-submit.
# This is useful for setting default environmental settings.

# Example:
# spark.master                     spark://master:7077
# spark.eventLog.enabled            true
# spark.eventLog.dir               hdfs://namenode:8021/directory
# spark.serializer                 org.apache.spark.serializer.KryoSerializer
# spark.driver.memory              5g
# spark.executor.extraJavaOptions  -XX:+PrintGCDetails -Dkey=value -Dnumbers="one two three"
spark.debug.maxToStringFields    150
```

Fixing the WARN Utils problem in spark-defaults.sh

Save the file and restart `spark-shell`.

Now, inspect the updated Spark configuration again. We updated the value of spark.debug.maxToStringFields in the spark-defaults.sh file. This change is supposed to fix the truncation problem reported by Spark. We will confirm imminently that the change we made caused Spark to update its configuration also. That is easily done by inspecting SparkConf.

Inspecting your SparkConf again

As before, invoking the getConf returns the SparkContext instance that stores configuration values. Invoking getAll on that instance returns an Array of configuration values. One of those values is an updated value of spark.debug.maxToStringFields:

```
sc.getConf.getAll
res4: Array[(String, String)] =
Array((spark.repl.class.outputDir,C:\Users\Ilango\AppData\Local\Temp\spark-
10e24781-9aa8-495c-a8cc-afe121f8252a\repl-c8ccc3f3-62ee-46c7-a1f8-
d458019fa05f), (spark.app.name,Spark shell),
(spark.sql.catalogImplementation,hive), (spark.driver.port,58009),
(spark.debug.maxToStringFields,150),
```

That updated value for spark.debug.maxToStringFields is now 150.

 spark.debug.maxToStringFields had a default value of 25 inside a private object called Utils.

Calculating statistics again

Run the invoke on the dataframe describe method and pass to it column names:

```
val dFrame2 =
dFrame1.describe("Id","SepalLengthCm","SepalWidthCm","PetalLengthCm","Petal
WidthCm","Species"
)
dFrame2: org.apache.spark.sql.DataFrame = [summary: string, Id: string ...
5 more fields]
```

The invoke on the describe method of DataFrame dfReader results in a transformed DataFrame that we call dFrame2. On dFrame2, we invoke the show method to return a table of statistical results. This completes the first phase of a basic yet important EDA:

```
val dFrame2Display= = dfReader2.show
```

The results of the statistical analysis are shown in the following screenshot:

summary	Id	SepalLengthCm	SepalWidthCm	PetalLengthCm	PetalWidthCm	Species
count	150	150	150	150	150	150
mean	75.5	5.843333333333335	3.0540000000000007	3.7586666666666693	1.1986666666666672	null
stddev	43.445367992456916	0.8280661279778637	0.43359431136217375	1.764420419952262	0.7631607417008414	null
min	1	4.3	2.0	1.0	0.1	Iris-setosa
max	150	7.9	4.4	6.9	2.5	Iris-virginica

Results of statistical analysis

We did all that extra work simply to demonstrate the individual data reading, loading, and transformation stages. Next, we will wrap all of our previous work in one line of code:

```
val dfReader =
spark.read.format("com.databricks.spark.csv").option("header",true).option(
"inferSchema",true).load("iris.csv")
dfReader: org.apache.spark.sql.DataFrame = [Id: int, SepalLengthCm: double
... 4 more fields]
```

That completes the EDA on `spark-shell`. In the next section, we undertake steps to implement, build (using SBT), deploy (using `spark-submit`), and execute our Spark pipeline application. We start by creating a skeletal SBT project.

Step 3 – creating an SBT project

Lay out your SBT project in a folder of your choice and name it `IrisPipeline` or any name that makes sense to you. This will hold all of our files needed to implement and run the pipeline on the Iris dataset.

The structure of our SBT project looks like the following:

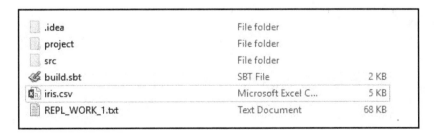

.idea	File folder	
project	File folder	
src	File folder	
build.sbt	SBT File	2 KB
iris.csv	Microsoft Excel C...	5 KB
REPL_WORK_1.txt	Text Document	68 KB

Project structure

We will list dependencies in the `build.sbt` file. This is going to be an SBT project. Hence, we will bring in the following key libraries:

- Spark Core
- Spark MLlib
- Spark SQL

The following screenshot illustrates the `build.sbt` file:

```
libraryDependencies ++= Seq(
  "org.apache.spark" %% "spark-core" % "2.2.1",
  "org.apache.spark" %% "spark-mllib" % "2.2.1",
  "org.apache.spark" %% "spark-sql" % "2.2.1",
  // Last stable release
  "org.scalanlp" %% "breeze" % "0.13.2",

  // Native libraries are not included by default. add this if you want them (as of 0.7)
  // Native libraries greatly improve performance, but increase jar sizes.
  // It also packages various blas implementations, which have licenses that may or may not
  // be compatible with the Apache License. No GPL code, as best I know.

  "org.scalanlp" %% "breeze-natives" % "0.13.2",

  // The visualization library is distributed separately as well.
  // It depends on LGPL code
  "org.scalanlp" %% "breeze-viz" % "0.13.2",
  "joda-time" % "joda-time" % "2.9.9",
  "org.scalatest"  %% "scalatest"   % "3.0.1"   % "test",
  "org.slf4j" % "slf4j-api" % "1.7.22",
  "org.slf4j" % "slf4j-simple" % "1.7.22"

)
```

The build.sbt file with Spark dependencies

The `build.sbt` file referenced in the preceding snapshot is readily available for you in the book's download bundle. Drill down to the folder `Chapter01` code under `ModernScalaProjects_Code` and copy the folder over to a convenient location on your computer.

Drop the `iris.csv` file that you downloaded in *Step 1 – getting the Iris dataset from the UCI Machine Learning Repository* into the root folder of our new SBT project. Refer to the earlier screenshot that depicts the updated project structure with the `iris.csv` file inside of it.

Step 4 – creating Scala files in SBT project

Step 4 is broken down into the following steps:

1. Create the Scala file `iris.scala` in
   the `com.packt.modern.chapter1` package.
2. Up until now, we relied on `SparkSession` and `SparkContext`, which `spark-shell` gave us. This time around, we need to create `SparkSession`, which will, in turn, give us `SparkContext`.

What follows is how the code is laid out in the `iris.scala` file.

In `iris.scala`, after the package statement, place the following `import` statements:

```
import org.apache.spark.sql.SparkSession
```

Create `SparkSession` inside a trait, which we shall call `IrisWrapper`:

```
lazy val session: SparkSession = SparkSession.builder().getOrCreate()
```

Just one `SparkSession` is made available to all classes extending from `IrisWrapper`. Create `val` to hold the `iris.csv` file path:

```
val dataSetPath = "<<path to folder containing your iris.csv
file>>\\iris.csv"
```

Create a method to build `DataFrame`. This method takes in the complete path to the Iris dataset path as `String` and returns `DataFrame`:

```
def buildDataFrame(dataSet: String): DataFrame = {
/*
  The following is an example of a dataSet parameter string:
"C:\\Your\\Path\\To\\iris.csv"
*/
```

Import the `DataFrame` class by updating the previous `import` statement for `SparkSession`:

```
import org.apache.spark.sql.{DataFrame, SparkSession}
```

Create a nested function inside `buildDataFrame` to process the raw dataset. Name this function `getRows`. `getRows` which takes no parameters but returns `Array[(Vector, String)]`. The `textFile` method on the `SparkContext` variable processes the `iris.csv` into `RDD[String]`:

```
val result1: Array[String] = session.sparkContext.textFile(<<path to
```

```
iris.csv represented by the dataSetPath variable>>)
```

The resulting RDD contains two partitions. Each partition, in turn, contains rows of strings separated by a newline character, `'\n'`. Each row in the RDD represents its original counterpart in the raw data.

In the next step, we will attempt several data transformation steps. We start by applying a `flatMap` operation over the RDD, culminating in the `DataFrame` creation. `DataFrame` is a view over `Dataset`, which happens to the fundamental data abstraction unit in the Spark 2.0 line.

Step 5 – preprocessing, data transformation, and DataFrame creation

We will get started by invoking `flatMap`, by passing a function block to it, and successive transformations listed as follows, eventually resulting in `Array[(org.apache.spark.ml.linalg.Vector, String)]`. A vector represents a row of feature measurements.

The Scala code to give us `Array[(org.apache.spark.ml.linalg.Vector, String)]` is as follows:

```
//Each line in the RDD is a row in the Dataset represented by a String,
which we can 'split' along the new //line character
val result2: RDD[String] = result1.flatMap { partition =>
partition.split("\n").toList }

//the second transformation operation involves a split inside of each line
in the dataset where there is a //comma separating each element of that
line
val result3: RDD[Array[String]] = result2.map(_.split(","))
```

Next, drop the `header` column, but not before doing a collection that returns an `Array[Array[String]]`:

```
val result4: Array[Array[String]] = result3.collect.drop(1)
```

The header column is gone; now import the `Vectors` class:

```
import org.apache.spark.ml.linalg.Vectors
```

Now, transform `Array[Array[String]]` into `Array[(Vector, String)]`:

```
val result5 = result4.map(row => (Vectors.dense(row(1).toDouble,
```

```
row(2).toDouble, row(3).toDouble, row(4).toDouble),row(5)))
```

The last step remaining is to create a final DataFrame

DataFrame Creation

Now, we invoke the `createDataFrame` method with a parameter, `getRows`. This returns `DataFrame` with `featureVector` and `speciesLabel` (for example, Iris-setosa):

```
val dataFrame = spark.createDataFrame(result5).toDF(featureVector,
speciesLabel)
```

Display the top 20 rows in the new dataframe:

```
dataFrame.show
+--------------------+------------------------+
|iris-features-column|iris-species-label-column|
+--------------------+------------------------+
|   [5.1,3.5,1.4,0.2]|            Iris-setosa|
|   [4.9,3.0,1.4,0.2]|            Iris-setosa|
|   [4.7,3.2,1.3,0.2]|            Iris-setosa|
....................
....................
+--------------------+------------------------+
only showing top 20 rows
```

We need to index the species label column by converting the strings Iris-setosa, Iris-virginica, and Iris-versicolor into doubles. We will use a `StringIndexer` to do that.

Now create a file called `IrisPipeline.scala`.

Create an object `IrisPipeline` that extends our `IrisWrapper` trait:

```
object IrisPipeline extends IrisWrapper {
```

Import the `StringIndexer` algorithm class:

```
import org.apache.spark.ml.feature.StringIndexer
```

Now create a `StringIndexer` algorithm instance. The `StringIndexer` will map our species label column to an indexed learned column:

```
val indexer = new StringIndexer().setInputCol
(irisFeatures_CategoryOrSpecies_IndexedLabel._2).setOutputCol(irisFeatures_
CategoryOrSpecies_IndexedLabel._3)
```

Step 6 – creating, training, and testing data

Now, let's split our dataset in two by providing a random seed:

```
val splitDataSet: Array[org.apache.spark.sql.Dataset
[org.apache.spark.sql.Row]] = dataSet.randomSplit(Array(0.85, 0.15),
98765L)
```

Now our new `splitDataset` contains two datasets:

- **Train dataset:** A dataset containing `Array[(Vector, iris-species-label-column: String)]`
- **Test dataset:** A dataset containing `Array[(Vector, iris-species-label-column: String)]`

Confirm that the new dataset is of size 2:

```
splitDataset.size
res48: Int = 2
```

Assign the training dataset to a variable, `trainSet`:

```
val trainDataSet = splitDataSet(0)
trainSet: org.apache.spark.sql.Dataset[org.apache.spark.sql.Row] = [iris-
features-column: vector, iris-species-label-column: string]
```

Assign the testing dataset to a variable, `testSet`:

```
val testDataSet = splitDataSet(1)
testSet: org.apache.spark.sql.Dataset[org.apache.spark.sql.Row] = [iris-
features-column: vector, iris-species-label-column: string]
```

Count the number of rows in the training dataset:

```
trainSet.count
res12: Long = 14
```

Count the number of rows in the testing dataset:

```
testSet.count
res9: Long = 136
```

There are 150 rows in all.

Step 7 – creating a Random Forest classifier

In reference to Step 5 - DataFrame Creation. This DataFrame 'dataFrame' contains column names that corresponds to the columns present in the DataFrame produced in that step

The first step to create a classifier is to pass into it (hyper) parameters. A fairly comprehensive list of parameters look like this:

- From 'dataFrame' we need the Features column name - **iris-features-column**
- From 'dataFrame' we also need the Indexed label column name - **iris-species-label-column**
- The `sqrt` setting for `featureSubsetStrategy`
- Number of features to be considered per split (we have 150 observations and four features that will make our `max_features` value 2)
- Impurity settings—values can be gini and entropy
- Number of trees to train (since the number of trees is greater than one, we set a tree maximum depth), which is a number equal to the number of nodes
- The required minimum number of feature measurements (sampled observations), also known as the minimum instances per node

Look at the `IrisPipeline.scala` file for values of each of these parameters.

But this time, we will employ an exhaustive grid search-based model selection process based on combinations of parameters, where parameter value ranges are specified.

Create a `randomForestClassifier` instance. Set the features and `featureSubsetStrategy`:

```
val randomForestClassifier = new RandomForestClassifier()
  .setFeaturesCol(irisFeatures_CategoryOrSpecies_IndexedLabel._1)
  .setFeatureSubsetStrategy("sqrt")
```

Start building `Pipeline`, which has two stages, `Indexer` and `Classifier`:

```
val irisPipeline = new Pipeline().setStages(Array[PipelineStage](indexer)
++  Array[PipelineStage](randomForestClassifier))
```

Next, set the hyperparameter `num_trees` (number of trees) on the classifier to 15, a `Max_Depth` parameter, and an impurity with two possible values of gini and entropy.

Build a parameter grid with all three hyperparameters:

```
val finalParamGrid: Array[ParamMap] = gridBuilder3.build()
```

Step 8 – training the Random Forest classifier

Next, we want to split our training set into a validation set and a training set:

```
val validatedTestResults: DataFrame = new TrainValidationSplit()
```

On this variable, set `Seed`, set `EstimatorParamMaps`, set `Estimator` with `irisPipeline`, and set a training ratio to `0.8`:

```
val validatedTestResults: DataFrame = new
TrainValidationSplit().setSeed(1234567L).setEstimator(irisPipeline)
```

Finally, do a fit and a transform with our training dataset and testing dataset. Great! Now the classifier is trained. In the next step, we will apply this classifier to testing the data.

Step 9 – applying the Random Forest classifier to test data

The purpose of our validation set is to be able to make a choice between models. We want an evaluation metric and hyperparameter tuning. We will now create an instance of a validation estimator called `TrainValidationSplit`, which will split the training set into a validation set and a training set:

```
val validatedTestResults.setEvaluator(new
MulticlassClassificationEvaluator())
```

Next, we fit this estimator over the training dataset to produce a model and a transformer that we will use to transform our testing dataset. Finally, we perform a validation for hyperparameter tuning by applying an evaluator for a metric.

The new `ValidatedTestResults DataFrame` should look something like this:

```
--------+
|iris-features-column|iris-species-column|label| rawPrediction|
probability|prediction|
 +--------------------+-------------------+-----+--------------------+
 | [4.4,3.2,1.3,0.2]| Iris-setosa| 0.0| [40.0,0.0,0.0]| [1.0,0.0,0.0]| 0.0|
 | [5.4,3.9,1.3,0.4]| Iris-setosa| 0.0| [40.0,0.0,0.0]| [1.0,0.0,0.0]| 0.0|
 | [5.4,3.9,1.7,0.4]| Iris-setosa| 0.0| [40.0,0.0,0.0]| [1.0,0.0,0.0]| 0.0|
```

Let's return a new dataset by passing in column expressions for `prediction` and `label`:

```
val validatedTestResultsDataset:DataFrame =
validatedTestResults.select("prediction", "label")
```

In the line of code, we produced a new `DataFrame` with two columns:

- An input label
- A predicted label, which is compared with its corresponding value in the input label column

That brings us to the next step, an evaluation step. We want to know how well our model performed. That is the goal of the next step.

Step 10 – evaluate Random Forest classifier

In this section, we will test the accuracy of the model. We want to know how well our model performed. Any ML process is incomplete without an evaluation of the classifier.

That said, we perform an evaluation as a two-step process:

1. Evaluate the model output
2. Pass in three hyperparameters:

```
val modelOutputAccuracy: Double = new MulticlassClassificationEvaluator()
```

Set the label column, a metric name, the prediction column `label`, and invoke evaluation with the `validatedTestResults` dataset.

Note the accuracy of the model output results on the testing dataset from the `modelOutputAccuracy` variable.

The other metrics to evaluate are how close the predicted label value in the `'predicted'` column is to the actual label value in the (indexed) label column.

Next, we want to extract the metrics:

```
val multiClassMetrics = new MulticlassMetrics(validatedRDD2)
```

Our pipeline produced predictions. As with any prediction, we need to have a healthy degree of skepticism. Naturally, we want a sense of how our engineered prediction process performed. The algorithm did all the heavy lifting for us in this regard. That said, everything we did in this step was done for the purpose of evaluation. Who is being evaluated here or what evaluation is worth reiterating? That said, we wanted to know how close the predicted values were compared to the actual label value. To obtain that knowledge, we decided to use the `MulticlassMetrics` class to evaluate metrics that will give us a measure of the performance of the model via two methods:

- Accuracy
- Weighted precision

The following lines of code will give us value of Accuracy and Weighted Precision. First we will create an accuracyMetrics tuple, which should contain the values of both accuracy and weighted precision

```
val accuracyMetrics = (multiClassMetrics.accuracy,
multiClassMetrics.weightedPrecision)
```

Obtain the value of accuracy.

```
val accuracy = accuracyMetrics._1
```

Next, obtain the value of weighted precision.

```
val weightedPrecsion = accuracyMetrics._2
```

These metrics represent evaluation results for our classifier or classification model. In the next step, we will run the application as a packaged SBT application.

Step 11 – running the pipeline as an SBT application

At the root of your project folder, issue the `sbt console` command, and in the Scala shell, import the `IrisPipeline` object and then invoke the `main` method of `IrisPipeline` with the argument `iris`:

```
sbt console
scala>
import com.packt.modern.chapter1.IrisPipeline
IrisPipeline.main(Array("iris")
Accuracy (precision) is 0.9285714285714286 Weighted Precision is:
0.9428571428571428
```

In the next section, we will show you how to package the application so that it is ready to be deployed into Spark as an Uber JAR.

Step 12 – packaging the application

In the root folder of your SBT application, run:

```
sbt package
```

When SBT is done packaging, the Uber JAR can be deployed into our cluster, using `spark-submit`, but since we are in standalone deploy mode, it will be deployed into `[local]`:

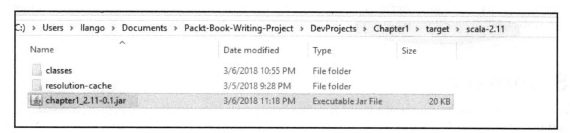

The application JAR file

The package command created a JAR file that is available under the target folder. In the next section, we will deploy the application into Spark.

Step 13 – submitting the pipeline application to Spark local

At the root of the application folder, issue the `spark-submit` command with the class and JAR file path arguments, respectively.

If everything went well, the application does the following:

1. Loads up the data.
2. Performs EDA.
3. Creates training, testing, and validation datasets.
4. Creates a Random Forest classifier model.
5. Trains the model.
6. Tests the accuracy of the model. This is the most important part—the ML classification task.

7. To accomplish this, we apply our trained Random Forest classifier model to the test dataset. This dataset consists of Iris flower data of so far not seen by the model. Unseen data is nothing but Iris flowers picked in the wild.

8. Applying the model to the test dataset results in a prediction about the species of an unseen (new) flower.

9. The last part is where the pipeline runs an evaluation process, which essentially is about checking if the model reports the correct species.

10. Lastly, pipeline reports back on how important a certain feature of the Iris flower turned out to be. As a matter of fact, the petal width turns out to be more important than the sepal width in carrying out the classification task.

That brings us to the last section of this chapter. We will summarize what we have learned. Not only that, we will give readers a glimpse into what they will learn in the next chapter.

Summary

In this chapter, we implemented an ML workflow or an ML pipeline. The pipeline combined several stages of data analysis into one workflow. We started by loading the data and from there on, we created training and test data, preprocessed the dataset, trained the `RandomForestClassifier` model, applied the Random Forest classifier to test data, evaluated the classifier, and computed a process that demonstrated the importance of each feature in the classification. We fulfilled the goal that we laid out early on in the *Project overview – problem formulation* section.

In the next chapter, we will analyze the **Wisconsin Breast Cancer Data Set**. This dataset has only categorical data. We will build another pipeline, but this time, we will set up the Hortonworks Development Platform Sandbox to develop and deploy a breast cancer prediction pipeline. Given a set of categorical feature variables, this pipeline will predict whether a given sample is benign or malignant. In the next and the last section of the current chapter, we will list a set of questions that will test your knowledge of what you have learned so far.

Questions

Here are a list of questions for your reference:

1. What do you understand by EDA? Why is it important?
2. Why do we create training and test data?
3. Why did we index the data that we pulled from the UCI Machine Learning Repository?
4. Why is the Iris dataset so famous?
5. Name one powerful feature of the random forest classifier.
6. What is supervisory as opposed to unsupervised learning?
7. Explain briefly the process of creating our model with training data.
8. What are feature variables in relation to the Iris dataset?
9. What is the entry point to programming with Spark?

Task: The Iris dataset problem was a statistical classification problem. Create a confusion or error matrix with the rows being predicted setosa, predicted versicolor, and predicted virginica, and the columns being actual species, such as setosa, versicolor, and virginica. Having done that, interpret this matrix.

2
Build a Breast Cancer Prognosis Pipeline with the Power of Spark and Scala

Breast cancer is the leading cause of death among women each year, leaving others in various stages of the disease. Lately, **machine learning** (ML) has shown great promise for physicians and researchers working towards better outcomes and lowering the cost of treatment. With that in mind, the **Wisconsin Breast Cancer Data Set** represents a combination of suitable features that are useful enough to generate ML models, models that are able to predict a future diagnostic outcome by learning from predetermined or historical breast mass tissue sample data.

Here is the dataset we refer to:

- UCI Machine Learning Repository: Breast Cancer Wisconsin (Original) Data Set
- UCI Machine Learning Repository: Breast Cancer Wisconsin (Diagnostic) Data Set
- Accessed July 13, 2018
- Website URL: `https://archive.ics.uci.edu/ml/datasets/Breast Cancer Wisconsin (Original)`

In this chapter, we will be focusing on implementing and training a logistic regression multiclass classifier for making a prediction on whether a breast cancer mass is malignant or not. The Wisconsin Breast Cancer Data Set is a classification task.

The overarching learning objective of this chapter is to be able to implement a Scala solution that will predict cancer outcomes. Starting from the **UCI Machine Learning Repository** breast cancer dataset, we will lean on the Spark ML library's ML APIs and its supporting libraries to build a breast cancer prediction pipeline.

The following list is a section-wise breakdown of individual learning outcomes for this chapter:

- Breast cancer classification problem
- Getting started
- Random Forest breast cancer pipeline
- LR breast cancer pipeline

Breast cancer classification problem

At the moment supervised learning is the most common class of ML problems in the business domain. In Chapter 1, *Predict the Class of a Flower from the Iris Dataset*, we approached the Iris classification task by employing a powerful supervised learning classification algorithm called **Random Forests**, which at its core depends on a categorical response variable. In this chapter, besides the Random Forest approach, we also turn to yet another intriguing yet popular classification technique, called **logistic regression**. Both approaches present a unique solution to the prediction problem of breast cancer prognosis, while an iterative learning process is a common denominator. The logistic regression technique occupies center stage in this chapter, taking precedence over Random Forests. However, both learn from a test dataset containing samples with predetermined measurements and compute a prediction on new, unseen data.

Before we proceed further, a quick note on ML terminology. The literature in this rapidly expanding field is sometimes seen to be replete with terms from other overlapping fields, leading to differing perceptions, even though two apparently different terms refer to the same thing or are mostly equivalent in regard to semantics. Sometimes, two terms that are often used interchangeably in the literature might actually be quite different; for example, the terms **multivariate** and **multivariable** are two such terms. We will avoid using multivariable in this chapter. That said, let's take up the Wisconsin Breast Cancer Data Set and understand the terms around it, prior to problem formulation and implementation.

First, we must download the dataset from the UCI Machine Learning Repository. It is available in the ModernScalaProjects_Code folder.

Breast cancer dataset at a glance

The Wisconsin Breast Cancer Data Set contains 699 rows of data. Each row corresponds to a single sample (the term **example** is sometimes used interchangeably with a **sample** in the ML literature) containing nine feature measurements of digitized images of a fine needle aspirate of a breast mass.

Before we dive into the details, here is a table listing the key characteristics of the 699 rows (instances) of the Wisconsin Breast Cancer Data Set:

Breast Cancer Wisconsin Dataset at a glance	
Classification technique	Multivariate
Total no of instances	699
Number of Attributes	10
Attribute Data Type	Integer
Attribute Names (Columns)	Sample Code Number
Number of classes (labels)	2
Cell Nuclei measurements (Attributes)	Sample Code number
	Clump Thickness
	Uniformity of Cell Size
	Uniformity of Cell Shape
	Marginal Adhesion
	Single Epithelial Cell Size
	Bare Nuclei
	Bland Chromatin
	Normal Nucleoli
	Mitoses
	Class

Breast cancer dataset characteristics

The preceding table lists nine cell nuclei attributes of the breast cancer dataset, where each attribute bears a single value. All of the nine cell nuclei attribute values are measurements that have been captured from digitized images of a certain sample. 699 of these breast cancer tissue samples, then, should constitute our ML experimental unit of 699 input vectors.

To reflect on what input vectors are, we invite readers to draw upon their previous experience with the Iris dataset supervised learning problem; this was a classification task characterized by two fundamental aspects:

- An input vector
- A response variable value Y with two possible outcomes for its input vector:
    - Y is represented by the class column and is sometimes known as a supervisory signal.
    - Two outcomes (for example, either heads or tails) implies more than one class label. An outcome represents a *classification*, as in a classification task.

The preceding two aspects are also shared by our breast cancer supervised learning problem—the task at hand. The following points describe the task at hand by offering more insight:

- It is a 699-input vector multiclass classification task. This task is characterized by historical (predetermined) categorical data and more than one dependent or outcome variable (or label).
- This task is performed on a dataset that has 699 observations/measurements (instances), where each observation row may be described further as follows:
    - Each row is composed of 10 attributes; each of these attributes is a predictor variable (inputs, X), which are also known as input variables (X)
    - Each of the 699 observations is historical or predetermined (with the exception of certain incomplete observations/rows), and represent (breast mass cell nuclei) characteristics of cell nuclei from a breast cancer tissue sample from a needle aspirate
    - There are 10 characteristics of the aforementioned breast mass cell nuclei; these are just the breast's mass cell nuclei measurements
- The classification task is also multidimensional, owing to the fact that 10 (input) attribute values exist as feature parameters that are passed into Model to carry out a diagnosis classification on the so-called target class.
- Each instance (row) in the breast cancer dataset represents measurements (from digitized images) made on breast mass tissue samples.
- The goal of the classification task is as follows:
    - To identify (or classify) the diagnosis on a new breast cancer sample as belonging to either of two diagnoses: malignant (cancerous) or benign (non-cancerous).

- To derive a predicted value for the response from the predictors by a process of learning (or fitting) a discrete number of targets or category labels (Y). The predicted value is a categorical response (outcome) variable (output Y), also known as a response or outcome variable (Y).
  - To learn a predictive function also known as a model; this computes a predictor function that predetermines the feature measurements on 10 attributes that will be able to classify or identify, the type of diagnosis (benign or malignant).

In `Chapter 1`, *Predict the Class of a Flower from the Iris Dataset*, we used a supervised learning classification algorithm called Random Forests. In this chapter, we will employ what is known as the logistic regression classification technique (a Spark ML algorithm). This will be the heart of our predictive analysis classification pipeline. To sum this up, a high-level view of the breast cancer classification task can be compartmentalized as follows:

- **The classifier algorithm**: This involves the creation of a discriminant function or model function that discovers patterns, relationships, or interactions between several independent variables and one dependent variable (indexed by the model to a binary dummy variable) that is either a nominal or ordinal variable
- **Predetermined features**: Measurements or observations that have been labeled malignant or otherwise
- **Predicted labels**: Labeling unseen data before arriving at a prediction on new, unseen data after a learning process

The end goal of logistical regression is to produce a model that is as well fitted (trained) as possible and one that emits a prediction. A prediction, of course, is a variable of interest.

The next section is a prelude to a broader discussion on the application of the logistic regression statistical technique.

Logistic regression algorithm

The **logistic regression (LR)** algorithm, which is employed when building a data pipeline in this chapter, is a fresh approach to making a prediction on whether a breast cancer mass is malignant or not.

At the outset, the key to understanding the LR algorithm boils down to this:

- "if (categorical) feature x = …", then it treats the label as an output that is something like this: "label =..".

- Speaking of categorical features, we may want to understand the relationship between two or more of them in the breast cancer dataset. In addition, we are also interested in building LR ML models as an efficient data inference to derive the concurrent effects of multiple categorical variables.

In the next section, we will present you with a high-level overview of the LR technique.

Salient characteristics of LR

The following table lists the salient characteristics of LR:

Logistic Regression	
It is a Statistical Technique	The technique helps analyze a dataset
It operates well on a dataset that contains more than one independent variable.	Each of these independent or input attribute value determines a prediction outcome
Its prediction outcome variable (dependent) is dichotomous	A dichotomous (output) variable can be: 1) Alabama (Red State) or California (Blue State) 2) Giant or tiny
Its dichotomous variable is a dummy, and is only measured in one of two ways: 1) Nominal measurement 2) Ordinal measurement	Dichotomous variables are identified as having 2 states that are mutually exclusive. Each state is represented as either a 0 or a 1, lending it the nature of a dummy variable
Its dichotomous variable is also known as a binary variable. That explains the term "Binary Logistic Regression"	A binary variable represents two possible results or outcomes. The flip of a coin produces 1) Heads 2) Tails

LR at a glance

The regression or classification model that we implement for the pipeline in this chapter is a specialized type of a generalized linear regression model called **binary logistic regression**.

Before we talk about binary logistic regression, we will take a step back, refer back to `Chapter 1`, *Predict the Class of a Flower from the Iris Dataset*, and remind ourselves of the different types of variables. One such variable type is that of a response variable, a variable whose changes are explained by a so-called explanatory variable. An explanatory variable is plotted on the *x* axis of a scatter plot, whereas the response variable plotted on the *y* axis is dependent on the former. The following diagram is an example of a scatter plot that, though not directly relevant to this chapter, has some significance:

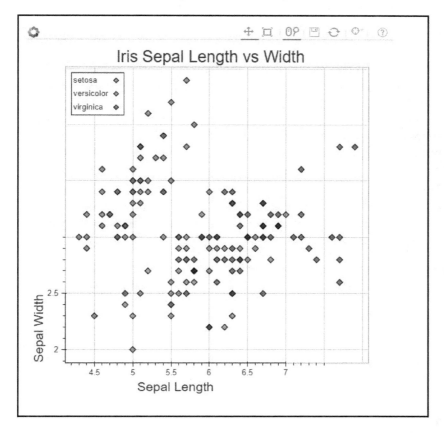

A scatter plot example

Going one step further, we get into the topic of linear regression. This type of prediction model takes a bunch of explanatory categorical values as hyperparameters that play a direct role in predicting expected response variable values. What are the odds of our response variable taking on a certain value? Those odds are represented in mathematical terms, which is a probability model that translates to a predictor function. A function like this does two things:

- Accepts more than one explanatory (or input) variable feature measurement
- Models the probabilities of response variables

Before we apply all of this to our breast cancer dataset, we will cite a (fictitious) example of a mathematics program admission process from the Case Western Reserve University. This process can be described in terms of the following points:

- It is supposed to be a fair, nondiscriminatory process, one that admits students coming from various categories or groups to academic programs.
- An admission process predictor model would predict the probability of the successful (or not) admission of a student, given that they belong to a certain gender, race, or economic background.
- An important question to pose is what are the odds of student A being successfully admitted into this program? In other words, how do we come up with a `StudentAdmission` predictor function (model) that will predict the odds of the `admission status` response variable taking a specific value?
- The `StudentAdmission` model receives a group of explanatory variables. This group consists of independent variables representing some characteristics of the individual. These are multiple feature measurements. Some features can include gender, race, income group, and many more.

All that being said, we want to know how binary logistic regression finds its niche as an extension of the linear regression model approach. Two examples of usage are described as follows:

- Consider, for example, that a binary logistic regression model simply predicts whether an incident (an event) took place or not. A researcher with earthquake data is interested in analyzing whether an earthquake is bound to happen sometime in the future. This kind of response variable is **discrete**. In other words, it is noncontinuous, static, or a one-time limited occurrence.

- The university admission process could be modeled as a binary logistic regression model, one that involves more than one explanatory variable or course. This model will predict the odds (or probability) of the response variable (`admission status`) taking a certain value. Taking this a step further, the predicted discrete value in the student admission process is a value of either 0 or 1.

Next, we will list assumptions that will help us formulate a logistical regression task.

Binary logistic regression assumptions

Here are some assumptions that are made for a binary logistic regression classification task:

- The dependent variable should be dichotomous, representing mutually exclusive states. There is more than one independent predictor variable.
- Correlations between predictor variables are represented by the elements of a correlation matrix. They can be no higher than 0.9.
- Outliers must be absent. Outlier presence or absence can be determined by transforming predictors into standardized statistical scores.

The only dataset that is relevant to us in this chapter is the breast cancer dataset. This is a classification task whose analysis solution will be a binary logistic regression. Before we get to that, we will present this as a much simpler dataset to illustrate the following:

- Independent variables
- Dependent variables
- Correlation matrix

In the next section, we will illustrate the bottom line of linear regression with a fictitious example from a survey on males and their luck with snagging the next date.

A fictitious dataset and LR

Here, we are going to present you with a fictitious dataset to merely present our case on LR so that it can be a candidate for our breast cancer dataset classification task.

The following example lists data that has been created by a dating website about male singles. Listed in the table is a dependent variable that represents whether the guy was lucky, which means they were able to work up to a second date with the same person within a week after the first date.

There are two independent variables, and they are as follows:

- Did the guy attend a dating workshop to firm up his dating skills?
- The second variable measures the guy's desperation on a desperation scale. The higher the score, the more desperate the guy is, with 100 being the most desperate.

The following dating survey table tabulates data pertaining to the dating logistical regression problem:

Individual	2nd Date	Dating Workshop	Coolness Score
1	1	1	80
2	0	1	85
3	0	1	65
4	0	0	60
5	1	0	70
6	1	1	75
7	1	0	78
8	1	0	65
9	1	0	87
10	0	0	60
11	0	1	55
12	0	1	58
13	0	1	40
14	0	0	35
15	0	1	70
16	1	1	69
17	1	1	81
18	1	0	35
19	1	0	65
20	1	0	55

Logistical regression example

An inspection of the dataset tells us that a little more than half of all single guys have had a second date in less than a week. This is assuming that the dating survey company does not possess any other background data on these singles and is applying the best techniques in this (fictitious) dating help industry.

Now, we want to know whether those in the **Workshop** group are more likely to have another date. Looking at the fourth column, **Cool**, greater coolness translates to a better chance of a second date:

	Date	Workshop	Cool
Correlation Coefficient			
Date	1		
Workshop	-3.1	1	
Cool	0.47	-.17	1
Mean	0.49	.36	52.52
Standard Deviation	.50	.50	9.35

Correlation coefficient table

Looking at the table for **Correlation Coefficients**, those men not in the **Workshop** were less likely to have another date and those with a higher **Cool** factor were more likely to have a second date.

A logistical regression applied on this dataset would have the following:

- Response (dependent) variable: **Date**
- Levels of measurement: **Mean** and **standard deviation**
- Regression function: **Logistic** or **logit**
- Total number of feature rows: **20**

At this point, we have given you a better understanding of LR. We will wade deeper into this topic in the next section. We talked about response variables and correlation coefficients, otherwise known as dichotomous variables, and got a good handle on all of these. However, we have not yet formulated the LR model in mathematical terms. We want to know if using linear regression for building a model is appropriate for the breast cancer classification task. As it turns out, we will not be able to apply linear regression models to the task at hand. Why we turned to LR and not linear regression is one of the points of discussion in the next section.

LR as opposed to linear regression

Before choosing between logistic and linear regression methods, here are a few pointers that reiterate or restate what we talked about in this chapter and `Chapter 1`, *Predict the Class of a Flower from the Iris Dataset*:

- A data scientist working on their experimental data unit is seeking to build a model. Naturally, the follow-up question might be why are they interested in building an (ML) model?
- One answer to the previous question might be that the model helps discover patterns or the underlying relationship between the predictor (explanatory or independent) variables and their response counterparts.

Speaking of response variables, response variables in a breast cancer dataset are categorical, as opposed to other ML classification tasks where the response variables are as follows:

- Continuous
- Unbounded

This brings us clarity, and with it the following working hypotheses:

The linear regression approach for our breast cancer classification task models may not work. After all, the response variable Y is neither continuous unbounded, or normally distributed. Before writing off the linear regression approach for our purposes, we will attempt such a formulation anyway, and in the process, shed more light on why LR is what we really want.

Formulation of a linear regression classification model

The basis for a mathematical formulation of a linear regression model may be broken down as follows:

- Left-hand side: The predicted variable.
- Right-hand side represented by y: A linear construct that is made up of coefficients, a predictor (independent variable), and the arithmetic operators + for addition and * for multiplication.
- Assuming there are four predictor variables, PX1, PX2, PX3, and PX4, each of these variables represents the so-called X.

At the outset, we could write an equation representing a linear regression model, as follows:

```
//y on the Left-Hand is the predicted variable, and PX1, PX2, PX3... are
predictor varibles (X)
y = LR0 + (LR1 * PX1) + (LR2 * PX2) + (LR3 * PX3) + (LR4 * PX4) + ......
```

There is a catch! Our new linear regression model is characterized by response variables that are actually **non-dichotomous**. Well, we could put up a stand and say that it is still possible to come up with an improved version of this equation, which will represent a linear regression model with dichotomous response variables. It turns out that such an improved linear model will not work in actuality, for two reasons:

- Our (dichotomous) response variables need to be arbitrarily assigned 0 and 1. This is because we want to represent two mutually exclusive categorical states. Those states can be either benign or malignant, respectively.
- The second reason has to do with the fact that because the response variable value Y is categorical, the predicted value is really the probability that this variable accepts a certain value, and not the value itself.

At this point, our thought process appears to be decidedly in favor of at least a regression model with dichotomous response variables, as opposed to a linear regression model. How so?

It may be that the model we are looking to build is a function of probabilities, an LR equation, distinguished by a left-hand-side representation of a logit of Y rather than Y itself. The next section will weave the ideas presented here and build a mathematical formulation of the LR as an equation.

Logit function as a mathematical equation

Continuing on from where we left off in the previous section, this section is an attempt at translating those ideas and conclusions into a newer narrative. The goal of this section is to have a high-level mathematical formulation for LR.

However, with LR being a much more complicated case, we will formulate a simpler equation for what is known as a logit function, logit model, or logit odds.

Without further ado, the logit function at a high level is expressed as `Logit(p)` and can be expanded to the mean logit of the odds of `Y`, rather than `Y` itself.

That said, here are a few mathematical concepts to help us understand and write a logit function:

- **Euler number**: Euler number (e) = 2.718228183
- **Natural logarithm**: If e can be raised to the power y, as in $e^y = x$, then the logarithm of x to the base e is $log_e(x) = y$

At this point, a formulation of the logit function becomes something like the following equation:

```
//Natural Logarithm of the probability that Y equals one of two values,
perhaps 0 and 1, each taken to //represent one of two mutually exclusive
states
Ln[p/(1-p)] = LR0 + (LR1 * PX1) + (LR2 * PX2) + (LR3 * PX3) + (LR4 * PX4)
```

Our newly-minted logit function is an equation based on the natural logarithm of the ratio of odds or probabilities. The logit function is a model, which is characterized by the following features:

- In this logit function, `Ln[p/(1-p)]`, `p/(1-p)` is called the odds of our sample being labeled as benign. For example, `Ln[p/(1-p)]` is the natural logarithm or log-odds, or simply the logit as `Ln[p/(1-p)]` varying between drop down -∞ to +∞.
- The logit function can be written as `fnLogistic(p) = ln(p/1-p)`, where p is between 0 and 1, and where 0 and 1 are the maximum and minimum values plotted on the *x* axis, for example, `fnLogistic(0.9) = 2.197224577336`.
- `LR0`, `LR1`, `LR2`, and so on are known as model coefficients or correlation coefficients. These model coefficients relate to the predictor (explanatory) variable of the predicted (response) variable.

- PX1, PX2, and PX3 are predictor variables.
- The logit function is also a **link function**. It is a link function because it links the natural log of the probabilities on the left of the logit function to the linear equation made up of predictor variables and their respective coefficients.
- p is said to be bounded between 0 and 1, which is the case here.

A typical logit function curve looks like this:

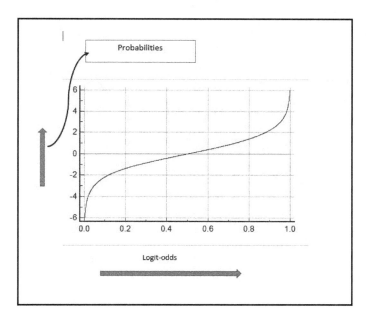

Logit model graph

 At this point, we haven't discussed LR, which is a little more complicated than the logit model.

An interpretation of the graph is as follows:

- The nonlinear graph will depict the following:
  - *x* axis: Logit values
  - *y* axis: Probabilities (or odds)
  - Looking at the graph, for a probability of **0**, the logit value is **0.5**

To recap, we started with linear regression and then progressed to a discussion on the logit model. Understanding what the logit function is sets the stage for LR in the context of the breast cancer classification task.

LR function

We said before that LR is harder than the logit function. However, the LR formulation, as we shall see, is a good fit for this problem. We want to make a prediction on the fate of a sample being either benign or malignant. In other words, a prediction on a particular breast cancer tissue sample can only take one of two mutually exclusive values, based on feature measurements such as clump thickness, uniformity of cell size, and many more. Each of these feature measurements can be X1, X2, and X3, respectively.

This brings us to the beginning of a formulation of the LR function.

The core concept behind the LR function is the so-called inverse function, which is written down as:

$$p = \frac{1}{1 + e^{-L}}$$

Here is a brief interpretation of the preceding equation:

p in the preceding equation is simply a function of feature measurements of breast cancer samples represented by X1, X2, X3, and many more.

Rewriting **p** as `fLogistic(X1,X2,..)`, we have a complete function definition as follows:

```
fLogistic(X1,X2,X3,..) = LR0 + (LR1 * PX1) + (LR2 * PX2) + (LR3 * PX3) +
...
```

It turns out that the logit function we discussed earlier and our logistic regression function are inverses of each other.

Important points to remember about logistic regression are as follows:

- There is a dichotomous response variable representing the odds of an outcome occurring or not
- A non-linear relationship between:
  - The categorical input (independent feature measurements) values plotted on the *x* axis. These are also known as predictor variables.

- The probabilities on the y-axis. These are predicted values.
- Very important: The coefficients LR0, LR1, and LR2 are computed from our training dataset. Our training dataset has known or predetermined input measurements and output labels.

At this point, we have what we need to switch focus to the Spark ML API for an implementation of the LR mathematical model that we just discussed.

In the next section, we will build two data pipelines:

- A pipeline using the Random Forests algorithm
- A pipeline using the LR method

We are familiar with Random Forests from Chapter 1, *Predict the Class of a Flower from the Iris Dataset*. LR is a proven method that is backed by established statistical techniques that ML has found very handy for solving binary classification problems.

The following *Getting started* section will get you started with the implementation process.

Getting started

The best way to get started is by understanding the bigger picture—gauging the magnitude of the work ahead of us. In this sense, we have identified two broad tasks:

- Setting up the prerequisite software.
- Developing two pipelines, starting with data collection and building a workflow sequence that could end with predictions. Those pipelines are as follows:
  - A Random Forests pipeline
  - A logistical regression pipeline

We will talk about setting up the prerequisite software in the next section.

Setting up prerequisite software

First, please refer back to the *Setting up the prerequisite software* section in Chapter 1, *Predict the Class of a Flower from the Iris Dataset,* to review your existing infrastructure. If need be, you might want to install everything again. The chances of you having to substantively change anything are slim.

However, here are the upgrades I recommend:

- JDK upgrade to 1.8.0_172, if you have not already done so
- Scala from 2.11.12 to an early stable version of 2.12
- Spark 2.2 to 2.3 where 2.3, is a major release with numerous bug fixes, which is why hence it is recommended

At the time of writing this book, Java 9 and 10 don't appear to work with Spark. That might change. For the purposes of this chapter, your local Spark shell will be the development environment of choice.

With the prerequisites out of the way, we are ready to jump right into developing pipelines. This journey starts in the *Implementation objectives* section.

Implementation objectives

We fulfilled our implementation objectives for Chapter 1, *Predict the Class of a Flower from the Iris Dataset*. In that chapter, early on, we developed the beginnings of a workflow process. This is depicted in the following diagram, which will help us frame the implementation objectives for this chapter as well:

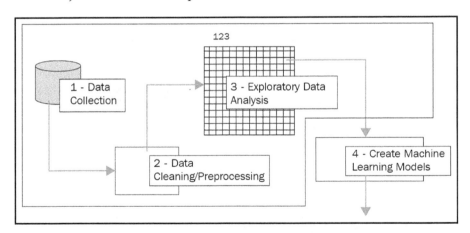

Stages in a preliminary workflow

Since the current chapter also deals with a multiclass classification task like the one before it, the four boxes that are shown in the preceding diagram are our guide to setting up implementation objectives for this chapter. The broad high-level objectives are:

- A **Data Collection** step followed by an **Exploratory Data Analysis** (**EDA**) step
- A **Data Cleaning/Preprocessing** step
- Handing off data to an algorithm; there are models to be trained (fitted) and predictions to be generated

This paves the way for a more complete list of implementation objectives, and they are:

- Getting the breast cancer dataset from the UCI Machine Learning Repository.
- Deriving a dataframe for EDA.
- Carrying out preliminary EDA in the Sandbox Zeppelin Notebook environment (or Spark shell), and running a statistical analysis.
- Developing the pipeline incrementally in Zeppelin and porting the code into IntelliJ. What this means is the following:
  - Creating a new Scala project in IntelliJ, or importing an existing empty project into IntelliJ, and creating Scala artifacts from code that was incrementally developed in the Notebook
  - Do not forget to wire up all the necessary dependencies in the `build` file
- Interpreting the results of the pipeline:
  - How well did the classifier perform?
  - How close are the predicted values to those in the original dataset?

Now, we will start working on these implementations one by one, starting with getting the Wisconsin Breast Cancer Data Set from the UCI Machine Learning Repository.

Implementation objective 1 – getting the breast cancer dataset

Head over to the UCI Machine Learning Repository website at `https://archive.ics.uci.edu/ml/datasets/bcw` and download the `Data` folder by clicking on **Data Folder**. Extract this folder someplace convenient and copy `bcw.csv` into the root of your project folder, which we will call `Chapter2`. At this point, `Chapter2` will be empty.

You may refer back to the project overview for an in-depth description of the breast cancer dataset. We depict the contents of the `bcw.data` file here as follows:

```
1000025,5,1,1,1,2,1,3,1,1,2
1002945,5,4,4,5,7,10,3,2,1,2
1015425,3,1,1,1,2,2,3,1,1,2
1016277,6,8,8,1,3,4,3,7,1,2
1017023,4,1,1,3,2,1,3,1,1,2
1017122,8,10,10,8,7,10,9,7,1,4
1018099,1,1,1,1,2,10,3,1,1,2
1018561,2,1,2,1,2,1,3,1,1,2
1033078,2,1,1,1,2,1,1,1,5,2
1033078,4,2,1,1,2,1,2,1,1,2
1035283,1,1,1,1,1,1,3,1,1,2
1036172,2,1,1,1,2,1,2,1,1,2
1041801,5,3,3,3,2,3,4,4,1,4
1043999,1,1,1,1,2,3,3,1,1,2
1044572,8,7,5,10,7,9,5,5,4,4
1047630,7,4,6,4,6,1,4,3,1,4
1048672,4,1,1,1,2,1,2,1,1,2
1049815,4,1,1,1,2,1,3,1,1,2
1050670,10,7,7,6,4,10,4,1,2,4
1050718,6,1,1,1,2,1,3,1,1,2
1054590,7,3,2,10,5,10,5,4,4,4
1054593,10,5,5,3,6,7,7,10,1,4
1056784,3,1,1,1,2,1,2,1,1,2
1057013,8,4,5,1,2,?,7,3,1,4
1059552,1,1,1,1,2,1,3,1,1,2
1065726,5,2,3,4,2,7,3,6,1,4
1066373,3,2,1,1,1,1,2,1,1,2
1066979,5,1,1,1,2,1,2,1,1,2
1067444,2,1,1,1,2,1,2,1,1,2
1070935,1,1,3,1,2,1,1,1,1,2
1070935,3,1,1,1,1,1,2,1,1,2
1071760,2,1,1,1,2,1,3,1,1,2
1072179,10,7,7,3,8,5,7,4,3,4
1074610,2,1,1,2,2,1,3,1,1,2
1075123,3,1,2,1,2,1,2,1,1,2
1079304,2,1,1,1,2,1,2,1,1,2
1080185,10,10,10,8,6,1,8,9,1,4
1081791,6,2,1,1,1,1,7,1,1,2
1084584,5,4,4,9,2,10,5,6,1,4
1091262,2,5,3,3,6,7,7,5,1,4
1096800,6,6,6,9,6,?,7,8,1,2
1099510,10,4,3,1,3,3,6,5,2,4
```

A snapshot of the breast cancer dataset with 699 rows

The breast cancer dataset that we just downloaded is multivariate, meaning it includes a set of more than one independent variable. Before performing any EDA on it, we need to create an abstraction over the dataset, which we call a dataframe. How we create a dataframe as a prelude to EDA is the goal of the next section.

Implementation objective 2 – deriving a dataframe for EDA

We downloaded the Wisconsin Breast Cancer data file into the `Chapter2` folder and renamed it `bcw.csv`. The process of `DataFrame` creation starts with loading the data.

We will invoke the `read` method on `SparkSession` as follows:

```
scala> val dfReader1 = spark.read
dfReader1: org.apache.spark.sql.DataFrameReader =
org.apache.spark.sql.DataFrameReader@3d9dc84d
```

The `read` method that has been returned produces `DataFrameReader`. Because our dataset is a CSV file, we want to tell Spark about it by invoking the `format` method on `DataFrameReader` by passing in the `com.databricks.spark.csv` format specifier string:

```
scala> val dfReader2 = dfReader1.format("com.databricks.spark.csv")
dfReader2: org.apache.spark.sql.DataFrameReader =
org.apache.spark.sql.DataFrameReader@3d9dc84d
```

At this point, `DataFrameReader` needs an input data source option in the form of a key-value pair. Invoke the `option` method with two arguments, a key `"header"` of type string and its value `true` of type Boolean:

```
scala> val dfReader3 = dfReader2.option("header", true)
dfReader3: org.apache.spark.sql.DataFrameReader =
org.apache.spark.sql.DataFrameReader@3d9dc84d
```

Next, the code is invoking the `option` method again (on the `DataFrameReader`) with an argument called `inferSchema` and a `true` value. With the `inferSchema` method call, we want Spark to figure out the schema of our input data source and return our `DataFrameReader`:

```
scala> val dfReader4 = dfReader3.option("inferSchema", true)
dfReader4: org.apache.spark.sql.DataFrameReader =
org.apache.spark.sql.DataFrameReader@3d9dc84d
```

Next, load `bcw.csv` by invoking the `load` method and passing it to the path to the dataset file. External data sources such as our dataset require a path for Spark to be able to load the data so that `DataFrameReader` can process the file and return the `DataFrame`, as follows:

```
scala> val dataFrame = dfReader4.load("\\bcw.csv")
dataFrame: org.apache.spark.sql.DataFrame = [id: int, clump_thickness: int
... 9 more fields]
```

We now have a breast cancer dataframe! This completes the *Implementation objective 2 – deriving a dataframe for EDA* section. Our next step is to run a preliminary statistical analysis.

Finally, before we move on to the next step, here is a view of the dataframe:

```
scala> dataFrame.show
+-------+---------------+---------------+----------------+----------------+--------------+-------------+---------------+------
|     id|clump_thickness|size_uniformity|shape_uniformity|marginal_adhesion|epithelial_size|bare_nucleoli|bland_chromatin|normal
_nucleoli|mitoses|class|
+-------+---------------+---------------+----------------+----------------+--------------+-------------+---------------+------
|1000025|              5|              1|               1|               1|             2|            1|              3|
      1|      1|    2|
|1002945|              5|              4|               4|               5|             7|           10|              3|
      2|      1|    2|
|1015425|              3|              1|               1|               1|             2|            2|              3|
      1|      1|    2|
|1016277|              6|              8|               8|               1|             3|            4|              3|
      7|      1|    2|
|1017023|              4|              1|               1|               3|             2|            1|              3|
      1|      1|    2|
|1017122|              8|             10|              10|               8|             7|           10|              9|
      7|      1|    4|
|1018099|              1|              1|               1|               1|             2|           10|              3|
      1|      1|    2|
|1018561|              2|              1|               2|               1|             2|            1|              3|
      1|      1|    2|
|1033078|              2|              1|               1|               1|             2|            1|              1|
      1|      5|    2|
|1033078|              4|              2|               1|               1|             2|            1|              2|
      1|      1|    2|
|1035283|              1|              1|               1|               1|             1|            1|              3|
```

Dataframe with raw data

It looks like we have data in our `DataFrame`, which is now ready for EDA.

Step 1 – conducting preliminary EDA

At this point, we will perform a fairly simple statistical analysis on our dataset. This will provide us with useful, though preliminary, statistical insights such as mean, median, range, and standard deviation, to name a few.

To proceed with the preliminary EDA, let's invoke the `describe` method with the required column names as parameters. This will give us a new `DataFrame` called `stats`. Invoking a `show` method on `stats` will produce a table of statistical results as follows:

```
scala> stats.show
+-------+------------------+------------------+------------------+------------------+------------------+------------------+------------------+------------------+---
|summary|                id|   clump_thickness|   size_uniformity|  shape_uniformity| marginal_adhesion|   epithelial_size|     bare_nucleoli|
nd_chromatin|   normal_nucleoli|           mitoses|             class|
+-------+------------------+------------------+------------------+------------------+------------------+------------------+------------------+------------------+---
|  count|               699|               699|               699|               699|               699|               699|               699|               699|
    699|               699|               699|
|   mean|1071704.0987124464|4.417739628040057|  3.1344778254649|3.2074391988555508|2.8068669527896994|3.216022889842632|3.5446559297218156|3.4
582403433476| 2.8669527896999571|1.5894134477825466|2.6895565092989986|
| stddev| 617095.7298192448|2.8157406585949933|3.0514591099542003|2.9719127672157133|2.855379239217023|2.214299886649047| 3.643857160492912|2.4
642523242512|3.0536338936127745| 1.715077942506795|0.9512753222121839|
|    min|             61634|                 1|                 1|                 1|                 1|                 1|                 1|                 1|
      1|                 1|                 2|
|    max|          13454352|                10|                10|                10|                10|                10|                10|                10|
     10|                10|                 4|
+-------+------------------+------------------+------------------+------------------+------------------+------------------+------------------+------------------+---
```

Statistical analysis

Although the output is ugly to look at and is mangled, we see statistical numbers such as the count, mean, standard deviation, minimum, and maximum. Yes, the dataset has 699 rows of continuous, discrete (or categorical) values.

Now that the preliminary exploratory data analysis is complete, we proceed to the next step, where we will load the dataset into Spark.

Step 2 – loading data and converting it to an RDD[String]

In this step, we will load the data again, but in a slightly different manner. The goal of this phase of the data analysis is to produce a DataFrame where the data has been read into an RDD[String]. First, we will need a path to the dataset:

```scala
scala> val dataSetPath =
"C:\\Users\\Ilango\\Documents\\Packt\\DevProjects\\Chapter2\\"
dataSetPath: String = C:\Users\Ilango\Documents\Packt\DevProjects\Chapter2\
```

We have just created dataSetpath. In the following code, we will pass the path to the dataset into the textFile method:

```scala
scala> val firstRDD = spark.sparkContext.textFile(dataSetPath +
"\\bcw.csv")
firstRDD: org.apache.spark.rdd.RDD[String] = C:\<<path to your dataset
file>>
 MapPartitionsRDD[1] at textFile at <console>:25
```

The textFile method returned an RDD[String]. To check if data was loaded into the RDD, we need to invoke the first method on firstRDD to give us the header content. We will leave this as an exercise for the reader.

Next, we want to know the number of partitions in our RDD:

```scala
scala> firstRDD.getNumPartitions
res7: Int = 2
```

The getNumPartitions method returned the number of partitions in firstRDD. Since an RDD allows us to work with data at a low level, we will continue to reorganize and massage this data as required.

In the next step, we want to inspect the RDD. We want to reorganize and repackage data into arrays.

Step 3 – splitting the resilient distributed dataset and reorganizing individual rows into an array

To split the dataset, we will start with the RDD partitions. It is helpful to think of an RDD partition in the following manner.

Each partition can be visualized as one long string consisting of rows of data separated by `"\n"`. We want to break down this long string into its constituent string, by splitting them along the `"\n"` separator. Shortly, we will try a `flatMap` operation on our RDD, `firstRDD`. Each constituent string is a `Row` that represents a row in the original dataset.

We will do `flatMap` and pass to it an anonymous function, which will be invoked on rows separated by a `"\n"` character, as follows:

```scala
scala> val secondRDD = firstRDD.flatMap{ row => row.split("\n").toList }
secondRDD: org.apache.spark.rdd.RDD[String] = MapPartitionsRDD[33] at
flatMap at <console>:27
```

The preceding code does a `flatMap` flattening operation, resulting in the creation of a new `RDD[String]` that will hold all of these strings (each string is a row in our dataset). At this point, we will `split` (along the comma between individual characters of that row) a `String` producing an `RDD[Array[String]]`:

```scala
scala> val rddArrayString = secondRDD.map(_.split(","))
rddArrayString: org.apache.spark.rdd.RDD[Array[String]] =
MapPartitionsRDD[34] at map at <console>:29
```

The `RDD[Array[String]]` naturally implies that the RDD contains more than one `Array[String]`. How many of these arrays are in this RDD?

```scala
scala> rddArrayString.count
res9: Long = 700
```

Invoking `count` on our RDD returns an array count of `700`, which is what it should be.

Step 4 – purging the dataset of rows containing question mark characters

Before we go any further, let's eyeball the raw dataset again. If you looked closely, you will notice that the dataset contains a ? character in some places. Actually, this character starts appearing in some rows in the seventh column, starting on the 25th row. The 25th row, with the ? character, is displayed in the following diagram. That them is a problem, which needs a solution.

Sometimes, a visual inspection of the dataset can reveal the presence of extraneous characters.

The following is a snapshot of the Wisconsin Breast Cancer Data Set with the ? character in the 25th row and the sixth column:

```
 2  1000025,5,1,1,1,2,1,3,1,1,2
 3  1002945,5,4,4,5,7,10,3,2,1,2
 4  1015425,3,1,1,1,2,2,3,1,1,2
 5  1016277,6,8,8,1,3,4,3,7,1,2
 6  1017023,4,1,1,3,2,1,3,1,1,2
 7  1017122,8,10,10,8,7,10,9,7,1,4
 8  1018099,1,1,1,1,2,10,3,1,1,2
 9  1018561,2,1,2,1,2,1,3,1,1,2
10  1033078,2,1,1,1,2,1,1,1,5,2
11  1033078,4,2,1,1,2,1,2,1,1,2
12  1035283,1,1,1,1,1,1,3,1,1,2
13  1036172,2,1,1,1,2,1,2,1,1,2
14  1041801,5,3,3,3,2,3,4,4,1,4
15  1043999,1,1,1,1,2,3,3,1,1,2
16  1044572,8,7,5,10,7,9,5,5,4,4
17  1047630,7,4,6,4,6,1,4,3,1,4
18  1048672,4,1,1,1,2,1,2,1,1,2
19  1049815,4,1,1,1,2,1,3,1,1,2
20  1050670,10,7,7,6,4,10,4,1,2,4
21  1050718,6,1,1,1,2,1,3,1,1,2
22  1054590,7,3,2,10,5,10,5,4,4,4
23  1054593,10,5,5,3,6,7,7,10,1,4
24  1056784,3,1,1,1,2,1,2,1,1,2
25  1057013,8,4,5,1,2,█,7,3,1,4
26  1059552,1,1,1,1,2,1,3,1,1,2
27  1065726,5,2,3,4,2,7,3,6,1,4
```

Dataset showing ? characters

Obviously, it is not just row 25th that has a ? character. There are likely other rows with the extraneous ? character that needs to be purged. One solution appears to be to invoke a `filter` operation on our `rddArrayString`:

```scala
scala> val purgedRDD = rddArrayString.filter(_(6) != "?")
purgedRDD: org.apache.spark.rdd.RDD[Array[String]] = MapPartitionsRDD[35]
at filter at <console>:31
```

As evident from the preceding code, we just ran the `filter` operation, which returned a new `RDD[Array[String]` that we called `purgedRDD`. Naturally, we may want to count the number of rows left in the dataset that we believe are relevant for data analysis. That is the goal of the next section.

Step 5 – running a count after purging the dataset of rows with questionable characters

We will now run `count` on our new `purgedRDD`:

```scala
scala> purgedRDD.count
res12: Long = 684
```

So, in the preceding code, we invoked the `count` method on `purgedRDD`. Spark returned a value of `684`. Apparently, 16 rows contained ? characters. After all, many datasets like this one need a preprocessing step or two. For now, we will proceed with the next steps in data analysis, secure in the knowledge that Spark will probably not report an error, especially at the point where we want a new two-column `DataFrame` containing a consolidated feature vector.

In the next section, we are going to get rid of `header`.

Step 6 – getting rid of header

Each of the inner arrays shown earlier holds rows that represent feature measurements, and a row representing the dataset `header`. The following line of code converts our RDD into an `Array`, containing arrays that themselves contain rows as strings:

```scala
//Drop the Array with the headers in it
scala> val headerRemoved = cleanedRDD.collect.drop(1)
headerRemoved: Array[Array[String]]
```

The `drop` method got rid of `header`. Next, we will move on and create a new `DataFrame`.

Step 7 – creating a two-column DataFrame

We are close. In this section, the goal is to create an input feature vector, and the steps are listed as follows:

1. Import the `Vectors` class.
2. Inside the `map` operation on the `Array`, we will iterate over each row of our header-free dataset. Then, we transform each row in turn, operating on every single column containing predetermined cell nuclei measurements. These columns are converted to doubles by using the `dense` method.
3. The `map` operation processes the entire dataset and produces `featureVectorArray`, a structure of type `Array[(Input Feature Vector, String representing the Class)]`:

```
//Step 1
scala> import org.apache.spark.ml.linalg.Vectors
import org.apache.spark.ml.linalg.Vectors

//Step 2
scala> val featureVectorArray = headerRemoved.map(row =>
(Vectors.dense(row(1).toDouble,..,row(10)))
featureVectorArray: Array[(org.apache.spark.ml.linalg.Vector,
String)]
```

Okay, we created `featureVectorArray`, an `Array` consisting of a set of (`Vector`, `String`) tuples. This `Array` is now ready to be converted into `DataFrame`. That is the goal of the next section.

Step 8 – creating the final DataFrame

The goal of this section is to create a final version of our analysis-ready `DataFrame`. The `createDataFrame` method available on `SparkSession` is suitable, and is shown as follows:

```
scala> val dataFrame = spark.createDataFrame(featureVectorArray)
dataFrame: org.apache.spark.sql.DataFrame = [_1: vector, _2: string]

//display the first 20 rows of the new DataFrame 'dataFrame'
//Readers are requested to run the show command and see what the contents
are, as an exercise
scala> dataFrame.show
+--------------------+---+
|  _1|  _2|
+--------------------+---+
```

```
|------------------------
|------------------------
|------------------------
|------------------------
Displaying 20 rows..
```

As seen earlier, the new `DataFrame` has two columns, which are not very readable named _1 and _2.

What we want is a renamed `DataFrame` with two readable columns as follows:

- A feature vector column that is named `bc-diagnosis-label-column` and a target variable label column named `bc-indexed-category-column`.
- By the way, a target variable in ML terminology denotes what is being predicted. For example, it could be a 0 for benign or 1 for malignant. Since a target variable is associated with the output, it can also be termed an outcome or output variable. Defining a target variable is an integral part of the binary classification model creation step; a target variable in statistics terminology is the same as a response variable.

To get a renamed `DataFrame`, we will transform it a little, and we will do this by creating two methods as follows:

```
//Features column
scala> def bcFeatures = "bc-diagnosis-label-column"
bcFeatures: String

//unindexed label column
scala> def bcDiagCategory = "bc-indexed-category-column"
bcDiagCategory: String
```

In the following line of code, invoke the `toDF` method:

```
;scala> val dataFrame2 = dataFrame.toDF(bcFeatures, bcDiagCategory)
dataFrame2: org.apache.spark.sql.DataFrame = [bc-diagnosis-label-column:
vector, bc-indexed-category-column: string]
```

Invoking the `toDF` method creates a `DataFrame` with the desired column names. Invoking `show` on `dataFrame2` will result in the following display:

```
scala> dataFrame2.show
+------------------------+--------------------------+
|bc-diagnosis-label-column|bc-indexed-category-column|
+------------------------+--------------------------+
|  --------------------| 2|
|  --------------------| 2|
|  --------------------| 2|
|  --------------------| 2|
|  --------------------| 2|
|  --------------------| 4|
|  --------------------| 2|
|  --------------------| 2|
|  --------------------| 2|
|  --------------------| 2|
|  --------------------
|  --------------------
|  --------------------
|  --------------------
|  --------------------
|  --------------------
|  --------------------
|  --------------------
|  --------------------
|  --------------------
+------------------------+--------------------------+
only showing top 20 rows
```

The preceding listing confirms that the `DataFrame` you wanted is what you got. In the next section, we will use this `DataFrame` to build a data pipeline with two algorithms:

- The Random Forest algorithm
- LR

We will build a Random Forest pipeline first.

Random Forest breast cancer pipeline

A good way to start this section off is to download the `Skeleton` SBT project archive file from the `ModernScalaProjects_Code` folder. Here is the structure of the `Skeleton` project:

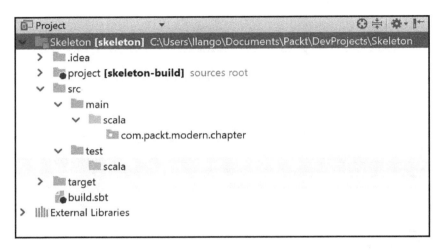

Project structure

Instructions to readers: Copy and paste the file into a folder of your choice before extracting it. Import this project into IntelliJ, drill down to the package `"com.packt.modern.chapter"`, and rename it `"com.packt.modern.chapter2"`. If you would rather choose a different name, choose something appropriate. The breast cancer pipeline project is already set up with `build.sbt, plugins.sbt,` and `build.properties`. You only need to make appropriate changes to the organization element in `build.sbt`. Once these changes are done, you are all set for development. For an explanation of dependency entries in `build.sbt`, please refer back to Chapter 1, *Predict the Class of a Flower from the Iris Dataset*. Unless we introduce new dependencies for this project, we will stick with the `build.sbt` that came bundled in the `Skeleton` project.

All that being said, we will now start the implementation. The first step will be to create Scala code files in IntelliJ. Note that the complete code is available in your downloaded folder, `ModernScalaProjects_Code`.

Step 1 – creating an RDD and preprocessing the data

Create a Scala file called `BreastCancerRfPipeline.scala` in the `com.packt.modern.chapter2` package. Up until now, we relied on `SparkSession` and `SparkContext`, which are what `spark-shell` gave us. We need to create our `SparkSession` now, which will give us `SparkContext`.

In `BreastCancerRfPipeline.scala`, after the package statement, place the following import statements:

```
import org.apache.spark.sql.SparkSession
```

Create a `SparkSession` inside a trait, which we shall call `WisconsinWrapper`:

```
lazy val session: SparkSession = { SparkSession .builder() .master("local")
.appName("breast-cancer-pipeline") .getOrCreate()
```

Just one `SparkSession` is made available to all classes extending from `WisconsinWrapper`. Create `val` to hold the `bcw.csv` file path:

```
val dataSetPath = "<<path to folder containing your Breast Cancer Dataset
file>>\\bcw.csv"
```

Create a method to build the `DataFrame`. This method takes in the complete path to the breast cancer dataset as a `String` and returns `DataFrame`:

```
def buildDataFrame(dataSet: String): DataFrame
```

Import the `DataFrame` class by updating the previous `import` statement for `SparkSession`:

```
import org.apache.spark.sql.{DataFrame, SparkSession}
```

Create a nested function inside `buildDataFrame` to process the raw dataset. Name this function `getRows`. The `getRows` function takes no parameters but returns `Array[(Vector, String)]`. The `textFile` method on the `SparkContext` variable processes `bcw.csv` into `RDD[String]`:

```
val result1: Array[String] = session.sparkContext.textFile(<<path to
bcw.csv represented by the dataSetPath variable>>)
```

The resulting RDD contains two partitions. Each partition, in turn, contains rows of strings separated by a newline character, `"\n"`. Each row in the RDD represents its original counterpart in the raw data.

In the next step, we will preprocess this RDD; this entails creating a single consolidated input `features` column out of the original four feature columns. We start this process by invoking `flatMap` and passing a function block to it. After successive transformations, which are listed in the following code, we should be able to create an array of type `Array[(org.apache.spark.ml.linalg.Vector, String)]`.

`Vector`, in this case, represents a row of feature measurements. The Scala code to give us `Array[(org.apache.spark.ml.linalg.Vector, String)]` is as follows:

```
val result2: RDD[String] = result1.flatMap { partition =>
partition.split("\n").toList }
val result3: RDD[Array[String]] = result2.map(_.split(","))
```

Next, drop the `header` column, but not before performing a `collect` that returns an `Array[Array[String]]`:

```
val result4: Array[Array[String]] = result3.collect.drop(1)
```

The `header` column is now eliminated. We will now import the `Vectors` class:

```
import org.apache.spark.ml.linalg.Vectors
```

Now, transform the `Array[Array[String]]` into `Array[(Vector, String)]`:

```
val result5 = result4.map(row =>
(Vectors.dense(row(1).toDouble,..toDouble),row(5)))
```

Now, we will invoke the `createDataFrame` method with a parameter called `getRows`. This returns a `DataFrame` with `featureVector` and `speciesLabel` (for example, bcw-Setos):

```
val dataFrame = spark.createDataFrame(result5).toDF(featureVector,
speciesLabel)
```

The new `DataFrame` contains two rows:

- A column named `bcw-features-column`
- A column named `bcw-species-label-column`

We need to index `species-label-column` by converting the "bcw-Setosa", "bcw-Virginica", and "bcw-Versicolor" strings into doubles. We will use a `StringIndexer` to do that.

Now, create a file called bcwPipeline.scala.

Create an object called bcwPipeline that extends our bcwWrapper trait:

```
object BreastCancerRfPipeline extends WisconsinWrapper { }
```

Import the StringIndexer algorithm class:

```
import org.apache.spark.ml.feature.StringIndexer
```

Now, create a StringIndexer algorithm instance. StringIndexer will map species-label-column to an indexed learned column:

```
val indexer = new
StringIndexer().setInputCol(bcwCategory).setOutputCol("indexedSpeciesLabel"
)
```

The indexer transforms the bcw type column into a column of type double. This is an example where a categorical variable is disguised as a quantitative variable.

Step 2 – creating training and test data

Now, let's split our dataset in two by providing a random seed:

```
val splitDataSet: Array[org.apache.spark.sql.
Dataset[org.apache.spark.sql.Row]] =
indexedDataFrame.randomSplit(Array(0.75, 0.25), 98765L)
```

The new splitDataset contains two datasets:

- The training Dataset is a dataset containing Array[(Vector, bcw-species-label-column: String)]
- The test Dataset is a dataset containing Array[(Vector, bcw-species-label-column: String)]

Confirm that the new Dataset is of size 2:

```
splitDataset.size
res48: Int = 2
```

Assign the training `Dataset` to the `trainSet` variable:

```
val trainDataSet = splitDataSet(0)
trainSet: org.apache.spark.sql.Dataset[org.apache.spark.sql.Row] = [bcw-
features-column: vector, bcw-species-label-column: string]
```

Assign the testing `Dataset` to the `testSet` variable:

```
val testDataSet = splitDataSet(1)
testSet: org.apache.spark.sql.Dataset[org.apache.spark.sql.Row] = [bcw-
features-column: vector, bcw-species-label-column: string]
```

Now, we will see how to create a Random Forest classifier.

Create a classifier and pass into it hyperparameters. We will set the following parameters first:

- A "`features`" column name
- An indexed "`label`" column name
- The number of features to be considered per split (we have 150 observations and four features) that will make our `max_features` 2

Since `bcw` is a classification problem, the '`sqrt`' setting for `featureSubsetStrategy` is what we need. In addition, we will pass in other parameters such as impurity, the number of trees to train, and many more, as follows:

- Impurity settings—values can be gini and entropy
- Number of trees to train (since the number of trees is greater than 1, we set the tree maximum depth, which is a number equal to the number of nodes)
- The required minimum number of feature measurements (sampled observations), also known as the minimum instances per node

This time, we will employ an exhaustive grid search-based model selection process, based on combinations of parameters, where parameter value ranges are specified. Create a `randomForestClassifier` instance. Set the features and `featureSubsetStrategy`:

```
val randomForestClassifier = new RandomForestClassifier()
  .setFeaturesCol(bcwFeatures_CategoryOrSpecies_IndexedLabel._1)
  .setFeatureSubsetStrategy("sqrt")
```

Start building a `Pipeline` that has two stages, an `indexer` and a `Classifier`:

```
val irisPipeline = new Pipeline().setStages(Array[PipelineStage](indexer)
++ Array[PipelineStage](randomForestClassifier)
```

Next, set the hyperparameter `num_trees` (number of trees) on the classifier to `15`, a `Max_Depth` parameter, and an impurity with two possible values of gini and entropy. Then, build a parameter grid with all three hyperparameters.

Step 3 – training the Random Forest classifier

Next, we will split our existing training set (the one used to train the model) into two:

- **Validation set**: This is a subset of the training dataset which is used to get a preliminary estimate of the effectiveness of the level of skillfulness attained by the model.
- **Training set**: A training set is that percentage of dataset that the model learns from. This learning process is called training the model. Also because the model learns from this data, the data is said fit the model.

We can accomplish a split by creating an instance of the `TrainValidationSplit` algorithm:

```
val validatedTestResults: DataFrame = new TrainValidationSplit()
.setSeed(1234567L) .setEstimatorParamMaps(finalParamGrid)
.setEstimator(irisPipeline)
```

On this variable, set a seed, set `EstimatorParamMaps`, set the `Estimator` with `bcwPipeline`, and finally set the training ratio to `0.8`.

Finally, do a fit and transform with our training `Dataset` and testing `Dataset`.

Great! Now, the classifier is trained. In the next step, we will apply this classifier to the testing data.

Step 4 – applying the classifier to the test data

The purpose of our validation set is to be able to make a choice between models. We want an evaluation metric as well as hyperparameter tuning. Now, we will create an instance of a validation estimator called `TrainValidationSplit`, which will split the training set into a validation set and a training set as follows:

```
validatedTestResults.setEvaluator(new MulticlassClassificationEvaluator())
```

Next, we will fit this estimator over the training dataset to produce a model and a transformer that we will use to transform our testing dataset. Finally, we will perform validation for hyperparameter tuning by applying an evaluator for a metric.

The new `ValidatedTestResults DataFrame` should contain the following columns, including three newly generated columns—`rawPrediction`, `probability`, and `prediction`, and some additional ones:

- `bcw-features-column`
- `bcw-species-column`
- `label`
- `rawPrediction`
- `probability`
- `prediction`

Next, let's generate a new dataset. Invoke the `select` method on the `validatedTestResults` dataset and pass the column expressions for `prediction` and `label` into it:

```
val validatedTestResultsDataset:DataFrame =
validatedTestResults.select("prediction", "label")
```

We will revisit these test results towards the close of this chapter, where we will be evaluating the classifier. At that point, we will explain how to interpret these results and how they tie into the main goal of this chapter predicting the class of a breast cancer mass diagnosis.

Step 5 – evaluating the classifier

In this section, we will evaluate the accuracy of the mode output results on the test result. Evaluation starts by creating an instance of `MulticlassEvaluator`:

```
val modelOutputAccuracy: Double = new MulticlassClassificationEvaluator()
```

Now, on `MulticlassEvaluationEvaluator`, we set the following:

- The `"label"` column
- A metric name
- The prediction column `label`

Next, we invoke the `evaluate` method with the `validatedTestResults` dataset. Note the accuracy of the model output results for the testing dataset from the `modelOutputAccuracy` variable. The other metric of note to evaluate is how close the predicted label value in the `predicted` column is to the actual label value in the (indexed) `"label"` column.

Next, we want to extract the metrics:

```
val multiClassMetrics = new MulticlassMetrics(validatedRDD2)
```

`MulticlassMetrics` includes two computed metrics that we extract by giving a reading of the `accuracy` and `weightedMetrics` variables.

Step 6 – running the pipeline as an SBT application

At the root of your project folder, issue the `sbt console` command, and in the Scala shell, import the `bcwPipeline` object and then invoke the `main` method of `bcwPipeline` with the `bcw` argument:

```
sbt console
scala>
import com.packt.modern.chapter2.BreastCancerRfPipeline
BreastCancerRfPipeline.main("bcw")
Accuracy (precision) is 0.9285714285714286 Weighted Precision is:
0.9428571428571428
```

The classifier reported on two metrics:

- Accuracy
- Weighted precision

In the next section, we will package the application.

Step 7 – packaging the application

In the root folder of your SBT application, we want to generate an Uber JAR. We will run the following command:

```
sbt package
```

This command generates an Uber JAR file, which can then be easily deployed into [local] in standalone deploy mode:

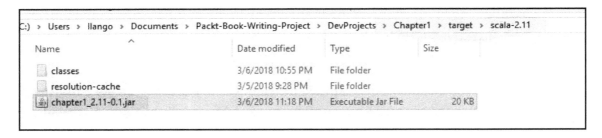

The application JAR file

The pipeline JAR file is available under the target folder. In the next section, we will deploy the application into Spark.

Step 8 – deploying the pipeline app into Spark local

At the root of the application folder, issue the spark-submit command with the class and JAR file path arguments, respectively. If everything went well, the application will do the following:

1. Load up the data.
2. Performs EDA.

3. Create training, test, and validation datasets.
4. Create a Random Forest classifier model.
5. Train the model.
6. Test the accuracy of the model, which is the most important part of the ML classification task.
7. To accomplish step 6, we apply our trained Random Forest classifier model to the test dataset, which is data that has not been seen by the model yet:

    • Unseen data could be likened to new data that the classifier needs to predict on
    • Our goal at the beginning of this was to classify the diagnosis of a breast cancer mass that is exemplified by specific features in the test dataset

8. Applying the model to the test dataset results in a prediction of the diagnosis.
9. The pipeline runs an evaluation process, which is all about checking the model reports the correct diagnosis.
10. Lastly, pipeline reports back on how important a certain feature of the breast cancer dataset turned out to be in relation to the others. As a matter of fact, it turns out that a certain feature is more important than others in carrying out the classification task.

The preceding summary listing concludes the Random Forests section and brings us to the beginning of a brand new section on the topic of creating a logistic regression pipeline.

LR breast cancer pipeline

Before getting down to the implementation of a logistic regression pipeline, refer back to the earlier table in section *Breast cancer dataset at a glance* where nine breast cancer tissue sample characteristics (features) are listed, along with one class column. To recap, those characteristics or features are listed as follows for context:

- **clump_thickness**
- **size_uniformity**
- **shape_uniformity**
- **marginal_adhesion**
- **epithelial_size**
- **bare_nucleoli**

- **bland_chromatin**
- **normal_nucleoli**
- **mitoses**

Now, let's get down to a high-level formulation of the logistic regression approach in terms of what it is meant to achieve. The following diagram represents the elements of such a formulation at a high level:

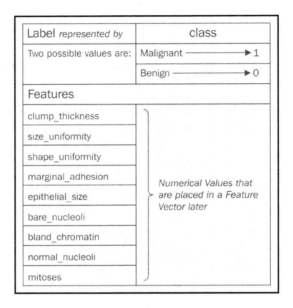

Breast cancer classification formulation

The preceding diagram represents a high-level formulation of a logistic classifier pipeline that we are aware needs to be translated into an implementation in Spark and Scala. Here are a few helpful points to get you started:

- What are some interesting attributes that we can choose to come up with predictions? Attributes or features are like `if` statements and the predicted label is the answer. For example, if it looks like a fish, is 100 feet long, and is a mammal, it must be a whale. We must identify those `if` statements or attributes with the express purpose of making predictions. Of course, a prediction must classify a tissue sample as either malignant or benign.

- Create a classifier model with LR.
- There is our class column in the breast cancer dataset, which represents the label. This column holds known (or predetermined) label values that `"label"` each feature measurement row with either malignant or benign.
- Thus, the entire dataset, an experimental unit of known labels for known measurements, is said to be labeled either malignant or benign.

In the next section, we will lay out our implementation objectives, what our implementation goals will be, and how we plan on implementing them.

Implementation objectives

We will kickstart this section by listing the following implementation objectives:

- **Implementation objective 1**: Depicting what we believe are fundamental pipeline building blocks, rough workflow stages in the actual pipeline, and where each block is visualized as being connected to the next, implying flow of data and the transformation of data. A state of connection implies a set of workflow stages placed in a sequence.
- **Implementation objective 2**: Core building blocks of the pipeline.
- **Implementation objective 3**: Spark ML Workflow for the breast cancer classification task.
- **Implementation objective 4**: Developing two pipeline stages and assigning an indexer and logit model to each of these stages.
- **Implementation objective 5**: Evaluating the binary classifier's performance.

Next, we get on with implementation objectives 1 and 2.

Implementation objectives 1 and 2

The following diagram depicts a **DataFrame** block that progresses through a transformation process into the **FeatureVector creation** block. A **Feature Vector** and an unindexed label (not shown in the following diagram for simplicity) make up a new (transformed) **DataFrame**. The **FeatureVector creation** block (or stage) is a precursor to **Classifier Model** creation. The last block is a **Prediction** stage where predictions are generated.

This is a succinct description of what is to be implemented in the code later:

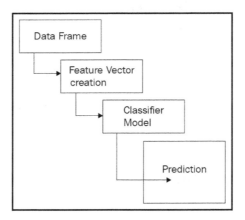

Core building blocks of the pipeline

The preceding diagram makes no mention of splitting the `DataFrame[Feature Vector and Label]` into two parts:

- A training dataset
- A testing dataset, which is input data on which the model is fitted (trained)

These two datasets are represented by a **training** block and a **testing** block in the diagram in the next section instead. Implementation objectives 1 and 2 were laid out in this section. Implementation objective 3 is laid out in the topic that follows.

Implementation objective 3 – Spark ML workflow for the breast cancer classification task

We will start working on implementation objective 3. This forms the basis for our logistic regression pipeline. This pipeline is divided into two functional areas—a training block depicted in the diagram as training, and a testing block depicted as testing.

We filled out the **training** block with four pipeline stages, which are as follows:

- **Loading Data**
- **Feature Extraction**
- **Model Fitting (Training)**
- **Evaluation**

Likewise, the testing block has four stages of its own:

- **Loading Data**
- **Feature Extraction**
- **Prediction**
- **Evaluation**

The two blocks don't appear to be all that different. However, there is more to it than meets the eye. We will now lay out a new ML workflow diagram in terms of the training, testing, and Spark ML components, as follows:

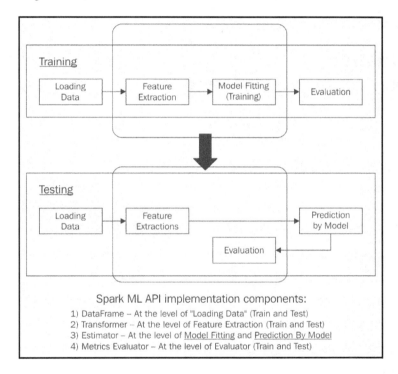

Spark ML workflow for the breast cancer classification task

An arrow from the training block to the testing block indicates a data transformation workflow starting in the training block and proceeding into the testing block.

Our preceding ML workflow diagram is a step forward. It is a precursor of sorts to the actual pipeline, whose implementation details will be laid out in *Implementation objective 4—coding steps for building the indexer and logit machine learning model* section.

At this point, we must note that the implementation critically depends on leveraging the following Spark ML API components:

- **DataFrame**
- **Transformer**
- **Estimator**
- **Metrics Evaluator**

Now, we have enough information to get to the next level that is *Implementation objective 4—coding steps for building the indexer and logit machine learning model* section where we will go through all the motions of building a two-stage pipeline.

Implementation objective 4 – coding steps for building the indexer and logit machine learning model

At the outset, fulfilling implementation objective 5 requires that we import the following. Create an empty Scala file in the following package and add the following imports in.

After all the imports are in, create a new Scala object called `BreastCancerLrPipeline` and have this class extend from the `WisconsinWrapper` trait:

```
package com.packt.modern.chapter2

import com.packt.modern.chapter2.WisconsinWrapper
import org.apache.spark.ml.classification.LogisticRegression
import org.apache.spark.ml.evaluation.{BinaryClassificationEvaluator,
MulticlassClassificationEvaluator}
import org.apache.spark.ml.{Pipeline, PipelineStage}
import org.apache.spark.mllib.evaluation.BinaryClassificationMetrics
import org.apache.spark.rdd.RDD
import org.apache.spark.sql.{DataFrame, Row}
```

The `WisconsinWrapper` trait contains code that creates a `SparkSession` for us. It also contains a method that takes in the dataset and creates a `DataFrame` from it. The imports also bring in the following, which is important for implementation tasks. For example, you will note that they are necessary for importing the Spark ML API for `LogisticRegression`, which is one of the algorithms used in binary classification. We needed APIs to compute binary classification metrics. That said, we will move on to the next task, where we talk more about our trait, `WisconsinWrapper`.

Extending our pipeline object with the WisconsinWrapper trait

WisconsionWrapper contains a trait called WisconsinWrapper, which contains the following code components:

- A SparkSession called lazy val
- A val representing the path to the breast cancer dataset, bcw.csv (this file is available in the root of the project folder)
- A tuple holding string representations of columns for "features" and "label" in DataFrame, which we will create shortly
- A method to build DataFrame. It takes in the fully qualified path to the dataset path with a method named buildDataFrame()

The Wrapper trait is depicted as follows, and includes all four code components:

```
trait WisconsinWrapper {

  //The entry point to programming Spark with the Dataset and DataFrame API.
  //This is the SparkSession

  lazy val session: SparkSession = {
    SparkSession
      .builder().getOrCreate()
  }


  val dataSetPath = "<<path to the folder containing the breast cancer csv file"

  val bcwFeatures_IndexedLabel = ("features","bcw-diagnoses-column", "label")

  /**
    *
    * @return a Dataframe with two columns. `features` contains the feature `Vector`s and `bcw-diagnoses-column`
    *         contains known values for diagnoses
    */

  def buildDataFrame(dataSet: String): DataFrame = {
    def getRows2: Array[(org.apache.spark.ml.linalg.Vector, String)] = {

    }
    //Create a dataframe by transforming an Array of a tuple of Feature Vectors and the Label

    val dataFrame = session.createDataFrame(getRows2).toDF(bcwFeatures_IndexedLabel._1, bcwFeatures_IndexedLabel._2)
    val bcFrameCached = dataFrame.cache
    bcFrameCached
    //dataFrame
  }
```

WisconsinWrapper

Readers may grab a copy of the `WisconsinWrapper` trait and paste this file into their SBT project. The SBT project is available under the `ModernScalaProjects_Code` folder.

Now, create a declaration for `object BreastCancerLrPipeline` as follows:

```
object BreastCancerLrPipeline extends WisconsinWrapper { }
```

We now have an empty `object` body, so we will add in an `import` for the `StringIndexer`.

Importing the StringIndexer algorithm and using it

We need the `StringIndexer` algorithm to index values in the `"label"` column. That is why `StringIndexer` is imported:

```
import org.apache.spark.ml.feature.StringIndexer
```

`StringIndexer` is an algorithm that can take a list of hyperparameters. Two such parameters are set as follows:

```
val indexer = new
StringIndexer().setInputCol(bcwFeatures_IndexedLabel._2).setOutputCol(bcwFe
atures_IndexedLabel._3)
```

We have created an `indexer` `StringIndexer` algorithm instance. The next step will be to fit the model on a new generic `DataFrame` that we will build using the `buildDataFrame` method:

```
val indexerModel = indexer.fit(dataSet)
val indexedDataFrame = indexerModel.transform(dataSet)
```

The resulting `StringIndexerModel` is transformed:

```
indexedDataFrame.show
```

The `show` method now displays the first 20 rows of the `DataFrame`:

```
+--------------------------+----------------------+-----+
|                  features|bcw-diagnoses-column |label|
+--------------------------+----------------------+-----+
|[5.0,1.0,1.0,1.0,...|                     2|  0.0|
|[5.0,4.0,4.0,5.0,...|                     2|  0.0|
|[3.0,1.0,1.0,1.0,...|                     2|  0.0|
|[6.0,8.0,8.0,1.0,...|                     2|  0.0|
|[4.0,1.0,1.0,3.0,...|                     2|  0.0|
|[8.0,10.0,10.0,8....|                     4|  1.0|
|[1.0,1.0,1.0,1.0,...|                     2|  0.0|
|[2.0,1.0,2.0,1.0,...|                     2|  0.0|
|[2.0,1.0,1.0,1.0,...|                     2|  0.0|
|[4.0,2.0,1.0,1.0,...|                     2|  0.0|
|[1.0,1.0,1.0,1.0,...|                     2|  0.0|
|[2.0,1.0,1.0,1.0,...|                     2|  0.0|
|[5.0,3.0,3.0,3.0,...|                     4|  1.0|
|[1.0,1.0,1.0,1.0,...|                     2|  0.0|
|[8.0,7.0,5.0,10.0...|                     4|  1.0|
|[7.0,4.0,6.0,4.0,...|                     4|  1.0|
|[4.0,1.0,1.0,1.0,...|                     2|  0.0|
|[4.0,1.0,1.0,1.0,...|                     2|  0.0|
|[10.0,7.0,7.0,6.0...|                     4|  1.0|
|[6.0,1.0,1.0,1.0,...|                     2|  0.0|
+--------------------------+----------------------+-----+
only showing top 20 rows
```

Result of the fit and transform of StringIndexer

There is a reason for the `"features"` column to coexist with `"bcw-diagnoses-column"`. The `"features"` that are present in the feature vector are attributes that are closely tied to the diagnosis of a certain tissue sample. `"bcw-diagnoses-column"` represents the class column in the original dataset. This is a binary classification problem where the category cannot have a numerical measure, so we must artificially assign a value of either 0 or 1. In this case, 2 and 4 are standing in for benign and malignant, respectively. The `"label"` column beside the `"features"` column bears two kinds of values:

- 0.0
- 1.0

The `StringIndexer` indexed values in the `"bcw-diagnoses-column"` from the original `DataFrame` are produced by the `buildDataFrame` method and are assigned values of 0.0 to 2.0 and 1.0 to 4.0, respectively.

Next, we will venture deeper into ML territory. As with any ML exercise, it is common to split a dataset into a training set and testing set. That is exactly what we will do in the next coding step.

Splitting the DataFrame into training and test datasets

We will split our `DataFrame` in two:

- Training set—75%
- Testing set—25%

The training set is used to train (fit) the model, and the remaining 25% will be put to use for testing:

```
val splitDataSet:
Array[org.apache.spark.sql.Dataset[org.apache.spark.sql.Row]] =
indexedDataFrame.randomSplit(Array(0.75, 0.25), 98765L)

//create two vals to hold TrainingData and TestingData respectively
val trainDataFrame = splitDataSet(0)
val testDataFrame = splitDataSet(1)
```

To verify that our split went well, we will run the `count` method on both the `trainDataFrame` and `testDataFrame` dataframes.
We will leave this as an exercise to the reader. Next, we will move on to creating a `LogisticRegression` classifier model and passing parameters into it.

Creating a LogisticRegression classifier and setting hyperparameters on it

The `LogisticRegression` classifier can take hyperparameters, which we will set by using the appropriate setter methods from the `LogisticRegression` API. Since Spark ML has support for elastic net regularization, we will pass this as a parameter first. We also want two additional parameters:

- The `"features"` column
- An indexed `"label"` column

```
val logitModel = new LogisticRegression() .setElasticNetParam(0.75)
.setFamily("auto") .setFeaturesCol(bcwFeatures_IndexedLabel._1)
.setLabelCol(bcwFeatures_IndexedLabel._3) .fit(trainDataSet)
```

What we just did was start the training process by creating an LR classifier model. We are now in a position to train our LR model on the training dataset by making an association between input feature measurements and their labeled output. To recap, we passed in a `"features"` column, a `"label"` column, and an elastic net coefficient.

Next, we will execute our model with a transformation operation and testing dataset data.

Running the LR model on the test dataset

We will now invoke the `transform` method on our `LogisticRegression` model:

```
//Next run the model on the test dataset and obtain predictions
val testDataPredictions = logitModel.transform(testDataSet)
```

The `transform` method invocation returns a new `DataFrame`. Not only that, that model transformation step resulted in three new columns:

- `rawPrediction`
- `probability`
- `predictions`

Next, we will display the first 25 rows of this `DataFrame`:

```
testDataPredictions.show(25)
```

See the following table to look at the displayed predictions, which were made by running our LR models on the test dataset:

```
+-----------------+---------------------+-----+--------------------+--------------------+----------+
|         features|bcw-diagnoses-column|label|       rawPrediction|         probability|prediction|
+-----------------+---------------------+-----+--------------------+--------------------+----------+
|[1.0,1.0,1.0,1.0,...|                   2| 0.0|[7.43601098731156...|[0.99941071489731...|       0.0|
|[1.0,1.0,1.0,1.0,...|                   2| 0.0|[7.08090265549135...|[0.99915969304957...|       0.0|
|[1.0,1.0,1.0,1.0,...|                   2| 0.0|[7.02267364088016...|[0.99910935503926...|       0.0|
|[1.0,1.0,1.0,1.0,...|                   2| 0.0|[7.41835610800472...|[0.99940022505386...|       0.0|
|[1.0,1.0,1.0,1.0,...|                   2| 0.0|[7.41835610800472...|[0.99940022505386...|       0.0|
|[1.0,1.0,1.0,1.0,...|                   2| 0.0|[7.00501876157331...|[0.99909350556530...|       0.0|
|[1.0,1.0,1.0,1.0,...|                   2| 0.0|[7.00501876157331...|[0.99909350556530...|       0.0|
|[1.0,1.0,1.0,1.0,...|                   2| 0.0|[7.00501876157331...|[0.99909350556530...|       0.0|
|[1.0,1.0,1.0,1.0,...|                   2| 0.0|[7.00501876157331...|[0.99909350556530...|       0.0|
|[1.0,1.0,1.0,1.0,...|                   2| 0.0|[7.00501876157331...|[0.99909350556530...|       0.0|
|[1.0,1.0,1.0,1.0,...|                   2| 0.0|[6.59168141514191...|[0.99863014749668...|       0.0|
|[1.0,1.0,1.0,1.0,...|                   2| 0.0|[6.59168141514191...|[0.99863014749668...|       0.0|
|[1.0,1.0,1.0,1.0,...|                   2| 0.0|[6.59168141514191...|[0.99863014749668...|       0.0|
|[1.0,1.0,1.0,1.0,...|                   2| 0.0|[6.59168141514191...|[0.99863014749668...|       0.0|
|[1.0,1.0,1.0,1.0,...|                   2| 0.0|[6.59168141514191...|[0.99863014749668...|       0.0|
|[1.0,1.0,1.0,1.0,...|                   2| 0.0|[6.59168141514191...|[0.99863014749668...|       0.0|
|[1.0,1.0,1.0,1.0,...|                   2| 0.0|[6.97383168999539...|[0.99906481605134...|       0.0|
|[1.0,1.0,1.0,1.0,...|                   2| 0.0|[5.70263257912325...|[0.99667393112928...|       0.0|
|[1.0,1.0,1.0,1.0,...|                   2| 0.0|[6.08478285397673...|[0.99772791535642...|       0.0|
|[1.0,1.0,1.0,1.0,...|                   2| 0.0|[5.6402584359674,...|[0.99646062136127...|       0.0|
|[1.0,1.0,1.0,1.0,...|                   2| 0.0|[7.40070122869787...|[0.99938954859514...|       0.0|
|[1.0,1.0,1.0,1.0,...|                   2| 0.0|[6.49399751337237...|[0.99848979346810...|       0.0|
|[1.0,1.0,1.0,2.0,...|                   2| 0.0|[3.01813679889347...|[0.95338679396620...|       0.0|
+-----------------+---------------------+-----+--------------------+--------------------+----------+
only showing top 25 rows
```

Three new columns resulting from model transformation

Spark's pipeline API provides us with the necessary tools to help us build a pipeline. A pipeline is a workflow and consists of a sequence of stages that we call pipeline stages. As we shall see later, each of these stages is executed in order.

That being said, we will now get on with the next order of business—creating a data pipeline with the following stages:

- A logit model
- An indexer

Building a breast cancer pipeline with two stages

Create the pipeline and add two stages to it as follows:

```
//Start building a Pipeline that has 2 stages, an Indexer and a Classifier
val wbcPipeline = new Pipeline().setStages(
                                Array[PipelineStage](indexer) ++
Array[PipelineStage](logitModel)
                                )
```

Next, let's do something with our pipeline. We can do the following things right away:

- Train the pipeline with the training dataset
- Run a `transform` operation with the test set data on our derived `pipelineModel`:

```
val pipelineModel = wbcPipeline.fit(trainDataSet)
```

Next, we will make predictions by running a `transform` operation on the `pipelineModel` with the testing dataset:

```
val predictions = pipelineModel.transform(testDataSet)
```

The next step focuses on obtaining quantifiable measures. These are key performance indicators, metrics that with facts and figures assess how each one of our algorithms fared. How do they stack up with respect to one another? What graphical evaluation tools are available that help us assess the performance of a certain algorithm contributing to a particular binary classification? To understand what it takes to perform this evaluation, we might want to ask the following question first: how close is the predicted value of a certain breast cancer sample to a predetermined label?

Implementation objective 5 – evaluating the binary classifier's performance

This section is all about obtaining evaluations, metrics, and supporting Spark ML APIs. In this section, we will go into depth on the importance of the evaluation step regarding quantifiable measures of effectiveness, as follows:

- Our breast cancer classification task is a supervised learning classification problem. In such a problem, there's a so-called **true output**, and a classifier or ML model generated prediction output for each individual feature measurement or data point in our breast cancer dataset.

- We have now turned our attention to evaluating the performance of our binary classification algorithm by deriving certain metrics. That said, the question is this: is pure accuracy enough to gauge the correctness of our classifier's evaluation effort? Here, pure accuracy is trying to simply tell whether the prediction was correct or not. Okay, what is a better method? We can employ a binary classification evaluator to evaluate the correctness and hence have a measure of the performance regarding this kind of accuracy.

- Circling back to the same topic of pure accuracy, the question to ask again is this: is this a good enough metric? It turns out that pure accuracy is not a great metric, because it does not take into account the type of error.

- For the aforementioned reason, we will derive better metrics, such as the **area under ROC curve (AUC)** and the **area under the precision recall curve (AUPCR)**. We will employ Spark's `BinaryClassificationMetrics` to compute such metrics for us.

Next, we will get on with the implementation part of the metric derivation process. First, we will create a `BinaryClassificationEvaluator`. We will reiterate this evaluator and evaluate predictions with a kind of metric or score that we will call pure accuracy:

```
val modelOutputAccuracy: Double = new BinaryClassificationEvaluator()
.setLabelCol("label") .setMetricName("areaUnderROC") //Area under Receiver
Operating Characteristic Curve .setRawPredictionCol("prediction")
.setRawPredictionCol("rawPrediction")
.evaluate(testDataPredictions)
```

We just computed a so-called pure accuracy score that we called `modelOutputAccuracy` in the preceding line of code. As an exercise, readers are invited to determine their pure accuracy score. The question they could pose is this: is this score useful? Is it a naive score?

With that accomplished, we will now turn our attention to the next task at hand, deriving a new dataframe by running a `select` operation on our predictions `DataFrame`:

```
val predAndLabelsDFrame:DataFrame = predictions.select("prediction",
"label")
println("Validated TestSet Results Dataset is:  " +
validatedTestResultsDataset.take(10))
```

We are not done yet. We will convert our `"predictions"` and `"label"` `DataFrame` that we derived in the preceding code to an `RDD[Double, Double]`:

```
val validatedRDD2: RDD[(Double, Double)] = predictionAndLabels.rdd.collect
{ case Row(predictionValue: Double, labelValue: Double) =>
(predictionValue,labelValue)
}
```

The RDD is now at hand. But why are we doing this? The answer is this: we talked about deriving better, meaningful, and not naive metric scores. We will now create a `BinaryClassificationMetrics` instance that we will call `classifierMetrics`:

```
val classifierMetrics = new BinaryClassificationMetrics(validatedRDD2)
```

`BinaryClassificationMetrics` provides us with tools to derive meaningful evaluation metrics for our breast cancer binary classification task. At its core, binary classification is an ML approach to classifying new, unclassified, incoming data under either of two mutually exclusive categories. For example, our classifier classified a breast cancer sample as either benign or malignant, but not both, of course. More specifically, the breast cancer binary classifier pipeline predicted the probability of a target breast cancer sample belonging to one of two outcomes, either benign or malignant. This looks like a straightforward yes or no-type prediction.

Sure, our model performed and did the heavy lifting. However, we want to put its performance to the test. To do that, we need numeric metrics that, if properly thought through and computed, will tell us the model's performance story in ways that are meaningful.

What are those measures and when do they assume relevance? When an experimental analysis unit is balanced—the number of breast cancer samples like our breast cancer dataset—the following measures assume relevance:

- **True Positive Rate (TPR)**: This is a ratio of the **true positives** (abbreviated as **TPs**) in the predicted output to the **false negatives** (abbreviated as **FNs**). Mathematically, it is represented as follows: $TPR = TPs / (TPs + FNs)$. TPR is known by the terms **Hit Rate, Recall**, or **Sensitivity**.
- **False Positive Rate (FPR)**: Mathematically, it is represented as $FPR = 1 - (TNs / (TNs + FPs))$, where **TNs** is a stand-in for **true negatives** and **FPs**, which is a stand-in for **false positives**.
- Before we proceed any further, some explanations are in order for TPs, TNs, FNs, and FPs:
    - True positives point to those predictions that turn out to be truly malignant
    - True negatives point to those predictions that turn out to be truly benign
    - False negatives point to those breast cancer samples that were wrongly labeled benign
    - False positives point to those breast cancer samples that were wrongly labeled malignant

- **Receiver Operating Characteristic (ROC) curve**: The area under this curve is a measure of binary classification performance. This curve is a graphical plot of FPR on the x axis and TPR on the y axis. A typical plot is shown later.
- **The area under the Precision-Recall (PR) curve**: This is a graphical plot of precision on the y axis and accuracy on the x axis. To plot the curve, we need computed (precision value, accuracy value) pairs. To compute these values, the following mathematical equations for accuracy and precision are applied as follows: Precision $= TPs / (TPs + FPs)$; Accuracy $= TPs / (TPs + FNs)$. The ROC curve is shown later, followed by the PR curve.

Both the ROC and PR curves represent binary classifier performance. How so? The area under the ROC curve becomes a measure of the binary classifier's performance. If a curve plotted for a particular algorithm snakes higher up to the top-right reading from left to right (the greater area under it), it has a lower **false positive rate**, making it a better classifier than a curve for a different algorithm that has a higher **false positive rate**. This is useful, though not necessarily the best metric. A typical ROC curve is shown as follows:

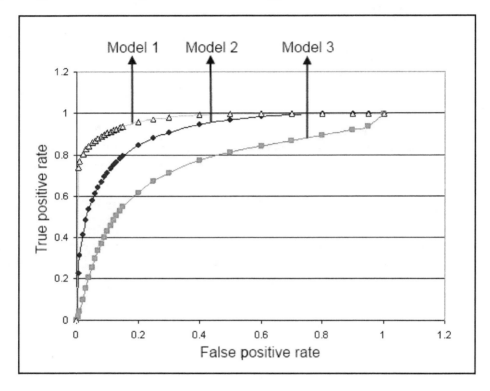

A typical ROC curve

The next metric that is worth mentioning is the so-called precision-recall curve or PR curve for short. This curve involves the computation of two separate metrics, precision and recall.

A PR curve is plotted with accuracy on the *x* axis and precision on the *y* axis. In this case, a particular algorithm fared better than others in its binary classification task if its curve snaked higher up towards the top-right. There are more TPs and considerably fewer FNs. This indicates a better classification.

This completes our discussion on binary classifier metrics, and their computation marks an important milestone regarding the breast cancer data analysis initiative.

Indeed, if the logit model we built performed well, the area under the ROC discriminant curve should represent a meaningful measure of prediction performance:

```
val accuracyMetrics = (classifierMetrics.areaUnderROC(),
classifierMetrics.areaUnderPR())

//Area under ROC
val aUROC = accuracyMetrics._1
println(s"Area under Receiver Operating Characteristic (ROC) curve:
${aUROC} ")
val aPR = accuracyMetrics._2
println(s"Area under Precision Recall (PR) curve: ${aPR} ")
```

The metrics are ready. Here are the results. Running the pipeline should generate the following metrics:

```
Area under Receiver Operating Characteristic (ROC) curve: 0.958521384053299
Area under Precision Recall (PR) curve: 0.9447563927932
```

That concludes our breast cancer classification task. In the previous section, on a Random Forests breast cancer pipeline, we showed you how to deploy your pipeline application into Spark. Likewise, in a similar fashion, we can deploy our logistic regression pipeline.

Summary

In this chapter, we learned how to implement a binary classification task using two approaches such as, an ML pipeline using the Random Forest algorithm and an secondly using the logistic regression method.

Both pipelines combined several stages of data analysis into one workflow. In both pipelines, we calculated metrics to give us an estimate of how well our classifier performed. Early on in our data analysis task, we introduced a data preprocessing step to get rid of rows that were missing attribute values that were filled in by a placeholder, ?. With 16 rows of unavailable attribute values eliminated and 683 rows with attribute values still available, we constructed a new DataFrame.

In each pipeline, we also created training, training, and validation datasets, followed by a training phase where we fit the models on training data. As with every ML task, the classifier may learn by rotating the training set details, a preponderant phenomenon called overfitting. We got around this problem by arriving at a reduced but optimal number of attributes. We did this by fitting our classifier models with various combinations of attributes.

In the next chapter, we will move our development efforts away from a local `spark-shell`. This time, we will take advantage of a Zeppelin Notebook running inside a **Hortonworks Development Platform (HDP)** Sandbox Virtual Machine.

To conclude this chapter, we will move on to the last section where we pose a set of questions to the reader.

Questions

We will now list a set of questions to test your knowledge of what you have learned so far:

- What do you understand by logistical regression? Why is it important?
- How does logistical regression differ from linear regression?
- Name one powerful feature of `BinaryClassifier`.
- What are the feature variables in relation to the breast cancer dataset?

The breast cancer dataset problem is a classification task that can be approached with other machine learning algorithms as well. Prominent among other techniques are **Support Vector Machine (SVM)**, **k-nearest neighbor**, and **decision trees**. When you run the pipelines developed in this chapter, compare the time it took to build a model in each case and how many of the input rows of the dataset were classified correctly by each algorithm.

This concludes this chapter. The next chapter implements a new kind of pipeline, which is a stock prediction task pipeline. We shall see how we can use Spark to work on larger datasets. Stock price prediction is not an easy problem to solve. How we shall tackle this is the subject of the next chapter.

Stock Price Predictions 3

The goal of this chapter is to predict the values of near-or long-term equity prices by using **machine learning** (**ML**). From an investor's perspective, investments (in equity) across several companies are stocks, while such investments in an individual company are shares. Most investors lean on a long-term investment strategy for the best returns. Investment analysts employ mathematical stock analysis models to help predict future stock prices or price movements in the long term. Such models factor in past equity prices and other indicators to perform a company's financial health evaluation.

The overarching learning objective of this chapter is to implement a Scala solution that will predict stock market prices. Starting from the stock price prediction dataset, we will use the Spark ML library's ML APIs to build a stock price prediction pipeline.

Here is the dataset we will refer to:

- Daily News for Stock Market Prediction | Kaggle.
- In-text: (Kaggle.com, 2018) Daily News for Stock Market Prediction.
- Kaggle. [online] Available at: https://www.kaggle.com/aaron7sun/stocknews [Accessed 27 Jul. 2018].

The following list is a section-wise breakdown of the individual learning outcomes in this chapter:

- Stock price binary classification problem
- Getting started
- Implementation objective

Stock price binary classification problem

Stock prices have a tendency to go up and down. We want to Spark ML and a Spark time-series library to explore historical stock price data going back a couple years and come up numbers like the average closing price. We also want our stock price prediction model to forecast what the stock price will be over the timeframe of a few days.

This chapter presents an ML methodology to reduce the complexity associated with stock price prediction. We will obtain a smaller set of optimal financial indicators by feature selection and employ a Random Forest algorithm to build a price prediction pipeline.

We must first download the dataset from the `ModernScalaProjects_Code` folder.

Stock price prediction dataset at a glance

We will use data from two sources:

- **Reddit worldnews**
- **Dow Jones Industrial Average (DJIA)**

The *Getting started* section that follows has two clear goals:

- Moving our development environment into a virtual appliance from a previous local Spark shell-centered development environment. This naturally implies setting up prerequisite resources.
- Attaining the preceding goal also implies being able to spin up a brand new Spark cluster, running inside the virtual appliance.

Getting started

In order to address the goals of this section, we will compile a resource list—a list of prerequisite software to be set up—before taking a shot at the first stated goal of setting up the **Hortonworks Development Platform** (HDP) Sandbox, a so-called virtual appliance from the Hortonworks organization. The virtual appliance overview section is helpful regarding this.

At its core, the HDP Sandbox is a robust data pipeline development environment. This appliance and its supporting ecosystem, like the underlying OS and the virtual machine configuration settings, make up the core of the development infrastructure.

The following is the resource list—the prerequisite software—that must be set or verified before proceeding further:

- A 64-bit host machine with support for hardware virtualization. To check for processor and motherboard support for virtualization, download and run a small utility called SecurAble. BIOS should be enabled or set to support virtualization.
- Host OS Windows 7, 8, or 10, macOS.
- Compatible browsers such as Internet Explorer 9, stable versions of Mozilla Firefox, Google Chrome, or Opera.
- At least 16 GB of RAM on the host machine.
- Supported virtualization applications need to be installed, such as Oracle VirtualBox Version 5.1 or above (this is our preferred virtualization application) or VMWare Fusion.
- The HDP Sandbox download file. This file is delivered as a virtual appliance with the **Open Virtualization Format Archive** (**OVA**) file.

In the next section, we will review the prerequisites on our resources list.

Support for hardware virtualization

Grab a copy of SecurAble from the `ModernScalaProjects_Code` folder. SecurAble is a small program that is able to tell you the following about your machine's processor:

- Confirm the presence or absence of 64-bit instructions on your host machine processor
- Whether there is hardware support for virtualization

To determine the preceding prerequisites, SecurAble will not make any changes to your machine. On running the SecurAble application file, it will present a screen that should like the following screenshot:

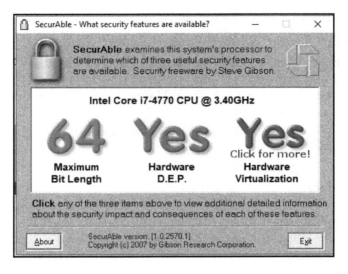

Screenshot of screen on running the SecurAble application file

Clicking on **64 Maximum Bit Length** makes SecurAble return the presence or absence of 64-bit processing, as shown in the following screenshot:

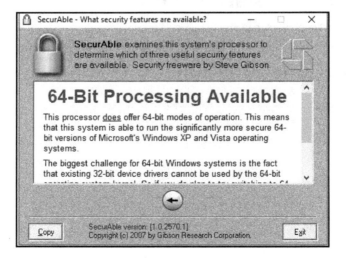

Screenshot of window displaying the presence or absence of 64-bit processing

The chipset on my Windows 64-bit machine is confirmed as offering a 64-bit mode of operation. Next, clicking on **Yes Hardware Virtualization** makes SecurAble report back that my processor does offer hardware support for virtualization, as shown in the following screenshot:

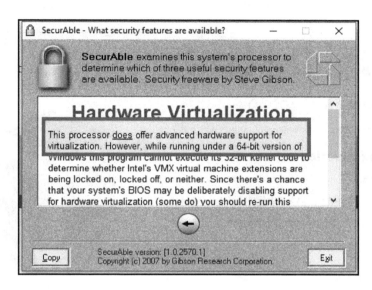

Screenshot of window displaying the hardware support for virtualization on SecurAble

If SecurAble reports back with the exact same results on your machine, it is likely that you have a host machine that can support Oracle VirtualBox. Note that at the BIOS level, support for virtualization is likely already set. If that is not the case, enable it. Note that SecurAble won't be able to report on BIOS support for the virtualization feature.

Ensure that the preceding prerequisites are satisfied before moving further. Next, take up prerequisite which is regarding installing a supported virtualization application that is able to host a virtual appliance.

Installing the supported virtualization application

The following are the steps to install the virtualization application:

1. Download the latest VirtualBox binaries from the Oracle VirtualBox website:

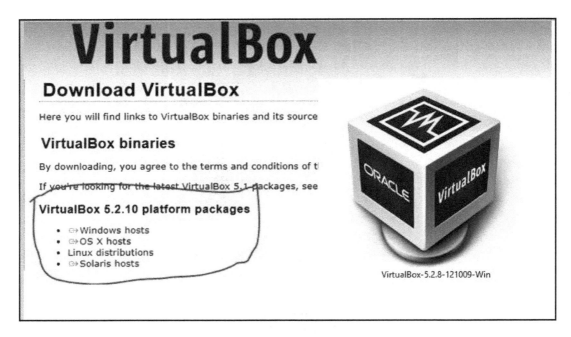

Screenshot of latest VirtualBox binaries

2. Double-click on the Oracle VirtualBox binary. The setup welcome screen presents itself as follows:

Screenshot of the setup window

3. Click **Next** on the welcome screen. In the new screen that presents itself, select where you want VirtualBox to be installed:

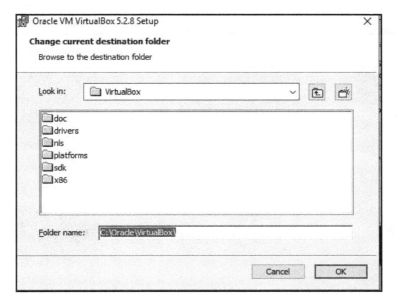

Screenshot of setup steps to place the folder

4. Click **OK** to move on to the **Ready to Install** screen:

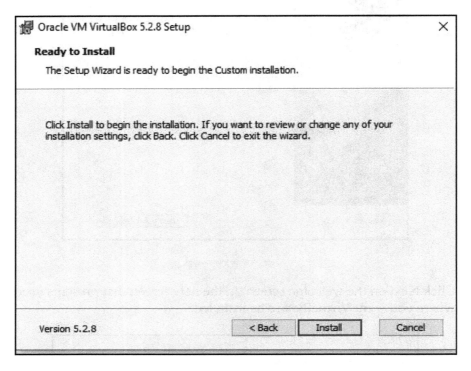

Screenshot of Ready for installation screen

5. Click **Install** and complete any self-explanatory steps needed to complete the installation. Once this process is complete, place a shortcut on your taskbar or on the desktop. Now, launch the VirtualBox application, as follows:

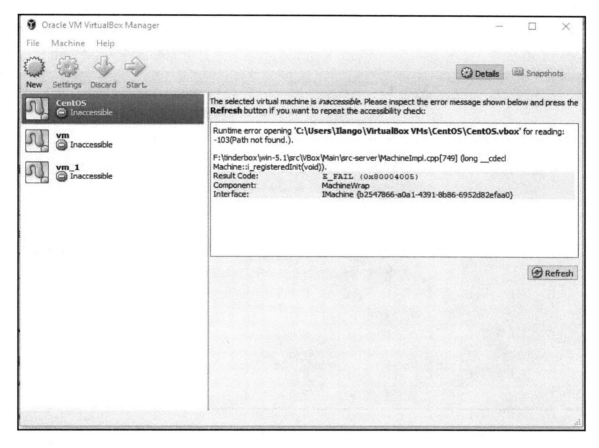

Screenshot of Ready for launch of VirtualBox application

You may optionally remove the inaccessible machines vm, vm_1, and CentOS as follows:

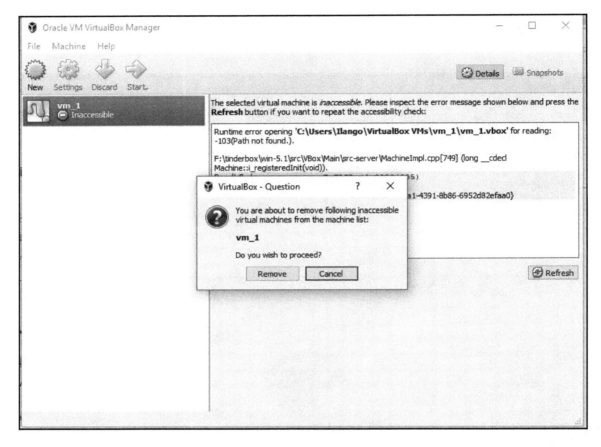

Screenshot displaying how to remove the inaccessible machines

6. Next, deselect the **Auto Capture Keyboard** option under **File | Preferences... | Input**:

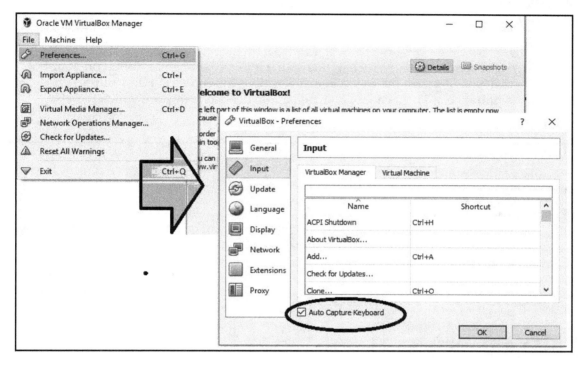

Screenshot of final steps to set the virtual machine

The virtual machine is now all set. In the next step, we will download and import the Sandbox into it.

Downloading the HDP Sandbox and importing it

The following are the steps to download the HDP Sandbox:

1. Head over to `https://hortonworks.com/downloads/#sandbox` and download the Hortonworks Sandbox virtual appliance file.

2. Move the Sandbox virtual appliance file into a convenient location on your host machine. Perform the following click actions in sequence: **File | Import Appliance....** Then, choose a virtual appliance file to import, which thereby imports the respective disk image:

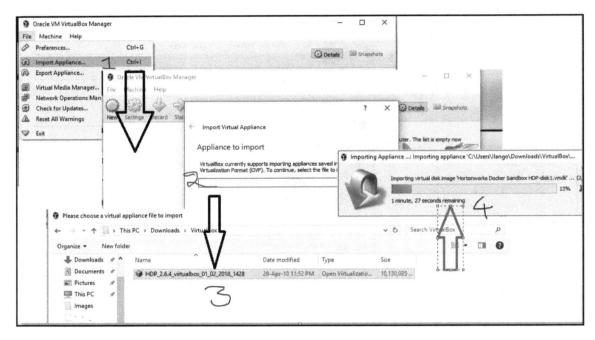

Steps to be performed to import the disk image

3. Next, let's tweak **Appliance settings** in the **Appliance settings** screen. Make sure you increase the available **RAM** to at least `10000  MB`. Leave the other default settings intact and click **Import**:

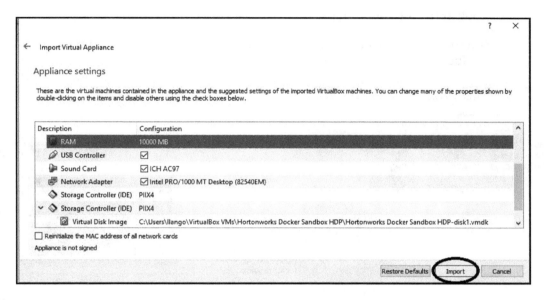

Screenshot to import the virtual appliance into Oracle VirtualBox

The virtual appliance has now been imported into Oracle VirtualBox. The following section offers a brief overview of the Hortonworks Sandbox virtual appliance.

Hortonworks Sandbox virtual appliance overview

The Hortonworks Sandbox is a virtual machine, or virtual appliance, which is delivered as a file with an `.ova` or `.ovf` extension. It appears as a bare machine to the host OS, and has the following components:

- A guest operating system that is treated as an application by the underlying host operating system
- The virtual appliance file we want is an `.ova` file, which is available in the `ModernScalaProjects_Code` folder under the virtual machines folder
- Applications that run in the guest OS

All that being said, we are done setting up prerequisites. Let's run the virtual machine for the first time.

Turning on the virtual machine and powering up the Sandbox

Let's take a look at the following steps:

1. Run the Oracle VirtualBox startup icon. The startup screen with a powered-off Sandbox appears as follows:

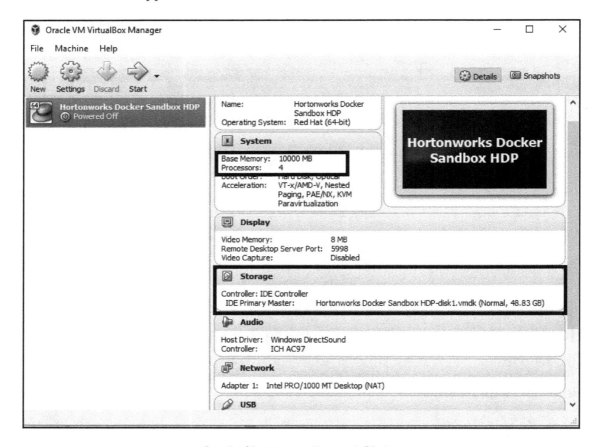

Screenshot of the startup screen with a powered-off Sandbox

The startup screen displays the updated Hortonworks Sandbox virtual appliance with its updated configuration. For example, our **Base Memory** is now **10000** MB.

2. Next, right-click on the Sandbox and click **Start | Normal Start**:

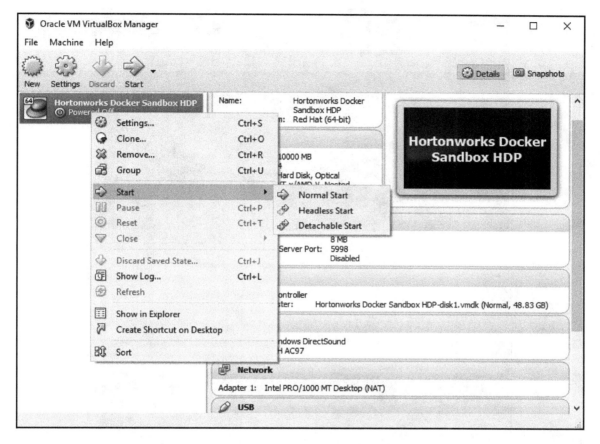

Screenshot of steps to be performed to get started

If everything went well, you should see the following **Hortonworks Docker Sandbox HDP [Running]** screen:

Screenshot of Hortonworks Docker Sandbox HDP [Running]

3. We want to log in to the Sandbox. *Alt + F5* takes you to the `sandbox-host login` screen as follows:

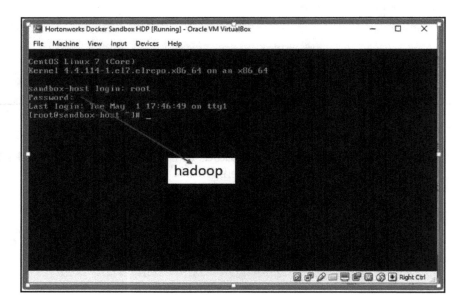

Screenshot displaying how to log in to the Sandbox

Sign in as `root` with a `Password` of `hadoop`.

4. Edit the `hosts` file, and map `127.0.0.1` to `sandbox-hdp.hortonworks.com`. On a Windows (host) machine, this is located under `C:\Windows\System32\drivers\etc`:

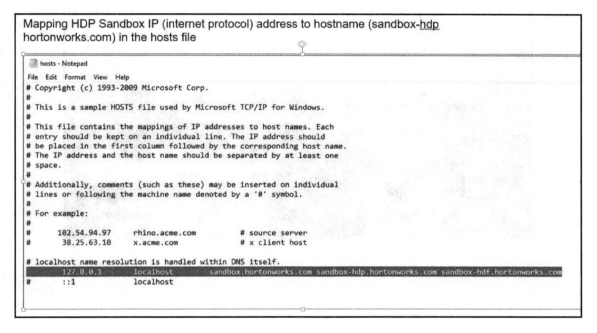

Screenshot displaying editing of host files

5. Save the updated `hosts` file and verify that these changes took effect before loading the URL as `sandbox-hdp.hortonworks.com:8888` in the browser.

6. Next, load the URL as `sandbox-hdp.hortonworks.com:4200` in your browser to launch the Sandbox web client. Change the default password from `hadoop` to something else. Note that the virtual appliance runs a CentOS Linux guest OS:

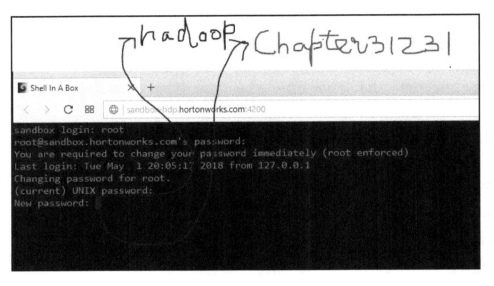

Screenshot to launch the Sandbox web client

In the next section, we will set up an SSH client for transferring files between the Sandbox and your local (host) machine.

Setting up SSH access for data transfer between Sandbox and the host machine

SSH stands for **Secure Shell**. We want to set up the SSH network protocol to establish a remote login and secure file transfers between our host machine and a virtual machine that's running the virtual appliance.

Two steps need to be followed:

- Set up PuTTY, a third-party SSH and Telnet client
- Set up WinSCP, a **Secure File Transfer Protocol** (**SFTP**) client for Windows

Setting up PuTTY, a third-party SSH and Telnet client

Let's take a look at the following installation steps of PuTTY:

1. The PuTTY installer, `putty-64bit-0.70-installer.exe`, is available in the `ModernScalaProjects_Code` folder. You can run it by double-clicking on the installer icon as follows:

putty-64bit-0.70-installer

PuTTY installer icon

2. Choose a destination folder to install PuTTY into and click **Next**:

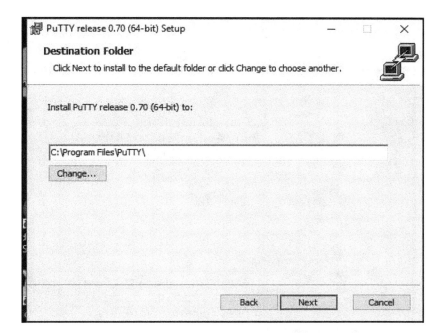

Screenshot to Install PuTTY

3. Select or deselect any product features you want to be installed:

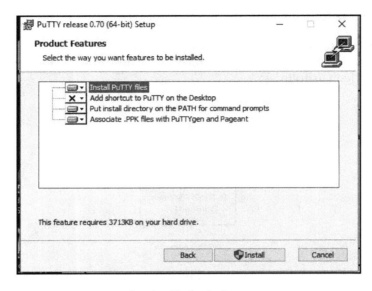

Screenshot of list of product features

4. Next, click **Install**. PuTTY and other supporting utilities will be installed:

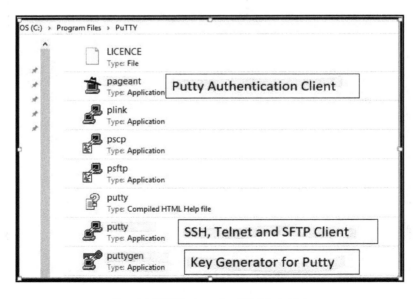

Screenshot of PuTTY and supporting utilities being installed

5. Run PuTTYgen. On the **PuTTY Key Generator** screen, press the **Generate** button and follow the onscreen instructions. Click on the **Save public key** button and save the generated public key into a file called `authorized_keys` in a convenient location, but not before typing in a passphrase:

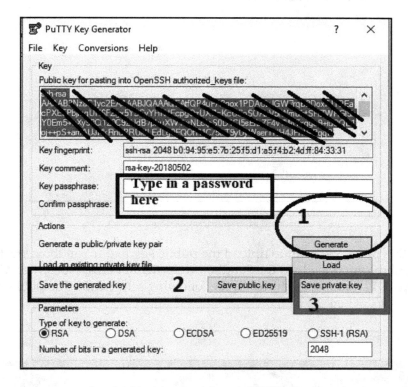

Screenshot of steps to be performed after running PuTTY Key Generator

6. Click on **Save private key**, which is marked by **3** in the preceding screenshot. This will let you save your private key in a convenient location. This could be the same as the public key location, as follows:

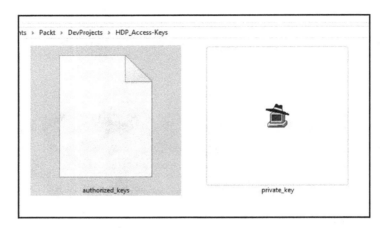

Screenshot of private key being saved in a convenient location

7. At this point, we want to upload the public key to our Sandbox. Start up the Sandbox, and then load the Sandbox web client like we did earlier. Carry out steps **1**, **2**, **3**, and **4**, as shown in the following screenshot. The public key is saved as `authorized_key`:

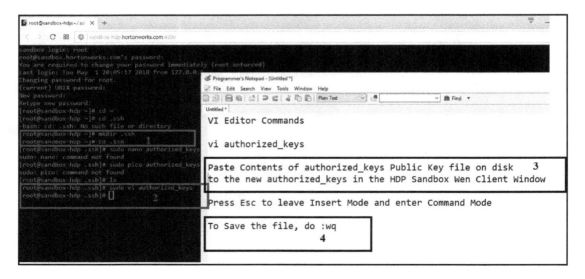

Screenshot displaying the upload of public key to our Sandbox

8. Dismiss PuTTYgen with **File | Exit**.
9. Open PuTTY and click on **Session**. We want to create and save a session. Follow the numbers in the following screenshot to set it up:
    1. Click on **Session** and select **Logging**
    2. Enter **Host Name** as our Sandbox
    3. Enter **Port** as 2222
    4. Then click on button **Save**

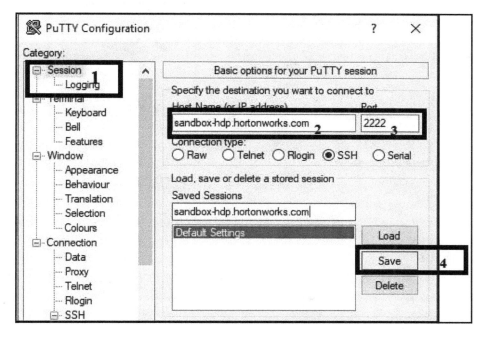

Screenshot displaying the steps to be performed for creating and saving the session

10. Save the session as `sandbox-hdp.hortonworks.com` (saved sessions) by clicking **Save**. Next, click on **Data** under **Connection** and enter the login name of the Sandbox. Do not click **Open** yet:

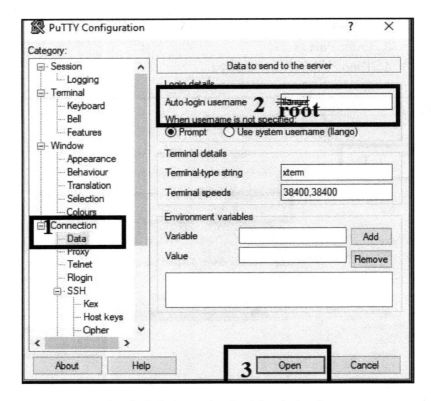

Screenshot showing the steps to be performed after saving the session

11. After entering the **Auto-login username**, click on **Connection | SSH |
Auth | Load the private key** after clicking on **Browse....** Load the private key and
click **Open**. This should establish an SSH connection with the Sandbox:

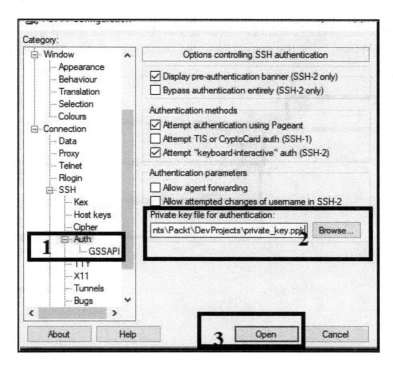

Screenshot of steps to be performed after entering the Auto-login username

Let's recap and summarize the steps we took so far to set up PuTTY, a third-party SSH and
Telnet client, and hence SSH access for data transfer between the Sandbox and the host
machine:

1. Click on **Session**. Enter the hostname under the **Host Name (or IP address)** field
   of the Sandbox virtual appliance and then select the appropriate SSH
   protocol. Moving on, navigate to **Connection | Data** and enter your login name
   for the Sandbox in the auto-login box.
2. Then, navigate to **Connection | SSH | Auth | Load the private key**.
3. Finally, click on **Session**. Load the saved session and click **Save**; this updates the
   session.

WinSCP is a popular graphical SSH client for Windows that makes it easy to transfer files
between the local (host) machine and the Sandbox. Let's set up WinSCP now.

Setting up WinSCP, an SFTP client for Windows

The following steps explain how to set up WinSCP:

1. The WinSCP binary file is available under
   the `ModernScalaProjects_Code` folder. Download it and run it. Once installed,
   launch WinSCP for the very first time. The **Login** screen presents itself as follows:

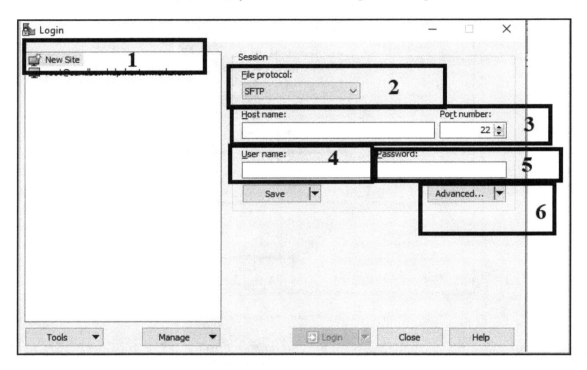

Screenshot of the login screen

Click on **New Site**, making sure that the **File protocol** is **SFTP**, and under **Host name**, you may enter the Sandbox hostname. Change the port from 22 to 2222. You might want to enter `root` under **User name** and the **Password** for the Sandbox WebClient. Next, click **6**, which takes us to the **Advanced Site Settings** screen:

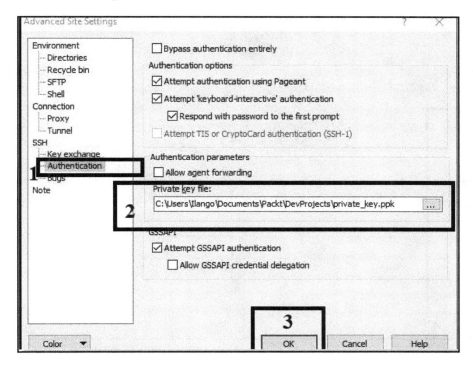

Screenshot of Advanced Site Settings screen

2. In the preceding **Advanced Site Settings** screen, drill down to **Authentication** under **SSH** and load the private key file. Click **OK**.

3. Now, launch WinSCP again. Clicking on **Login** should establish a connection with the Sandbox and you should be able to transfer files back and forth as follows:

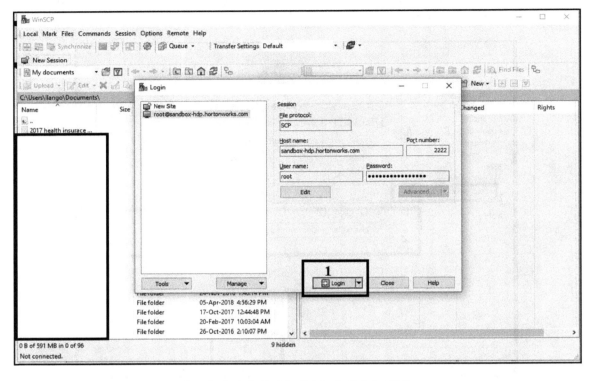

Screenshot showing Sandbox being able to transfer files back and forth

4. After the connection is established, the resulting screen should look as follows:

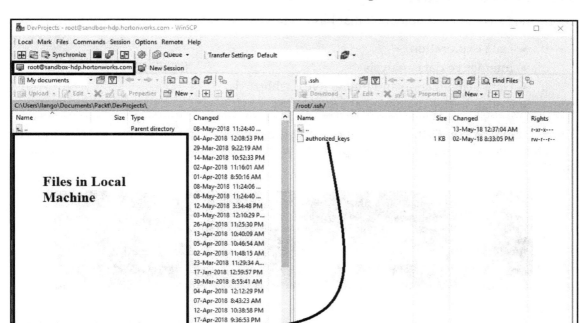

Screenshot of screen after the connection is establiashed

In the next step, we will move on to Sandbox configuration updates.

Updating the default Python required by Zeppelin

The Sandbox boasts a fully-fledged Spark development environment with one notable difference from our previous local Spark development environment: Zeppelin Notebook.

What is Zeppelin?

Zeppelin is a web-based notebook that has the following features:

- Data exploration
- Interactive data analysis
- Data visualization and interactive dashboards
- Collaborative document sharing

Zeppelin depends on Python 2.7 or above, but the Sandbox itself only supports Version 2.6. Therefore, we are going to have to replace 2.6 with 2.7. Before we go any further, let's check our Python version:

Screenshot displaying the python version

That's right! We need to get rid of Python 2.6 with Python 2.7 and bring the Notebook up to date.

The steps to accomplish this are summarized as follows:

- Set up the Anaconda data science environment. You can simply set up a lighter version of Anaconda, which would be Miniconda with Python 2.7. Miniconda brings with it many popular data science packages.
- Set up any packages that do not come packaged with Miniconda. Make sure that you have SciPy, NumPy, Matplotlib, and Pandas. Sometimes, we can simply pass a Spark/Scala `DataFrame` into Python on Pyspark to produce visualizations quickly.

Work through the following steps:

1. The first step is to download the installer for Miniconda and run it as follows:

Screenshot displaying the installer for Miniconda

Go through the installation process. It is straightforward. Once the installation is complete, restart the web client to allow changes to take effect. Now, log back in to the Sandbox with `root` and your secret password.

2. To check whether we do have a new, upgraded Python, issue the `python` command as follows:

Screenshot displaying how to issue the Python command

Voila! We have a new Python version: 2.7.14.

In the next section, we will update the Zeppelin instance using curl.

Updating our Zeppelin instance

Following steps need to be performed to update the Zeppelin instance:

- Install curl, if not installed already
- Update your Zeppelin instance with the latest and greatest notebooks from Hortonworks

Please follow the steps to install curl:

1. Run the `curl --help` command:

```
[root@sandbox-hdp ~]# curl -V/ --version
sh2/1.4.2.7 (x86_64-redhat-linux-gnu) libcurl/7.19.7 NSS/3.27.1 zlib/1.2.3 libidn/1.18 libs
Protocols: tftp ftp telnet dict ldap ldaps http file https ftps scp sftp

Features: GSS-Negotiate IDN IPv6 Largefile NTLM SSL libz
[root@sandbox-hdp ~]# curl -V/ --version
sh2/1.4.2.7 (x86_64-redhat-linux-gnu) libcurl/7.19.7 NSS/3.27.1 zlib/1.2.3 libidn/1.18 libs
Protocols: tftp ftp telnet dict ldap ldaps http file https ftps scp sftp

Features: GSS-Negotiate IDN IPv6 Largefile NTLM SSL libz
[root@sandbox-hdp ~]# 
```

Screenshot displaying how to run the curl --help command

2. The `curl --help` command confirms that we have curl already installed. Let's try updating Zeppelin now:

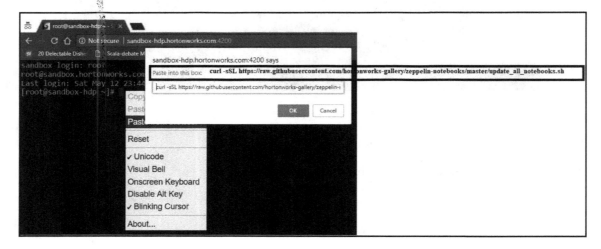

Screenshot displaying updating of Zeppelin

3. Run the `curl` command to update the Zeppelin instance with the latest notebooks. The following screenshot shows the updated Zeppelin instance:

```
[root@sandbox-hdp ~]# curl -sSL https://raw.githubusercontent.com/hortonworks-gallery/zeppelin-not
ebooks/master/update_all_notebooks.sh
if [ -d "/usr/hdp/current/zeppelin-server/notebook" ]; then
  NOTES_DIR="/usr/hdp/current/zeppelin-server/notebook"
else
  NOTES_DIR="/usr/hdp/current/zeppelin-server/lib/notebook"
fi

cd $NOTES_DIR
OLD_DIR=`date +%Y%m%d-%H%M%S`
mkdir old_${OLD_DIR}
mv 2* old_${OLD_DIR}/
rm -rf zeppelin-notebooks/
git clone -q --progress https://github.com/hortonworks-gallery/zeppelin-notebooks.git
/bin/mv -f zeppelin-notebooks/* ./
chown -R zeppelin:hadoop *
echo Restarting Apache Zeppelin...
/usr/hdp/current/zeppelin-server/lib/bin/zeppelin-daemon.sh restart &> /dev/null
echo Done!
[root@sandbox-hdp ~]# sudo -u zeppelin -E sh
sh-4.1$
```

Screenshot displaying updated Zeppelin instance

Now, let's go back to `hdp.hortonworks.com:8888`.

Launching the Ambari Dashboard and Zeppelin UI

The following are the steps required to launch Ambari and Zeppelin:

1. Click on the **Launch Dashboard** button and log in as `maria_dev` to navigate to the Ambari dashboard:

Screenshot displaying navigation through the Ambari dashboard

2. Clicking on **Zeppelin UI** under **Quick Links** takes us to the Zeppelin UI, as follows:

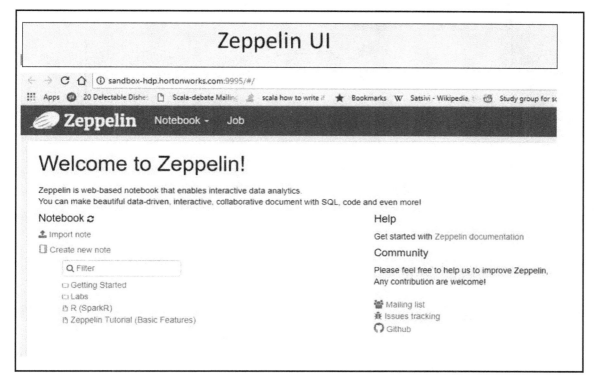

Screendhot of Zeppelin UI page

The Zeppelin UI runs on port 9995. For our Zeppelin Notebook to work with Spark 2 and Python 2.7, the Spark and Python interpreters need updating.

Updating Zeppelin Notebook configuration by adding or updating interpreters

The following steps need to be performed to update the Zeppelin notebook:

1. We need to update the interpreters, including a Spark 2 interpreter and adding a Python interpreter.

2. On the Zeppelin UI page, click on **anonymous** | **Interpreter** as follows:

Screenshot to perform steps on the Zeppelin UI page

Clicking on the **Interpreter** link takes us to the interpreter's page. First, we will update the Spark 2 interpreter.

Updating a Spark 2 interpreter

The following are the steps involved in updating the Spark 2 interpreter:

1. We will update the SPARK_HOME property as follows:

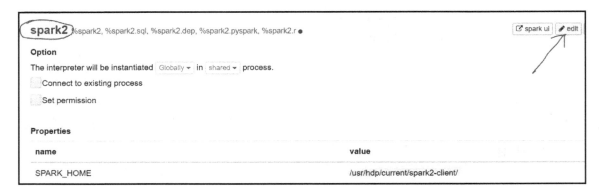

Screenshot displaying how to update the SPARK_HOME property

2. Next, we will update the `zeppelin.pyspark.python` property to point to the new Python interpreter:

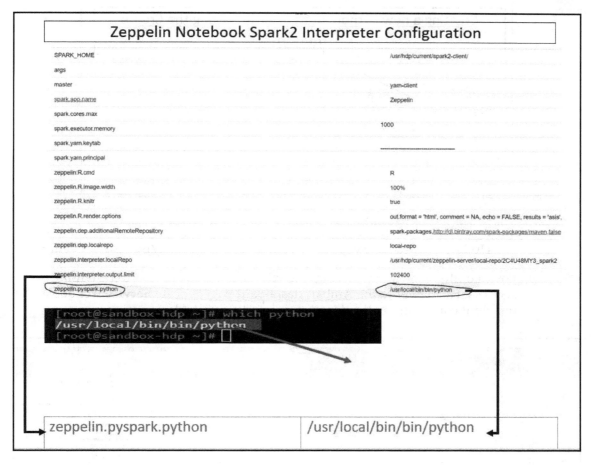

Screenshot displaying how to update the zeppelin.pyspark.python property

3. Next, let's create a new Python interpreter as follows:

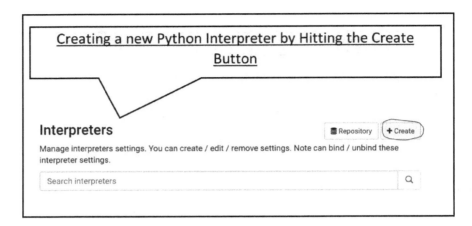

Screenshot to create a new Python interpreter

Update `zeppelin.pyspark.python` to `/usr/local/bin/bin/python`.

4. For all of these interpreter changes to take effect, we will need to restart the services. Head over to the Ambari dashboard page. Locate **Service Actions** at the top-right corner and in the dropdown, select **Restart All**:

Screenshot displaying final step for Zeppelin Notebook to be ready for development

At this point, the Zeppelin Notebook is ready for development.

Implementation objectives

The goal of this section will be to get started with developing a data pipeline using the Random Forests algorithm.

List of implementation goals

The following implementation objectives are the same and cover both the Random Forests pipeline and linear regression. We will perform preliminary steps such as **Exploratory Data Analysis (EDA)** once and develop specific implementation code that pertains to a particular pipeline. Therefore, the implementation objectives are listed here as follows:

- Get the stock price dataset.
- Carry out preliminary EDA in the Sandbox Zeppelin Notebook environment (or Spark shell), and run a statistical analysis.
- Develop the pipeline incrementally in Zeppelin, and port the code into IntelliJ. This means doing the following:
  1. Create a new Scala project in IntelliJ, or import an existing empty project into IntelliJ, and create Scala artifacts from code that was incrementally developed in the Notebook.
  2. Do not forget to wire up all the necessary dependencies in the `build.sbt` file.
  3. Interpret the results of the pipeline, such as how well the classifier performed. How close are the predicted values to those in the original dataset?

In the next subsection, we will download the stock price dataset.

Step 1 – creating a Scala representation of the path to the dataset file

The stock price dataset is available in the `ModernScalaProjects_Code` folder. Grab a copy and upload it to the Sandbox, then place it in a convenient location as follows:

```scala
scala> val dataSetPath = "\\<<Path to the folder containing the Data
File>>"
scala> val dataFile = dataSetPath + "\\News.csv"
```

In the next step, let's create a **resilient distributed dataset (RDD)**.

Step 2 – creating an RDD[String]

Invoke the `textFile` method of `sparkContext`, which is supplied by Spark in the Sandbox:

```scala
scala> val result1 = spark.sparkContext.textFile(dataSetPath + "News.csv")
result1: org.apache.spark.rdd.RDD[String] = C:\<<Path to your own Data
File>>\News.csv MapPartitionsRDD[1] at textFile at <console>:25
```

The resultant RDD, `result1`, is a partitioned structure. In the next step, we will iterate over these partitions.

Step 3 – splitting the RDD around the newline character in the dataset

Invoke a `flatMap` operation over the `result1` RDD, and split each partition around its `"\n"` (end of the line) character as follows:

```scala
scala> val result2 = result1.flatMap{ partition =>
partition.split("\n").toList }
result2: org.apache.spark.rdd.RDD[String] = MapPartitionsRDD[2] at flatMap
at <console>:27
```

Each `partition` is after a string. In the next step, we will transform the `result2` RDD.

Step 4 – transforming the RDD[String]

Invoke a `map` operation over the `result2` RDD. Each line in this RDD (a row of data) consists of stock price headline data separated by a comma, as follows:

```scala
scala> val result2A = result2.map(_.split(","))
result2A: org.apache.spark.rdd.RDD[Array[String]] = MapPartitionsRDD[3] at
map at <console>:29
```

The resultant RDD, `result2A`, is an `RDD[Array[String]]`. The RDD consists of an array of strings, where each string represents a row.

Step 5 – carrying out preliminary data analysis

This step is broken down into a set of smaller steps. The process starts with the creation of `DataFrame`.

Creating DataFrame from the original dataset

Load the stock price dataset file again by specifying an appropriate `option` for Spark to automatically infer the schema of the dataset before it can create the `DataFrame`, as follows:

```
scala> val spDataFrame =
spark.read.format("com.databricks.spark.csv").option("delimiter",
",").option("header", "true").option("inferSchema",
"true").load("News.csv")
spDataFrame: org.apache.spark.sql.DataFrame = [Date: string, Label: int ...
5 more fields]
```

The resultant structure, `spDataFrame`, is `DataFrame`.

Dropping the Date and Label columns from the DataFrame

`Date` and `Label` are columns we may exclude for now as follows:

```
scala> val newsColsOnly = spDataFrame.drop("Date", "Label")
newsColsOnly: org.apache.spark.sql.DataFrame = [Top1: string, Top2: string
... 23 more fields]
```

The resultant structure is a new `DataFrame` that consists of all 25 top headlines.

Having Spark describe the DataFrame

Invoke the `describe` and `show` methods in that order to give us a visual of the first 20 rows as follows:

```
scala> val expAnalysisTestFrame = spDataFrame.describe("TopHeadline1",
"TopHeadline2", "TopHeadline3","TopHeadline4","TopHeadline5", TopHead.....)
expAnalysisTestFrame: org.apache.spark.sql.DataFrame = [summary: string,
TopHeadline: string ... 25 more fields]

scala> newsColsOnly.show
```

In the next step, let's add a new column to the `DataFrame`, an `expAnalysisTestFrame`, called `AllMergedNews`.

Adding a new column to the DataFrame and deriving Vector out of it

Let's perform the following steps to add a new column and derive `Vector`:

1. Create a new `DataFrame` by creating a new `AllMergedNews` column in place of the `Top1` column, which is done by invoking the `withColumn` method as follows:

```
scala> val mergedNewsColumnsFrame =
newsColsOnly.withColumn("AllMergedNews",
newsColsOnly("TopHeadline1"))
mergedNewsColumnsFrame: org.apache.spark.sql.DataFrame =
[TopHeadline1: string, TopHeadline2: string ... 23 more fields]
```

2. Next, transform the `mergedNewsColumns DataFrame` into `Vector` as follows:

```
scala> import org.apache.spark.sql.functions
import org.apache.spark.sql.functions

scala> val mergedFrameList = for (i <- 2L to newsColsOnly.count() +
1L) yield mergedNewsColumnsFrame.withColumn("AllMergedNews",
functions.concat(mergedNewsColumnsFrame("AllMergedNews"),
functions.lit(" "), mergedNewsColumnsFrame("Top" + i.toString)))
mergedFrameList:
scala.collection.immutable.IndexedSeq[org.apache.spark.sql.DataFram
e] = Vector([Top1: string, Top2: string ... 4 more fields], [Top1:
string, Top2: string ... 4 more fields])
```

3. In the next step, we simply derive the `mergedFinalFrame DataFrame` from `mergedFrameList`:

```
scala> val mergedFinalFrame = mergedFrameList(0)
mergedFinalFrame: org.apache.spark.sql.DataFrame = [Top1: string,
Top2: string ... 4 more fields]
```

At this point, we have `DataFrame` that needs some preprocessing. Let's start by getting rid of stop words.

Removing stop words – a preprocessing step

The stop words we want to be eliminated are words such as *a, an, the,* and *in*. **Natural Language Toolkit (NLTK)** comes to the rescue as follows:

```
import org.apache.spark.ml.feature.StopWordsRemover
import org.apache.spark.ml.param.StringArrayParam
```

```
val stopwordEliminator = StopWordsRemover(new
StringArrayParam("words","..."), new StringArrayParam("stopEliminated", "..."))
```

The next step is going to be using the `transform` operation.

Transforming the merged DataFrame

The `mergedFinalFrame DataFrame` is passed into the `transform` method. This NLTK step gets rid of all stop words that were not necessary for our analysis:

```
val cleanedDataFrame = stopwordEliminator.transform(mergedFinalFrame)
 cleanedDataFrame.show()
+------------+-----+--------------------+--------------------+
| Date|label|  words|    stopEliminated|
+------------+-----+--------------------+--------------------+
| 09 09 09|  0|[Latvia, downs, ...|[Latvia, downs, ...|[Latvia downs, d...|
|11 11 09 09|  1|[Why, wont, Aust...|[wont, Australia, N...|[wont Australia,
Au...|
+------------+-----+--------------------+--------------------+
```

In the next step, we will use a feature transformer called `NGram`.

Transforming a DataFrame into an array of NGrams

What is an n-gram? It is simply a sequence of items such as letters, words, and so on (as in our dataset). Our dataset resembles a corpus of text. It is an ideal candidate for processing into an array of n-grams, which is an array consisting of words from the latest version of our dataset, devoid of stop words:

```
//Import the feature Transformer NGram
import org.apache.spark.ml.feature.NGram

//Create an N-gram instance; create an N-Gram of size 2
val aNGram = new NGram(new StringArrayParam("stopRemoved".."), new
StringArrayParam("ngrams", n=2)

// transform the cleanedDataFrame (the one devoid of stop words)
val cleanedDataFrame2 = aNGram.transform(cleanedDataFrame)

//display the first 20 rows
 cleanedDataFrame2.show()
+------------+-----+--------------------+----------------------+--------------
-------+
| Date|label|  words|  stopEliminated| Ngrams|
+------------+-----+--------------------+----------------------+--------------
-------+
```

```
    | 09 09 09| 0|[Latvia, downs, ...|[Latvia, downs, ...|[Latvia downs,
d...|
    |11 11 09 09| 1|[Why, wont, Aust...|[wont, Australia, N...|[wont
Australia, Au...|
    +----------+-----+--------------------+--------------------+--------------
-------+
```

In the next step, we will create a new dataset by adding a column called `ndashgrams`.

Adding a new column to the DataFrame, devoid of stop words

Derive a new `DataFrame` by adding a new column called `ndashgrams` to
`DataFrame cleanedDataFrame2` as follows:

```
cleanedDataFrame3 = cleanedDataFrame2.withColumn('ndashgrams', ....)

cleanedDataFrame3.show()
```

```
    +----------+-----+--------------------+--------------------+--------------
-------+
    | Date|label|  words| stopEliminated| Ngrams|
    +----------+-----+--------------------+--------------------+--------------
-------+
    | 09 09 09| 0|[Latvia, downs, ...|[Latvia, downs, ...|[Latvia downs, d...|
    |11 11 09 09| 1|[Why, wont, Aust...|[wont, Australia, N...|[wont
Australia, Au...|
    +----------+-----+--------------------+--------------------+--------------
-------+
```

The next step gets more interesting. We will apply what is known as a count vectorizer.

Constructing a vocabulary from our dataset corpus

Why `CountVectorizer`? We need one to construct a vocabulary of certain terms regarding our stock price corpus:

```scala
import org.apache.spark.ml.feature.CountVectorizer

//We need a so-called count vectorizer to give us a CountVectorizerModel
that will convert our 'corpus' //into a sparse vector of n-gram counts

 val countVectorizer = new CountVectorizer
//Set Hyper-parameters that the CountVectorizer algorithm can take
countVectorizer.inputCol(new StringArrayParam("NGrams")
countVectorizer.outputCol(new StringArrayParam("SparseVectorCounts")
//set a filter to ignore rare words
countVectorizer.minTF(new DoubleParam(1.0))
```

`CountVectorizer` generates a `CountVectorizerModel`, which can convert our corpus into a sparse vector of n-gram token counts.

Training CountVectorizer

We want to train our `CountVectorizer` by passing into it our latest version of the dataset as shown in the following code snippet:

```
cleanedDataFrame3 = countVectorizer.fit(cleanedDataFrame2)

cleanedDataFrame3.show()
| Date|label|  words|  stopEliminated| NGrams| SparseVectorCounts|
| 09 09 09| 0|[Latvia, downs, ...|[Latvia, downs, ...|[Latvia downs, d...|
|11 11 09 09| 1|[Why, wont, Aust...|[wont, Australia, N...|[wont Australia,
Au...|
   +-----------+-----+--------------------+--------------------+-------------
-------+--------------------
```

Using StringIndexer to transform our input label column

Now, let's index our `label` input in the dataset using `StringIndexer` as follows:

```
import org.apache.spark.ml.feature.StringIndexer

val indexedLabel = new StringIndexer(new StringArrayParam("label"), new
StringArrayParam("label2"), ...)

cleanedDataFrame4 =
indexedLabel.fit(cleanedDataFrame3).transform(cleanedDataFrame3)
```

Next, let's drop the input label column `label`.

Dropping the input label column

Invoke the `drop` method on `DataFrame` `cleanedDataFrame4` as follows:

```
val cleanedDataFrame5 = cleanedDataFrame4.drop('label')
DataFrame[Date: string, words: array<string>, stopRemoved: array<string>,
ngrams: array<string>, countVect: vector, label2: double]

cleanedDataFrame5.show()

| Date|label|  words|  stopEliminated| NGrams| SparseVectorCount|label2|
| 09 09 09| 0|[Latvia, downs, ...|[Latvia, downs, ...|[Latvia downs, d...|
```

```
|11 11 09 09| 1|[Why, wont, Aust...|[wont, Australia, N...|[wont Australia,
Au...|
   +-----------+-----+-------------------+-------------------+--------------
--------+-------------------+------+
```

Next, let's add a new column called `label2` in place of the dropped `label` column.

Adding a new column to our DataFrame

This time, invoke the `withColumn` method to add in the `label2` column as a replacement for `label1`:

```
val  cleanedDataFrame6 = cleanedDataFrame5.withColumn('label',
cleanedDataFrame.label2)
cleanedDataFrame6.show()

| Date|label|  words|  stopRemoved|  ngrams|  countVect|label2|
| 09 09 09| 0|[Latvia, downs, ...|[Latvia, downs, ...|[Latvia downs, d...|
|11 11 09 09| 1|[Why, wont, Aust...|[wont, Australia, N...|[wont Australia,
Au...|
   +-----------+-----+-------------------+-------------------+--------------
--------+-------------------+------+
```

Now, it is time to divide our dataset into a training set and a test set.

Dividing the DataSet into training and test sets

Let's split the dataset into two datasets. 85% of the dataset will be the training dataset and the remaining 15% will be the testing dataset, as follows:

```
//Split the dataset in two. 85% of the dataset becomes the Training
(data)set and 15% becomes the testing (data) set
val finalDataSet1:
Array[org.apache.spark.sql.Dataset[org.apache.spark.sql.Row]] =
cleanedDataFrame6.randomSplit(Array(0.85, 0.15), 98765L)
println("Size of the new split dataset " + finalDataSet.size)

//the testDataSet
val testDataSet = finalDataSet1(1)

//the Training Dataset
val trainDataSet = finalDataSet1(0)
```

Let's create a `StringIndexer` to index the `label2` column.

Creating labelIndexer to index the indexedLabel column

Let's create `labelIndexer` now. This will create a new indexed input and output the columns `label` and `indexedLabel`, as follows:

```
val labelIndexer = new
IndexToString().setInputCol("label").setOutputCol("indexedLabel").fit(input
)
```

Next, let's `transform` our indexed labels back to the original labels that were not indexed.

Creating StringIndexer to index a column label

The following will help us create a `StringIndexer` to index the `label` column:

```
val stringIndexer = new
StringIndexer().setInputCol("prediction").setOutputCol("predictionLabel")
```

In the next step, we will create `RandomForestClassifier`.

Creating RandomForestClassifier

Let's create `randomForestClassifier` now and pass in the appropriate hyperparameters as follows:

```
val randomForestClassifier = new
RandomForestClassifier().setFeaturesCol(spFeaturesIndexedLabel._1)
.setFeatureSubsetStrategy("sqrt")
```

We have a classifier now. Now, we will create a new pipeline and create stages, with each stage holding the indexers that we have just created.

Creating a new data pipeline with three stages

Let's create the appropriate imports first, as follows:

```
import org.apache.spark.ml.classification.RandomForestClassifier
import org.apache.spark.ml.evaluation.MulticlassClassificationEvaluator
import org.apache.spark.ml.param._
import org.apache.spark.ml.tuning.{ParamGridBuilder, TrainValidationSplit}
import org.apache.spark.ml.{Pipeline, PipelineStage}
```

Let's start building a pipeline now. This is a pipeline that has three stages, which are `StringIndexer`, `LabelIndexer`, and `randomForestClassifier`.

Creating a new data pipeline with hyperparameters

The following steps need to be performed to create a new data pipeline:

1. Create a new pipeline with the following three stages:

```
val soPipeline = new Pipeline().
setStages(Array[PipelineStage](labelIndexer) ++
Array[PipelineStage](randomForestClassifier)) ++
Array[PipelineStage](stringIndexer)]
```

2. Create a hyperparameter called NumTrees as follows:

```
//Lets set the hyper parameter NumTrees
val rfNum_Trees = randomForestClassifier.setNumTrees(15)
println("Hyper Parameter num_trees is: " + rfNum_Trees.numTrees)
```

3. Create a hyperparameter tree called MaxDepth and set it to 2 as follows:

```
//set this default parameter in the classifier's embedded param map
val rfMax_Depth = rfNum_Trees.setMaxDepth(2)
println("Hyper Parameter max_depth is: " + rfMax_Depth.maxDepth)
```

It is time to train the pipeline.

Training our new data pipeline

We have a pipeline that is ready to be trained on the training dataset. Fitting (training) also runs the indexers, as follows:

```
val stockPriceModel = pipeline.fit(trainingData)
```

Next, run a transformation operation on our stockPriceModel and generate stock price predictions.

Generating stock price predictions

The following steps need to be performed to generate stock price predictions:

1. Run the `stockPriceModel` transformation operation on our test dataset as follows:

   ```
   // Generate predictions.
   val predictions = stockPriceModel.transform(testData)
   ```

2. Let's display the relevant columns of our `predictions DataFrame` as follows:

   ```
   predictions.select("predictedLabel", "label", "features").show(5)
   ```

3. Finally, we want to evaluate the accuracy of our model, its ability to generate predictions, or in other words, find out how close the generated output was to the predictor labels, as follows:

   ```
   modelOutputAccuracyEvaluator: Double = new
   MulticlassClassificationEvaluator()
   .setLabelCol("indexedLabel")
   .setPredictionCol("prediction")
   .setMetricName("precision")

   val accuracy = modelOutputAccuracyEvaluator.evaluate(predictions)
   ```

Before we wind up this chapter, there are other metrics that we can evaluate. We leave this as an exercise for the reader.

Using the `MulticlassMetrics` class in the Spark ML API, it is possible to generate metrics that can tell us how close the predicted label value in the predicted column is to the actual label value in the `label` column.

Readers are invited to come up with two more metrics:

- Accuracy
- Weighted precision

There are many other ways to build ML models to predict stock prices and help investors build their long-term investment strategy. For example, linear regression is another commonly used but fairly popular method for predicting stock prices.

Summary

In this chapter, we learned how to leverage the Random Forests algorithm to predict stock prices based on historical trends.

In next chapter, we will create a spam classifier. We will start with two datasets, one representing ham and the other, spam dataset.

Questions

Here are a list of few questions:

1. What do you understand by linear regression? Why is it important?
2. How does linear regression differ from logistic regression?
3. Name one powerful feature of the binary classifier.
4. What are the feature variables in relation to the stock price dataset?

Building a Spam Classification Pipeline

4

Two pillars of Google's Gmail service stand out. These are an **Inbox** folder, receiving benign or wanted email messages, and a **Spam** folder, receiving unsolicited, junk emails, or simply spam.

The emphasis of this chapter is on identifying spam and classifying it as such. It explores the following topics concerning spam detection:

- What are the techniques of separating spam from ham?
- If spam filtering is one suitable technique, how can it be formalized as a supervised learning classification task?
- Why is a certain algorithm better than another for spam filtering, and in what respect?
- Where are the tangible benefits of effective spam filtering most felt?

This chapter implements a spam filtering data analysis pipeline.

Implementing a spam classifier with Scala and **machine learning** (**ML**) is the overall learning objective of this chapter. Starting from the datasets we created for you, we will rely on the Spark ML library's machine learning APIs and its supporting libraries to build a spam classification pipeline.

The following list is a section-wise breakdown of the individual learning outcomes:

- Introduction to the spam classification problem
- The project's problem formulation
- Implementing the spam binary classification pipeline using the various algorithms
- The goal is to start with `DataFrame` and proceed towards analysis

Spam classification problem

Any email service should process incoming mail intelligently. This could be classifications that produces two distinct, sorted streams of email, ham and spam. Email processing at the sentry level entails a smart vetting process—a classification task that produces two distinct, sorted streams of email—ham and spam. Gmail's sophisticated spam filtering engine filters out spam by a classification process, fulfilling, in a proverbial sense, the separation of the wheat from the chaff.

Spam can be a pernicious phenomenon in our daily lives, which is intimately tied to an increasingly connected world. For example, a binary classification is an ongoing deceptive link to apparently innocent looking websites hosting malware. Readers can learn why a spam filter can minimize problems spam can cause. These are summarized as follows:

- Unethical companies harvest email addresses from the web and send out a flood of bulk emails to people. A Gmail user, say, `gmailUser@gmail.com`, is enticed to click on an innocent-looking website masquerading as a popular website people commonly recognize as reputable. One kind of vile intention is to trap the user into giving up personal information on entering a supposedly popular reputable website.

- Another spam email like the one sent out by operators of a shady website, `frz7yblahblah.viral.sparedays.net`, is preying on people's predilection for making easy money. For example, the innocent looking link contains a deceptive link to some shady website hosting malware, a rootkit virus for example. A rootkit is very hard to remove. It is a virus that embeds itself into your OS kernel. It can be so elusive and potentially destructive that a remote hacker can gain control of your system, and before you know it, your network may come to a grinding halt. Several man hours will be lost and, if you are a company, revenue will be lost as well.

The following is a screenshot of a spam email sitting in Gmail's **Spam** folder, indicative of phishing. **Phishing** refers to deliberate attempts at maliciously gaining fraudulent access to personal information by deception, as shown in the following screenshot:

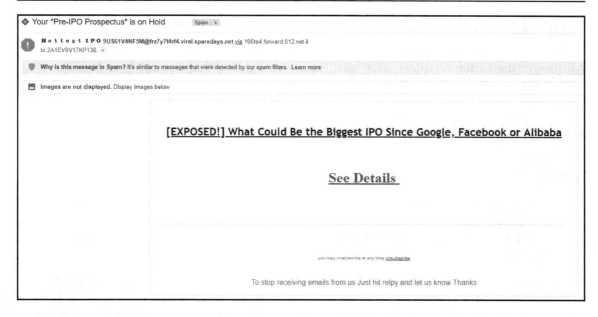

An example of a spam email

In the next section, we will explore a handful of topics that are relevant to the development of the spam classification pipeline.

Relevant background topics

The following topics are reviewed in this section prior to developing the spam classifier:

- Multidimensional data
- Importance of features
- Classification task
- Individual feature importance in relation to another feature
- Term frequency-inverse document frequency (TF-IDF)
- Hashing trick
- Stop word removal
- Normalization

In the next section, we will talk more about each topic.

Multidimensional data

Multidimensional data is data bearing more than one feature. We have dealt with many features in the earlier chapters. That said, let's restate this with an example, explaining what a feature means and why features are such a big deal.

Features and their importance

Each feature in a multidimensional dataset is a contributing factor in arriving at a prediction:

- A prediction is to be made on a new sample; for example, a new breast cancer mass sample belonging to a certain individual
- Each contributing factor has a certain feature importance number or feature weight

Some features are more important than others in contributing to the final prediction. In other words, a (final) prediction is made on what category a new sample belongs to. For example, in the breast cancer dataset in `Chapter 2`, *Build a Breast Cancer Prognosis Pipeline with Spark and Scala*, the Random Forest algorithm can be used to estimate feature importance. In the following list the top-most features have the highest weight; the feature at the bottom of the list has the lowest weight (in order of decreasing importance):

1. **Uniformity_of_Cell_Size**
2. **Uniformity_of_Cell_Shape**
3. **Bare_Nuclei**
4. **Bland_Chromatin**
5. **Single_Epithelial_Cell_Size**
6. **Normal_Nucleoli**
7. **Clump_Thickness**
8. **Marginal_Adhesion**
9. **Mitosis**

This means that the first feature has the most impact on the final predicted outcome, second feature has the second biggest impact, and so on.

We have just covered features, feature importance, weight, and so on. This exercise has laid the groundwork for this chapter.

In the following section, we will look at classification.

Classification task

Classification implies a categorization action, a task involving categories. A classification task then typically denotes a supervised learning technique that lets us categorize a new sample previously unseen (such as an Iris flower, whose species we do not know yet). By categorizing, we allude to the fact that the classification task is tagging an unseen sample with one of the predicted labels in the training dataset.

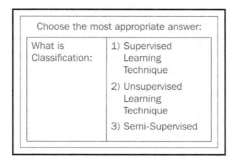

What is classification?

Before we move on the to next question, we will draw your attention to the term **training dataset**. In the next topic on classification outcomes, we discuss classification outcomes as binary or categorical and explain supporting concepts like **target** variable.

Classification outcomes

Up until `Chapter 3`, *Stock Price Predictions*, we worked with ML problems related to classification as a supervised learning technique. The classification tasks were data-centered (data as in samples, observations, or measurements) for which you already know the target answer. That brings us to the term **target variable**. This is another commonly-used alternative name for the **response variable**, a term from statistics. A target variable, in the ML context, is the variable that is typically the output or outcome. For example, it could be a binary outcome variable with only two classification outcomes—0 or 1. With that point made, we know that data for which the target answer is readily known or predetermined is called **labeled data**.

The classification task developed in this chapter is all about supervised learning, where an algorithm is teaching itself to learn from the labeled samples that we provide. A notable example from a previous chapter is the breast cancer dataset, which is also a supervised learning classification task. In that chapter, we classified breast cancer samples in two categories—benign and malignant. These are the two classification outcomes, outcome values that we can use to label or tag so-called training data that an algorithm will be trained on. On the other hand, unlabeled data is a new breast cancer sample data waiting to be diagnosed. More pertinently, a new incoming corpus possibly containing both ham and spam contains unlabeled data. Based on labeled samples from the training set, you could try to classify the unlabeled samples.

Two possible classification outcomes

Spam filtering is a binary classification task, an ML task that generates predicted values that only contain one of two possible classification outcomes. In this chapter, we will set out to build a spam classifier. Labels in the spam classification set belong to a finite set consisting of text from two types of emails, spam and ham. The binary classification task then becomes one of predicting the (output) label from previously unseen data. Deciding whether an email is spam or not, therefore, become a binary classification problem. By convention, we assign the ham mutually exclusive state a value of 1, and 0 for the other state, spam. In the next section, we will formulate the spam classification problem at hand. This will give us an overview of the project as well.

Project overview – problem formulation

In this chapter, the stated goal is to build a spam classifier, one that is capable of distinguishing spam terms in email messages that are mixed in with regular or expected email content as well. It is important to know that spam messages are email messages that are sent out to multiple recipients with the same content, as opposed to regular messages. We start with two email datasets, one that represents ham and one that represents spam. After stages of preprocessing, we fit the model on a training set, say 70% of the entire dataset.

This application is a typical spam filtering application in the sense that it works on text. We then put algorithms to work that help the ML process detect words, phrases, and terms most likely found in spam emails. Next, will go over the ML workflow at a high level in relation to spam filtering.

The ML workflow is as follows:

- We will be developing a pipeline that will use dataframes
- A dataframe contains a `predictions` column and another column containing preprocessed text
- The classification process involves transformation operations—one `DataFrame` is transformed into another
- Our pipeline runs a series of stages, involving TF-IDF, a hashing trick, stop word removal, and Naive Bayes algorithms

In essence, the spam filtering or classification problem is a supervised learning task, where we supply labeled data to the pipeline. A natural language processing step in this task entails labeled feature data being converted into a bag of feature vectors.

At this point, we can lay out the steps needed to build the spam classifier:

# 1	Read in both Ham and Spam datasets
# 2	Create a Ham dataset that contains enough samples of spam and regular e-mails
# 3	A Feature Extraction step converts the email text corpus into useful features for training e.g. remove stop words, words frequency. Then we are able to evaluate these features with attribute selection technique.
# 4	Our combined dataset is split in two in a 80-20 ration as: • Training set, and a Testing set
# 5	We then set up a Pipeline consisting of multiple stages: • Tokenize the sentence (message features) of the dataset • Convert each dataset's words into feature vectors • Train a Regression Model
# 6	Make predictions on the test dataset
# 7	We finally use the trained model to classify Spam and Ham in new e-mails from the "wild"

Steps needed to build the spam classifier

The steps described in the preceding list are useful and help us come up with an outline of the spam classifier.

The following diagram represents a formulation of the spam classification problem:

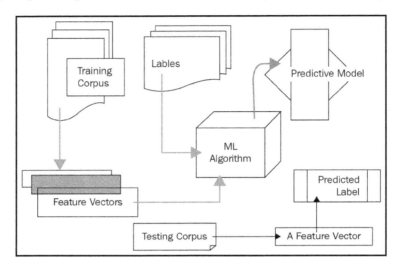

Spam classifier outline

Here is a refresher on the following topics:

- Stop words
- Punctuation marks
- Regular expressions

We want to eliminate two categories of text in our spam and ham datasets. These are as follows:

- Punctuation marks may be characterized in three categories:
    - Terminal points or marks
    - Dashes and hyphens
    - Pausing points, or marks

- Stop words.

The following is a representative list of punctuation marks:

Punctuation Marks			
Terminal Marks	**Pausing Marks**	**Dashes and Hyphens**	**Others**
The period .	Comma ,	Hypen (-)	Angle Brackets < >
Question Mark ?	Semicolon ;		Slash /
Exclamation Point !	Colon :		Parantheses ( )
			Braces { }
			Apostrophe ‘
			Square Brackets [ ]
			Quotation Marks “
The list is only representative, it covers commonly used punctuation marks			

Punctuation marks

We covered a list of commonly encountered punctuation marks in a text corpus that we want to be removed from our spam and ham datasets.

We also need to remove stop words—words that are common. Our spam classifier will remove these in the preliminary preprocessing steps.

Here is a representative list of stop words:

#	Stop Word	
1	A	All these words are so-called Function words. They have limited meaning, and occur throughout a corpus or text document frequently
2	About	
3	Also	
4	And	
5	Another	**Other stop words are:**
6	The	1) At 2) For
7	Is	3) To 4) On 5) With
8	It	6) From
Note:		
The above list is by means complete. It is however representative of what our Stop Word Remover will get rid of.		

A representative list of stop words

The following is a representative list of regular expressions to help with punctuation mark removal. A spam corpus can be daunting. Regular expressions can get as complex as can be in order to cope with spam:

A regular expression is a ASCII character-set based combination of alphanumeric characters and symbols. The purpose of a regex is to serve as a "matching template" in a corpus text	
Regular Expression	**What it does, when used in the classifier: Finds, matches and used in code to remove:**
[0-9]	**Single Digit Numbers between 0 and 9, 0 and 9 included**
1[0-9][1-9][0-9]	**Matches a number in the range:** 1010-1999
/[^A-Za-z0-9]+/g	Notes: **/ - Indicates the start of an expression** Caret ^ and $ are anchors marking start and end of an expression (a sequence of characters) **A-Z matches a character in the range A-Z** a-z **matches a character in the range** a-z 0-9 **matches a character (number) in the range of numbers** 0-9 **+ Matches one or more of characters matched by the previous regular expression tokens** **/ indicates the end of the regular expression**
This is only a small representative set of a vast vocabulary of regular expressions. It is intended to inform the user about the potential of regular expressions. Sophisticated Spam Classifiers may use complex regular expressions as required to stop Spam.	

Some relevant regular expressions

In the *Getting started* section, we will get started implementing the project.

Getting started

In order to get started, download the dataset from the `ModernScalaProjects_Code` folder and drop it into the root folder of your project.

Setting up prerequisite software

You may use your existing software setup from previous chapters. Apache Log4j 2 Scala API is the notable exception. This is a Scala wrapper over Log4j 2, which is an upgraded `Logger` implementation of Log4j version 1.x (the version provided by Spark).

Simply override the existing Log4j from Spark (version 1.6) with Log4j 2 Scala by adding in appropriate entries in the `build.sbt` file.

The following table lists two choices of prerequisite software:

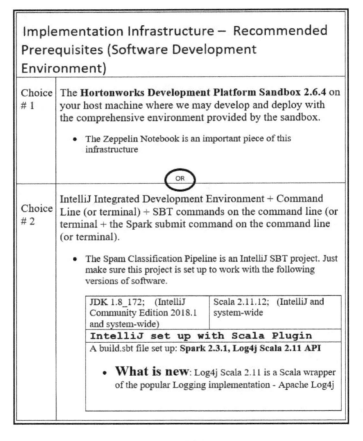

Implementation Infrastructure – Recommended Prerequisites (Software Development Environment)	
Choice # 1	The **Hortonworks Development Platform Sandbox 2.6.4** on your host machine where we may develop and deploy with the comprehensive environment provided by the sandbox. • The Zeppelin Notebook is an important piece of this infrastructure OR
Choice # 2	IntelliJ Integrated Development Environment + Command Line (or terminal) + SBT commands on the command line (or terminal + the Spark submit command on the command line (or terminal). • The Spam Classification Pipeline is an IntelliJ SBT project. Just make sure this project is set up to work with the following versions of software.

JDK 1.8_172; (IntelliJ Community Edition 2018.1 and system-wide)	Scala 2.11.12; (IntelliJ and system-wide)
IntelliJ set up with Scala Plugin	
A build.sbt file set up: **Spark 2.3.1, Log4j Scala 2.11 API**	
• **What is new**: Log4j Scala 2.11 is a Scala wrapper of the popular Logging implementation - Apache Log4j	

Implementation infrastructure

Download the dataset from the `ModernScalaProjects_Code` folder and drop it into the root folder of your project.

Spam classification pipeline

The most important development objective of this chapter is to perform spam classification tasks with the following algorithms:

- Stop word remover
- Naive Bayes
- Inverse document frequency
- Hashing trick transformer
- Normalizer

The practical goal of our spam classification task is this: Given a new incoming document, say, a collection of random emails from either **Inbox** or **Spam**, the classifier must be able to identify spam in the corpus. After all, this is the basis of an effective classifier. The real-world benefit behind developing this classifier to give our readers experience of developing their own spam filters. After learning how to put together the classifier, we will develop it.

The implementation steps are in the next section. This takes us straight into the development of Scala code in a Spark environment. Given that Spark allows us to write powerful distributed ML programs such as pipelines, that is exactly what we will set out to do. We will start by understanding the individual implementation steps required to reach our goal.

Implementation steps

The spam detection (or classification) pipeline involves five stages of implementation, grouped by typical ML steps that are needed. These are as follows:

1. Loading data
2. Preprocessing data
3. Extracting features
4. Training the spam classifier
5. Generating predictions

In the next step, we will set up a Scala project in IntelliJ.

Step 1 – setting up your project folder

Here is what the project looks like in IntelliJ:

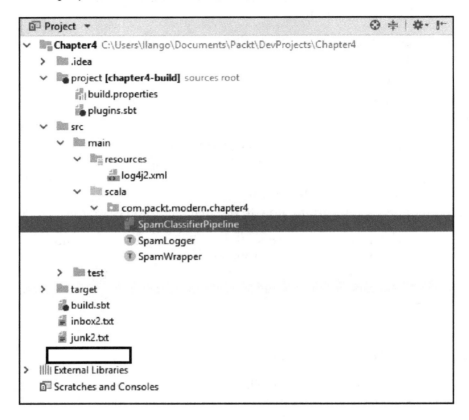

Project outline in IntelliJ

In the next section, we will upgrade the `build.sbt` file.

Step 2 – upgrading your build.sbt file

Here is the upgraded `build.sbt` file. What is new here? Remember, earlier, we talked about a new `Logging` library. Those new entries you see in the following screenshot are the new dependencies you need to move from Log4j 1.6 to the new Scala wrapper for Log4j 2:

```
libraryDependencies ++= Seq(
  "org.apache.spark" %% "spark-core" % "2.3.1",
  "org.apache.spark" %% "spark-mllib" % "2.3.1",
  "org.apache.spark" %% "spark-sql" % "2.3.1",
  "org.apache.logging.log4j" %% "log4j-api-scala" % "11.0",
  "org.apache.logging.log4j" % "log4j-scala" % "11.0" pomOnly(),
  "org.apache.logging.log4j" % "log4j-api" % "2.11.0",
  "org.apache.logging.log4j" % "log4j-core" % "2.11.0" % Runtime
)
```

New entries in the build.sbt file

In the next section, we will start with the Scala code, starting with a trait.

Step 3 – creating a trait called SpamWrapper

In IntelliJ, using **File** | **New** | **Scala** class, create an empty Scala trait called `SpamWrapper` in a file called `SpamWrapper.scala`.

First things first. At the top of the file, we will set up the following imports for implementing classes to take advantage of this trait:

- `SparkSession`—the entry point to programming with Spark
- The appropriate Log4J library imports, so that we can dial down logging messages from Spark:

These are the minimum imports. Next, create an empty `trait`. The following is an updated trait:

```
trait SpamWrapper {   }
```

Inside the `SpamWrapper` trait, create a `SparkSession` instance called `session`. At this point, here is a refresher on Spark:

- We need a `SparkSession` object instance to be the entry point to programming with Spark.
- We do not need a separate `SparkContext`. This is provided by `SparkSession`. The underlying context is available to us easily as `session.sparkContext`.
- To create a `SparkSession` object instance or get an existing `SparkSession`, a builder pattern is used.
- The `SparkSession` instance is available for the entire time frame of a Spark job.

Here is the updated `SpamWrapper` trait:

```
package com.packt.modern.chapter4

import org.apache.spark.sql.SparkSession
import org.apache.logging.log4j.scala.Logging
import org.apache.logging.log4j.Level


trait SpamWrapper extends Logging{

    //The entry point to programming Spark with the Dataset and DataFrame API.
    //This is the SparkSession

    lazy val session: SparkSession = {
      SparkSession
        .builder()
        .master( master = "local")
        .appName( name = "spam-classifier-pipeline")
        .getOrCreate()
    }

      //logger.getLogger("org").setLevel(Level.OFF)
    //logger.getLogger("akka").setLevel(Level.OFF)
      logger.apply(Level.OFF, "org")
      logger.apply(Level.OFF, "akka")


  }
```

SpamWrapper trait with SparkSession value

To recap, we create a `val` called `session` that our pipeline class will use. Of course, this will be the entry point to programming with Spark to build this spam classifier.

Step 4 – describing the dataset

Download the dataset from the `ModernScalaProjects_Code` folder. It consists of two text files:

- `inbox.txt`: Ham emails (I created this file from my Gmail **Inbox** folder)
- `junk.txt`: Spam emails (I created this out of spam from my Gmail **Spam** folder)

Drop these files into the root of your project folder. In the next section, we will describe the dataset.

Description of the SpamHam dataset

Before we present the actual dataset, here are a few real-world spam samples:

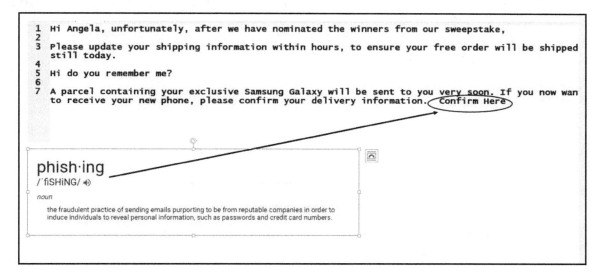

Spam email with phishing example

Here is an example of regular or wanted mail, also known as ham:

Hi there,

Thank you for being part of the Lightbend community. We wanted to let you know that we have made some updates to Lightbend's Privacy Policy and Cookie Policy in preparation for the EU's Data Protection Regulation that will be effective on May 25, 2018.

Changes include:

- Greater transparency into what type of data is being collected, processed and disclosed
- Detailed instructions on how to access, correct or delete your personal information
- The new Cookie Policy explains what type of cookies are being used as part of our services and allows users to more easily restrict sharing of personal data

At Lightbend, we are strongly committed to protecting the privacy of personal data that we maintain about Lightbend clients, employees and other individuals interested in the Reactive and Fast Data journey.

Thank you for your continued support.

If you have any questions, please contact us at privacy@lightbend.com.

Regards,

Lightbend Team

A perfectly normal email from Lightbend

The following is a glimpse into the actual dataset used in our spam-ham classification task. There are two datasets:

- `inbox.txt`: A ham dataset compiled from a small collection of regular emails from my **Inbox** folder
- `junk.txt`: A spam dataset compiled from a small collection of junk email from my **Spam/Junk** folder

Here is the regular dataset:

```
Hi Fellow Little Hills Toastmasters:
This coming Tuesday we are going to
take some time in the meeting to get
everyone up and running in Pathways.
If you are interested in being a
part of this, please bring your laptop
or tablet.  I look forward to seeing
you there.
Thanks, Kat
User Name: xyzstl
Dear Ilango,
Here's a summary of your Barclaycard
Ring Mastercard® account activity in
the past week. To view your purchases
at any time, please log in to
www.BarclaycardUS.com
and select View activity and
statements. Questions? Please log in
to our servicing site
and send a secure message. Please
remember to review your statement to
see
transactions, payments, and other
important account information and
disclosures.
Your Weekly Snapshot since 06/17/2018
Recent Payments & Credits: $0.00
Recent Charges: $0.00
Statement Balance: $0.00
Top 10 Resume Writing Tips for 2018 -
DailyWritingTips
```

A portion of the regular email dataset

Here is the spam dataset:

```
bitte achten Sie auf den
Zahlungseingang.
Mit besten Grüßen
Kavin Kumar Krishnamurthy
we are having issue with our
subscribers Ilangowrites
If you would like to unsubscribe,
please use this link
Re your message. click here
Unsubsrcibe From Mailing List
There's a small issue, Angela
Hi Angela, unfortunately, after we
have nominated the winners from our
sweepstake, we realized that there is
an issue related for your order.
Please update your shipping
information within hours, to ensure
your free order will be shipped still
today.
Hi do you remember me?
Delivery Status:
Confirmation Pending
Shipping Contractor:
UPS
Order destination:
Angela Baggett
A parcel containing your exclusive
Samsung Galaxy will be sent to you
very soon. If you now want to receive
your new phone, please confirm your
delivery information.
Confirm Here
```

A portion of the spam dataset

The preceding email wants you to confirm here. This is an attempt at phishing. This completes our description of our datasets. In the next step, we will proceed with data preprocessing. We need a new Scala object called `SpamClassifierPipeline`.

Step 5 – creating a new spam classifier class

We will create a new Scala file called `SpamClassifierPipeline.scala`. First of all, we need the following imports:

```
package com.packt.modern.chapter4

import org.apache.spark.ml.classification.NaiveBayes
import org.apache.spark.ml.{Pipeline, PipelineStage}
import org.apache.spark.sql.{DataFrame, DataFrameNaFunctions, Row, SparkSession}
import org.apache.spark.ml.feature.{HashingTF, IDF, Normalizer, Tokenizer}
import org.apache.spark.rdd.RDD
import org.apache.spark.sql.types._
import org.apache.spark.sql.functions.explode
```

Required imports

Now that the imports have been created, let's create an empty `SpamClassifierPipeline` object in the same package as the `SpamWrapper` trait, as follows:

```
object SpamClassifierPipeline extends App with SpamWrapper {   }
```

A prototype spam classifier is ready. We need to create code in it to do such things as preprocessing the data and, of course, much more. In the next step, we will list the necessary preprocessing steps to take up.

Step 6 – listing the data preprocessing steps

There is a purpose to preprocessing. In most data analytics tasks, the question that begs to be asked is—is our data necessarily usable? The answer lies in the fact that most real-world datasets need preprocessing, a massaging step meant to give data a new usable form.

With the spam and ham datasets, we identify two important preprocessing steps:

1. Removing punctuation marks:

   - Processing punctuation using regular expressions

2. Removing stop words

In the next step, we will write Scala code for two regular expressions, expressions that are fairly simple and only address a small subset of spam. However, it's a start.

In the next step, we will load our datasets into Spark. Naturally, we want a ham dataframe and a spam dataframe. We will take up the task of creating a ham dataframe first. Both our ham and spam datasets are ready for preprocessing. That brings us to the next step.

Step 7 – regex to remove punctuation marks and whitespaces

Here is a regular expression for our immediate needs:

```
val punctRegex = raw"[^A-Za-z0-9]+"
```

`raw` is a method in the string interpolation `StringContext` class of the standard Scala library.

Our corpus is likely to contain trailing and leading whitespaces which are sometimes ill-formatted. For example, we will run into whitespaces where lines are indented too much. To get rid of whitespaces, we will use regular expressions. This will work with the anchors, the hat `^`, and the `$` sign to extract the text without whitespaces. The updated regular expression now looks like this:

```
//matches whitespaces and punctuation marks
val regex2 = raw"[^A-Za-z0-9\s]+"
```

We just created a regular expression, `regex2`, a whitespace, and punctuation remover. Very soon, we will need this `regex2`. In the next section, we will create a new ham dataframe after applying the first of a few essential preprocessing steps—removing punctuation.

Step 8 – creating a ham dataframe with punctuation removed

We will have the regex work on each row of our ham **resilient distributed dataset** (RDD) and then use the `replaceAll` method. The underlying regex engine will use the regex to conduct a search and match on our ham corpus to come up with matched occurrences, as follows:

```
val hamRDD2 = hamRDD.map(_.replaceAll(regex2, "").trim)
hamRDD2: org.apache.spark.rdd.RDD[String] = inbox.txt MapPartitionsRDD[1]
at textFile at <console>:23
```

The `replaceAll` method kicked in and replaced all occurrences of whitespaces and punctuation. In the next step, we will convert this RDD into a dataframe.

We created a new ham RDD with leading and trailing whitespaces, and with punctuation removed. Let's display this new ham dataframe:

```
hamRDD3.take(10)
println("The HAM RDD looks like: " + hamRDD3.collect())
```

We created a new ham dataframe. We need to transform this dataframe by assigning a `label` of `0.0` to each ham sentence. We shall do that in the next step:

```
case class LabeledHamSpam(label: Double, mailSentence: String)
```

Therefore, we will create a case called `LabeledHamSpam` to model a sentence as a feature with a `Double` `label`. Next, create a new ham RDD that has exactly four partitions.

Creating a labeled ham dataframe

We will repartition our ham datafame and apply a `transform` operation to each `"Ham sentence"` in the ham dataframe, as follows:

```
val hamRDD3: RDD[LabeledHamSpam] = hamRDD2.repartition(4).map(w =>
LabeledHamSpam(0.0,w))
```

We repartitioned and created a new RDD that is structured as a row of ham sentences labeled with `0.0`. Now, display the first `10` rows of the new ham RDD:

```
hamRDD3.take(10)
println("The HAM RDD looks like: " + hamRDD3.collect())
```

So, we assigned `0.0` for all ham sentences. It is time to create the spam RDD:

```
val spamRDD = session.sparkContext.textFile(spamFileName)
spamRDisDset: org.apache.spark.rdd.RDD[String] = junk2.txt
MapPartitionsRDD[3] at textFile at <console>:23
```

Repeat the same set of preprocessing steps for the spam dataset as well.

Step 9 – creating a spam dataframe devoid of punctuation

We will use the same `LabeledHamSpam` case class to assign a `Double value` of `1.0` for spam sentences, as follows:

```
/*
Replace all occurrences of punctuation and whitespace
*/
val spamRDD2 = spamRDD.map(_.replaceAll(regex2, "").trim.toLowerCase)
/*
Repartition the above RDD and transform it into a labeled RDD
*/
val spamRDD3 = spamRDD2.repartition(4).map(w => LabeledHamSpam(0.0,w))
```

In the next step, we want a combined dataframe containing both spam and ham dataframes.

Step 10 – joining the spam and ham datasets

In this step, we will use the ++ method to join both dataframes in a `Union` operation:

```
val hamAndSpamNoCache: org.apache.spark.rdd.RDD[LabeledHamSpam] = (hamRDD3
++ spamRDD3)
hamAndSpam: org.apache.spark.rdd.RDD[LabeledHamSpam] = UnionRDD[20] at
$plus$plus at <console>:34
```

In the next section, let's create a dataframe, with two columns:

- A row containing `feature sentences` with punctuation removed
- A predetermined `label` column

Check for the following code snippet for better understanding:

```
val hamAndSpamDFrame" = hamAndSpam.select(hamAndSpam("punctLessSentences"),
hamAndSpam("label"))
dataFrame2: org.apache.spark.sql.DataFrame = [features: string, label:
double]
```

We created the new dataframe. Let's display this:

```
hamAndSpamDFrame.show
+--------------------+-----+
| lowerCasedSentences|label|
+--------------------+-----+
|this coming tuesd...| 0.0|
|pin free dialing ...| 0.0|
|regards support team| 0.0|
| thankskat| 0.0|
|speed dialing let...| 0.0|
|keep your user in...| 0.0|
| user name ilangostl| 0.0|
|now your family m...| 0.0|
```

Next, let's run the following optional checks:

- The schema of the dataframe
- Columns present in the dataframe

Here is how we will print out the schema:

```
hamAndSpamDFrame.printSchema
  root
  |-- features: string (nullable = true)
  |-- label: double (nullable = false)
```

They look good! Let's read off the `columns` now:

```
hamAndSpamDFrame.columns
res23: Array[String] = Array(features, label)
```

Up until now, we have created a dataframe that was punctuation-free, but not necessarily free of rows that contain null values. Therefore, in order to drop any rows containing null values, we will need to import the `DataFrameNaFunctions` class, that is, if you have not already imported it:

```
import org.apache.spark.sql.DataFrameNaFunctions

val naFunctions: DataFrameNaFunctions = hamAndSpamDFrame.na
```

In order to drop nulls from the punctuation-free dataframe, there is a column called `punctFreeSentences`. We will invoke the `drop()` method as shown in the following code:

```
val nonNullBagOfWordsDataFrame =
naFunctions.drop(Array("punctFreeSentences"))
```

The call to the `drop` method in the preceding code causes any rows of sentences that contain null values to be dropped. If you so wish, display the first 20 rows of the dataframe:

```
println("Non-Null Bag Of punctuation-free DataFrame looks like this:")
```

Display the dataframe. The following code will help you do just that:

```
nonNullBagOfWordsDataFrame.show()
```

At this point, a good next step relates to tokenizing punctuation-free rows, which also feature what we want to be tokenized. Tokenizing the current dataframe is the focus of the next section. Tokenizing brings us one step closer to the next preprocessing step—removing stop words.

Step 11 – tokenizing our features

Tokenizing is simply an operation executed by an algorithm. It results in the tokenization of each row. All the following terms define tokenization:

- Breaking up
- Splitting

The appropriate term appears to be the second term in the preceding list. For each row in the current dataframe, a tokenizer splits a `feature` row into its constituent tokens by splitting it along separating whitespaces. Each resulting Spark supplies two tokenizers:

- `Tokenizer` from the package `org.apache.spark.ml`
- `RegexTokenizer` from the same package

Both tokenizers are transformers. A transformer in Spark is an algorithm that accepts an input column as a (hyper) parameter and spits out a new `DataFrame` with a transformed output column, as follows:

```
import org.apache.spark.ml.feature.Tokenizer

val mailTokenizer = new
Tokenizer().setInputCol("lowerCasedSentences").setOutputCol("mailFeatureWor
ds")
mailTokenizer: org.apache.spark.ml.feature.Tokenizer = tok_0b4186779a55
```

Calling the `transform` method on `mailTokenizer` will give us a newly transformed dataframe:

```
val tokenizedBagOfWordsDataFrame: DataFrame =
mailTokenizer2.transform(nonNullBagOfWordsDataFrame)
```

The resulting dataframe, `tokenizedBagOfWordsDataFrame`, is a tokenized non-null bag of lowercased words. It looks like this:

```
+--------------------+-----+--------------------+
| lowerCasedSentences|label| mailFeatureWords|
+--------------------+-----+--------------------+
|This coming tuesd...| 0.0|[this, coming, tu...|
|Pin free dialing ...| 0.0|[pin, free, diali...|
|Regards support team| 0.0|[regards, support...|
| Thanks kat| 0.0| [thankskat]|
|Speed dialing let...| 0.0|[speed, dialing, ...|
|Keep your user in...| 0.0|[keep, your, user...|
| User name ilangostl| 0.0|[user, name, ilan...|
|Now your family m...| 0.0|[now, your, famil...|
```

The important thing to notice here is that a row in the transformed column, `mailFeatureWords`, resembles an array of words. Readers will not fail to notice that there are words in `mailFeatureWords` known as stop words. These are words that do not significantly contribute to our spam classification task. These words can be safely eliminated by Spark's `StopWordRemover` algorithm. In the next step, we will see how to put `StopWordRemover` to work.

Step 12 – removing stop words

First, make sure you have the `StopWordRemover` import in the `SpamClassifierPipeline` class. Next, we will create an instance of `StopWordRemover` and pass into it a (hyper) parameter column, `mailFeatureWords`. We want an output column that is devoid of stop words:

```
val stopWordRemover = new
StopWordsRemover().setInputCol("mailFeatureWords").setOutputCol("noStopWord
sMailFeatures")
```

Just like with `mailTokenizer`, we call the `transform` method to get a new `noStopWordsDataFrame`:

```
val noStopWordsDataFrame =
stopWordRemover.transform(tokenizedBagOfWordsDataFrame)
```

The resulting dataframe, a tokenized, non-null bag of lowercase words with no stop words looks like this:

```
noStopWordsDataFrame.show()
+-----------------------+-----+
|noStopWordsMailFeatures|label|
+-----------------------+-----+
|   coming|  0.0|
|  tuesday|  0.0|
|    going|  0.0|
|     take|  0.0|
|     time|  0.0|
|  meeting|  0.0|
|      get|  0.0|
| everyone|  0.0|
|  running|  0.0|
| pathways|  0.0|
```

In the next step, we will do a second transformation on our current dataframe:

```
import session.implicits._

val noStopWordsDataFrame2 =
noStopWordsDataFrame.select(explode($"noStopWordsMailFeatures").alias("noSt
opWordsMailFeatures"),noStopWordsDataFrame("label"))
```

The exploded, tokenized non-null bag of lowercase words with no stop words looks like this:

```
noStopWordsDataFrame2.show()
```

This completes data preprocessing. This sets the stage for feature extraction, an extremely important ML step.

Step 13 – feature extraction

In this step, we will extract the features of this dataset. We will do the following:

- Creating feature vectors
- Creating features entails converting the text into bigrams of characters using an n-gram model
- These bigrams of characters will be hashed to a length `10000` feature vector
- The final feature vector will be passed into Spark ML

Check out the following code snippet:

```
import org.apache.spark.ml.feature.HashingTF

val hashMapper = new HashingTF().setInputCol("words").
setOutputCol("noStopWordsMailFeatures").setOutputCol("mailFeatureHa
shes").setNumFeatures(10000)
hashFeatures: org.apache.spark.ml.feature.HashingTF =
hashingTF_5ff221eac4b4
```

Next, we will `transform` the featured version of the `noStopWordsDataFrame`:

```
val featurizedDF = hashMapper.transform(noStopWordsDataFrame)

//Display the featurized dataframe
featurizedDF1.show()
```

With a hash-featured and tokenized non-null bag of lowercased words with no stop words, this `DataFrame` looks like this:

```
+--------------------+-----+--------------------+--------------------+--------------------+
| lowerCasedSentences|label|    mailFeatureWords|noStopWordsMailFeatures|  mailFeatureHashes|
+--------------------+-----+--------------------+--------------------+--------------------+
|this coming tuesd...| 0.0|[this, coming, tu...| [coming, tuesday,...|(10000,[380,855,1...|
|pin free dialing ...| 0.0|[pin, free, diali...| [pin, free, diali...|(10000,[1073,1097...|
|regards support team| 0.0|[regards, support...| [regards, support...|(10000,[468,695,9...|
|            thankskat| 0.0|         [thankskat]|         [thankskat]|(10000,[5652],[1.0])|
|speed dialing let...| 0.0|[speed, dialing, ...| [speed, dialing, ...|(10000,[1097,3245...|
|keep your user in...| 0.0|[keep, your, user...| [keep, user, info...|(10000,[2904,5813...|
| user name ilangostl| 0.0|[user, name, ilan...| [user, name, ilan...|(10000,[15,742,58...|
|now your family m...| 0.0|[now, your, famil...| [family, member, ...|(10000,[1094,1181...|
|click on link bel...| 0.0|[click, on, link,...| [click, link, ent...|(10000,[847,1719,...|
|hi fellow little ...| 0.0|[hi, fellow, litt...| [hi, fellow, litt...|(10000,[1960,3391...|
|for every person ...| 0.0|[for, every, pers...| [every, person, r...|(10000,[855,1073,...|
|we look forward t...| 0.0|[we, look, forwar...| [look, forward, s...|(10000,[7923,9504...|
|thank you for cho...| 0.0|[thank, you, for,...| [thank, choosing,...|(10000,[763,768,1...|
|anbei die steuerb...| 0.0|[anbei, die, steu...| [anbei, die, steu...|(10000,[1409,1576...|
|we are having iss...| 0.0|[we, are, having,...|            [issue]|(10000,[6748],[1.0])|
|re your message c...| 0.0|[re, your, messag...| [re, message, click]|(10000,[1719,2425...|
|hi do you remembe...| 0.0|[hi, do, you, rem...|     [hi, remember]|(10000,[1960,5685...|
|                 ups| 0.0|              [ups]|              [ups]|(10000,[2525],[1.0])|
|        confirm here| 0.0|     [confirm, here]|          [confirm]|(10000,[5943],[1.0])|
|      angela baggett| 0.0|   [angela, baggett]|  [angela, baggett]|(10000,[6290,9622...|
+--------------------+-----+--------------------+--------------------+--------------------+
only showing top 20 rows
```

Dataframe with hash-featured and tokenized non-null bag of lowercase words

At this point, we are ready to create training and test sets.

Step 14 – creating training and test datasets

This step is important because we are going to create a model that we want to train with a training set. One way to create a training set is to partition the current dataframe and assign 80% of it to a new training dataset:

```
val splitFeaturizedDF = featurizedDF.randomSplit(Array(0.80, 0.20), 98765L)
splitFeaturizedDF1:
Array[org.apache.spark.sql.Dataset[org.apache.spark.sql.Row]] =
Array([filteredMailFeatures: string, label: double ... 2 more fields],
[filteredMailFeatures: string, label: double ... 2 more fields])
```

Now, let's retrieve the training set:

```
val trainFeaturizedDF = splitFeaturizedDF(0)
```

The testing dataset follows. Here is how we will create it:

```
val testFeaturizedDF = splitFeaturizedDF(1)
```

We need to go one step further. A modified version of the training set that has the following columns removed is needed:

- `mailFeatureWords`
- `noStopWordsMailFeatures`
- `mailFeatureHashes`

Here is the new training set, after doing `drop` on the preceding columns:

```
val trainFeaturizedDFNew =
trainFeaturizedDF1.drop("mailFeatureWords","noStopWordsMailFeatures","mailF
eatureHashes")

trainFeaturizedDFNew.show()
```

The invocation of the `show()` method results in the following display of the new training dataset:

```
+--------------------+-----+
| lowerCasedSentences|label|
+--------------------+-----+
|pin free dialing ...|  0.0|
|regards support team|  0.0|
|this coming tuesd...|  0.0|
|speed dialing let...|  0.0|
| user name ilangostl|  0.0|
|for every person ...|  0.0|
|hi fellow little ...|  0.0|
|thank you for cho...|  0.0|
|we look forward t...|  0.0|
|anbei die steuerb...|  0.0|
|     angela baggett|  0.0|
|        confirm here|  0.0|
|hi do you remembe...|  0.0|
|re your message c...|  0.0|
|                 ups|  0.0|
|we are having iss...|  0.0|
|weve received you...|  0.0|
|content of your o...|  0.0|
|delivery address ...|  0.0|
|   order destination|  0.0|
+--------------------+-----+
only showing top 20 rows
```

Training dataframe

The next important step right before training (fitting) the model is what is known as **inverse document frequency (IDF)**. Spark provides an estimator called IDF that will compute the IDF for us. The IDF is an algorithm that will train (fit) models on our current dataframe:

```
val mailIDF = new
IDF().setInputCol("mailFeatureHashes").setOutputCol("mailIDF")
```

Now we will pass in our `featurizedDF` dataframe into the `fit` method on the IDF algorithm. This will produce our model:

```
val mailIDFFunction = mailIDF.fit(featurizedDF)
```

The next step is a normalizing step. A `normalizer` normalizes the scales for the different `features` so that different-sized articles are not weighted differently:

```
val normalizer = new
Normalizer().setInputCol("mailIDF").setOutputCol("features")
```

Let's use the Naive Bayes algorithm now. Initialize it and pass into it the hyperparameters it needs:

```
val naiveBayes = new
NaiveBayes().setFeaturesCol("features").setPredictionCol("prediction")
```

Now it's time to create the pipeline and set up all the stages in it. These are as follows:

- `StopWordRemover`
- `HashingTF`
- `mailIDF`
- `normalizer`
- `naiveBayes`

The code snippet sets up the stages as follows:

```
val spamPipeline = new
Pipeline().setStages(Array[PipelineStage](mailTokenizer2) ++
Array[PipelineStage](stopWordRemover) ++
Array[PipelineStage](hashMapper) ++
Array[PipelineStage](mailIDF) ++
Array[PipelineStage](normalizer) ++
Array[PipelineStage](naiveBayes)
```

Fit the pipeline to the training documents:

```
val mailModel1 = spamPipeline1.fit(trainFeaturizedDFNew)
```

Make predictions on the test dataset:

```
val rawPredictions =
mailModel1.transform(testFeaturizedDF.drop("mailFeatureWords","noStopWordsM
ailFeatures","mailFeatureHashes"))
```

Now we will display generated raw predictions:

```
rawPredictions.show(20))
```

Note that they are not two tables. It is one table broken in two for visual clarity:

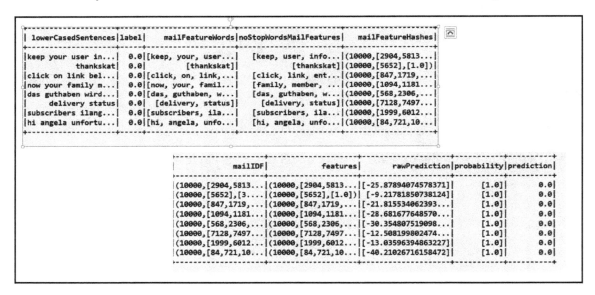

Raw predictions table

This is the final step, where we only want to show the relevant columns in the predictions table. The following line of code will drop those columns that are not required:

```
val predictions = rawPredictions.select($"lowerCasedSentences",
$"prediction").cache
```

Display the final `predictions` table. We only need the first and the last column. The `label` column is the predictions the model generated:

```
predictions.show(50)
```

It displays predictions as follows:

```
Displaying Predictions as below:
+--------------------+----------+
| lowerCasedSentences|prediction|
+--------------------+----------+
|keep your user in...|       0.0|
|           thankskat|       0.0|
|click on link bel...|       0.0|
|now your family m...|       0.0|
|das guthaben wird...|       0.0|
|     delivery status|       0.0|
|subscribers ilang...|       0.0|
|hi angela unfortu...|       0.0|
+--------------------+----------+
```

Predictions

We are done, so `stop` the `session`:

```
session.stop()
```

Summary

In this chapter, we created a spam classifier. We started with two datasets, one representing ham and the other, spam. We combined both datasets into one combined corpus that we put through a set of preprocessing steps, as mentioned in the *Implementation steps* section.

In the next chapter, we will build on some of the techniques learned so far to create a fraud detection ML application.

Questions

Here are 10 questions that will help to reinforce all of the learning material presented in this chapter:

1. Is the spam classification task a binary classification task?
2. What was the significance of the hashing trick in the spam classification task?
3. What is hashing collision and how is it minimized?
4. What do we mean by inverse document frequency?
5. What are stop words and why do they matter?
6. What is the role played by the Naive Bayes algorithm in spam classification?
7. How do you use the `HashingTF` class in Spark to implement the hashing trick in your spam classification process?
8. What is meant by the vectorization of features?
9. Is there a better algorithm that you can think of to implement the spam classification process?
10. What are the benefits of spam filtering, and why do they matter in business terms?

Further reading

The following paper is a comprehensive work that deserves reading:

https://www.sciencedirect.com/science/article/pii/S2405882316300412

Build a Fraud Detection System

5

In this chapter, we are going to develop an algorithm based on the Gaussian Distribution function using Spark ML. We will apply the algorithm to detect fraud in transactions data. This kind of algorithm can be applied toward building robust fraud detection solutions for financial institutions, such as banks, which handle great quantities of online transactions.

At the heart of the Gaussian Distribution, the function is the notion of an **anomaly**. The fraud detection problem is only a classification task but in a very narrow sense. It is a balanced supervised learning problem. The term *balanced* refers to the fact that the positives in the dataset are of a small number in relation to the negatives. On the other hand, an anomaly detection problem is typically not balanced. The dataset contains a significantly small number of anomalies (positives) in relation to the negatives. The fraud detection problem is a prime example of an anomaly detection problem. This is a problem where the dataset has a small number of outliers or data points whose values depart considerably from normal, to-be-expected values.

The overarching learning objective of this chapter is to implement a Scala solution that will predict fraud in financial transactions. We will lean on the Spark ML library's APIs and its supporting libraries in order to build a fraud detection prediction application.

In this chapter, we will cover the following topics:

- Fraud detection problem
- Project overview—problem formulation
- Getting started
- Implementation steps

Fraud detection problem

The fraud detection problem is not a supervised learning problem. We have an unbalanced class situation in our fraud detection scenario. What do we have to say about the importance of the F1 score in relation to the target variable? First, the target variable is a binary label. The F1 score is relevant to our fraud detection problem because we have an unbalanced class, where one class is practically more important than the other. What do we mean by that? The bottom line of the fraud detection classification process concerns whether a certain instance is fraudulent, and getting the classifier to classify or label this instance correctly as fraudulent. The emphasis is not on labeling an instance as non-fraudulent.

To reiterate, there are two classes in our fraud detection problem:

- Fraudulent
- Non-fraudulent

That said, we will now look at the dataset that this implementation depends upon

Fraud detection dataset at a glance

Download the dataset from the `ModernScalaProjects_Code` download folder.

Here is what the dataset looks like:

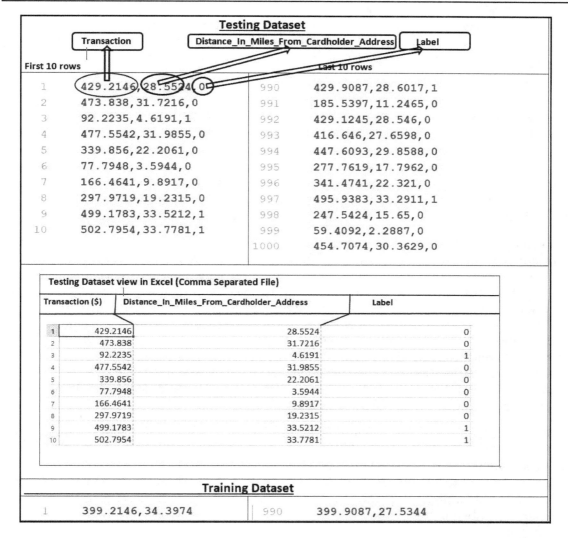

Testing Dataset

| Transaction | Distance_In_Miles_From_Cardholder_Address | Label |

First 10 rows   Last 10 rows

1	429.2146, 28.5524, 0	990	429.9087, 28.6017, 1
2	473.838, 31.7216, 0	991	185.5397, 11.2465, 0
3	92.2235, 4.6191, 1	992	429.1245, 28.546, 0
4	477.5542, 31.9855, 0	993	416.646, 27.6598, 0
5	339.856, 22.2061, 0	994	447.6093, 29.8588, 0
6	77.7948, 3.5944, 0	995	277.7619, 17.7962, 0
7	166.4641, 9.8917, 0	996	341.4741, 22.321, 0
8	297.9719, 19.2315, 0	997	495.9383, 33.2911, 1
9	499.1783, 33.5212, 1	998	247.5424, 15.65, 0
10	502.7954, 33.7781, 1	999	59.4092, 2.2887, 0
		1000	454.7074, 30.3629, 0

Testing Dataset view in Excel (Comma Separated File)

	Transaction ($)	Distance_In_Miles_From_Cardholder_Address	Label
1	429.2146	28.5524	0
2	473.838	31.7216	0
3	92.2235	4.6191	1
4	477.5542	31.9855	0
5	339.856	22.2061	0
6	77.7948	3.5944	0
7	166.4641	9.8917	0
8	297.9719	19.2315	0
9	499.1783	33.5212	1
10	502.7954	33.7781	1

Training Dataset

| 1 | 399.2146, 34.3974 | 990 | 399.9087, 27.5344 |

The dataset that our fraud detection system is built on

The Gaussian Distribution function is the basis for our algorithm.

So, is the F1 score important? Yes. The F1 score cannot be ignored (in the case of a balanced class situation, the F1 score is not necessarily important). It is the measure of an ML binary classification's process accuracy.

There is an F1 score for each class (one for fraudulent and the other for non-fraudulent). Therefore, if we want to compute the F1 score, we need to ensure that the F1 score is associated with the fraudulent class.

Fraud detection in the context of ML is a classification technique method that allows us to build models that attempt to detect outliers. Flagging outliers leads us to do what is needed to address fraud. For example, if I swiped my card in Portland, Maine, on a whale watching vacation in a location more than 1,000 miles away from where I live, it is possible that an underlying fraud detection algorithm associated with my credit card will flag **fraud**. The distance, in this case, led the algorithm to claim that the said transaction at a certain seafood establishment place on Maine's waterfront was fake. This is a simple use case. There are other financial transactions that this algorithm is trained to monitor and flag fraud.

For example, imagine a situation where Kate lost her card, and some random person picked that card up on the street (let us assume that Kate wasn't aware that she had lost her card until a day later) and tried to fill up his truck's gas tank with about $50 worth of gas. Even though this transaction was carried out, assuming that this person that attempted to use her card somehow got past the zip code check, Kate's credit card's fraud detection ML algorithm will flag as a suspicious transaction. Most likely, the algorithm will simply kick in and cause the transaction to fail or, even if that does not happen, she would get a call from the credit card company asking her where she used the card recently. In this case scenario, she got that call from the credit card company because the fraud detection algorithm flagged that particular transaction as suspicious, a fraudulent incident that requires the credit card company to take action.

A fraud detection system deals with massive amounts of data. A fraud detection classifier, as described in this chapter, will sift through a dataset of transaction data and process it. Spark's streaming capabilities allow us to detect outliers, samples in our dataset whose values do not fall within a normal, anticipated range of values. Detecting such values and generating a set of predictions flagging fraud is the emphasis of the fraud detection problem described in this chapter.

We will evaluate the performance of the algorithm and look at whether it flags or tags non-fraudulent samples as fraudulent or fraudulent samples as fraudulent, by computing metrics, such as precision, recall, and a harmonic mean of the precision and recall, known as the F1 score.

Precision, recall, and the F1 score

The following are important:

- The F1 measure
- Error term

In terms of a mathematical function, an F1 score can be defined mathematically as:

```
2 * precision recall / precision + recall
```

We will talk a little about the F1 score or measure. The error term is denoted by the Epsilon symbol (ε). Central to all this is the labeled input points in our unbalanced dataset. We are going to optimize the Epsilon parameter. How exactly do we do this? Let's first find the best possible F1 score. What is an Epsilon? In statistics, it is an **error term**. A measurement may deviate from its expected value. For example, it be the mean height of all males in a certain population. What is its purpose? We may denote an arbitrarily small, positive number as ε. Before computing the Epsilon, let's persist the testing dataframe. We have the following tasks cut out for us:

- Write a function to help us calculate the best Epsilon and the best F1 score
- Understand what the F1 score is

The maximum possible value that the F1 measure can take is 1. It denotes the level of correctness of the classification process by the classifier, that is, the proportion of samples or instances that are classified with a high degree of correctness or precision. It also tells us how robust (or not) the classifier is—whether the classifier missed classifying only a small number of samples or more. The F1 score is like a balanced mean between the precision and recall.

F1 becomes more important in an unbalanced class situation. It is a more practical measure than **accuracy**. Even though accuracy is more intuitive, and because of the fact that both false positives and false negatives are considered, a weighted score such as F1 becomes more meaningful in understanding the degree of correctness of the classifier.

Feature selection

Carefully selecting features is a crucial step in the formulation of a fraud detection program. Selecting many features or features, that does not contribute in a meaningful way, may impact the performance or skew predictions.

So, if we wish to flag fraudulent transactions, we should start small and build a system with two features only that we deem to meaningfully contribute to the classification. We choose two features that we represent in the dataset as columns of double values in a comma-separated file. These features are as follows:

- **Transaction**: Money spent on buying a certain commodity or service
- **Distance**: A geographical distance from the address of the cardholder on file, or a general distance outside of the perimeter defined by the zip code of the cardholder

That said, the goal for our fraud detection algorithm is that, with the feature selection process in place, we want to process the data, crunch all of the data points in our dataset, and flag potential fraud. This is a good place to bring in the Gaussian Distribution function, the basis for how we implement our fraud detection model. We need to talk a little more about this equation. It will help us understand exactly what our algorithm does and why it does what it does. In the next section, we will talk about the Gaussian Distribution function.

The Gaussian Distribution function

The Gaussian Distribution function is also known as a **bell curve** or a **normal distribution curve**. The bell curve has the following characteristics:

- This kind of distribution (of data) is said to be a continuous distribution.
- Data is spread out in this curve so that it converges around the bell portion (the highest point) of the curve, rather than to the left or the right. This center at the highest point is also the mean of the curve.
- The highest point on the bell curve corresponds to the highest probability of an occurrence and, as the curve tapers off, the probability of occurrences slides down to positions on either side of the curve on its slopes.
- Because of this property, the bell curve is also known as a normal distribution curve. All it needs are the standard deviation and the (population) mean.
- In a normal distribution, the three statistics, mean, mode and median, all bear the same value.
- The normal distribution curve is plotted with values of probability densities (a.k.a. normal frequencies). Referring to the figure present in *Project overview—problem formulation* section, the following are the meanings of the symbols in the equation:
  - μ = Mean of the population
  - σ = Standard deviation

- x = Plotted on the *x* axis, this represents a continuous random variable
- e = Natural logarithmic base, with a value of 2.71
- π = 3.1415

- The mean is simply a net value that is equal to the sum of all values of the data points, divided by the number of data points.
- It is to be noted that *y* is nothing but f(x) or p(x), the values of which are plotted on the *y* axis of the bell curve.

The following diagram illustrates a bell curve:

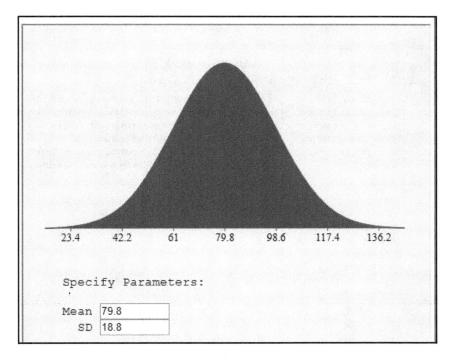

Bell curve

Non-fraudulent data comprises the bulk of our data. Such data is clustered in or close to the peak of the bell curve. In general terms, the top of the bell curve represents an event or a data point with the highest probability of occurrence. The tapering edges of the curve are where anomalies or outliers indicating fraud are found.

We mentioned fraud detection as a classification problem in a sense. It falls under the banner of anomaly detection. The table that follows describes the fundamental differences between a classification task and an anomaly detection task:

Property #	Classification	Anomaly Identification
1		It is not immediately apparent upfront or by casual inspection that data is either "regular", "expected", "within a certain range" or something that is unexpected represents a significant deviation The proportion of data with an unexpected value in comparison with those with regular or expected value is really small
2	Both Classification and Anomaly identification tasks perform classification in a sense, but the differences set them apart	
	Categories in a Classification task are clear cut. For example, a Breast Cancer sample is either Benign or Malignant	As opposed to a Classification task, there are no distinct categories available. In the case of finance transaction, it is harder to have an algorithm make straightforward predictions, because finance transactions can be arbitrary occurrences between one person and the next. Spending habits of different people make an Anomaly Identification task not so trivial.
3	The number of samples that are "positive" make up much higher proportion of the data. For example, we may have many breast cancer samples that are "malignant".	The number of anomalies indicating "Potential Fraud" are small.

Classification versus anomaly identification task

Looking at the preceding table, it is clear that the reasons that stand out to justify the use of an anomaly identification system are as follows:

- Samples that may be anomalous in one dataset may not be anomalous when they are new, incoming samples in another dataset of financial transactions.
- On the other hand, consider a breast cancer sample in an experimental unit of breast cancer samples that are classified as **malignant**. If the same sample is an incoming sample to experimental unit 2, the result of the classification will be the same.

Where does Spark fit in all this?

Whether you run Spark locally or in an environment where you have a cluster operating several distributed nodes, Spark will ramp up. In a local Spark environment, Spark will treat CPU cores as resources in a cluster.

The Gaussian Distribution algorithm is worth looking into. Let's see what our approach should be in the following section.

Fraud detection approach

The following diagram illustrates the high-level architecture for our fraud detection pipeline:

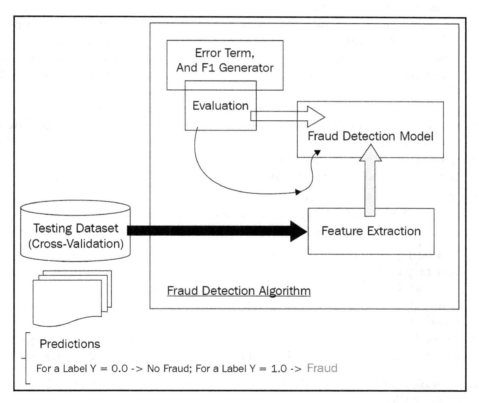

High-level architecture for the fraud detection pipeline

The following is a quick overview of the fraud detection process:

1. First, we compute statistics on the training set, which serves as a cross-validation dataset. We are interested in the mean and standard deviation from the statistical numbers.

2. Next, we want to compute the net **probability density function** (PDF) for each sample in our cross-validation set.

3. We derive the net probability density as a product of the individual probability densities.

4. Inside the algorithm, we compare a PDF value with an **Error Term** value to determine whether that sample represents an outlier, a potential **Fraud** transaction.

5. We optimize our classification process by having the algorithm executed on a cross-validation dataset.

6. As part of the optimization process, our algorithm computes the best possible value for the **Error Term**, an optimal value for the **Error Term** (denoted by an Epsilon) corresponding to a computed value of the **F1** score that is the highest. The algorithm, after repeated iterations, will come up with this highest score of the Epsilon.

7. A look at the dataset tells us that the most transaction data points fall within the range of 55-105 dollars. These transactions occurred within a radius of two to seven miles.

8. Spark will run this fraud detection program and extract a certain number of potential **Fraud** data points, for example, a good split dataset to use.

9. A breakup of the dataset could be as follows:
   - 65% as training examples to train the model on
   - 35% as a cross-validation set with instances of potential fraud in it

10. Evaluating the performance of our fraud detection algorithm is not done by the accuracy metric. The reason lies in the fact that if only a handful of samples exist that should be flagged as fraudulent, the algorithm that successfully flagged non-fraudulent samples may fail to flag the ones that are indeed potentially fraudulent.

11. Instead, we will compute the precision and recall metrics and, consequently, the F1 measure as a way to evaluate the performance of the fraud detection classifier.

Now we will look at an overview of our project, where we formulate the problem at hand, mostly in mathematical terms.

Project overview – problem formulation

Here is a helpful flowchart formulates the fraud detection problem at hand:

Understand what mathematical equation our Fraud Detection System will be based upon.

Choose the right features that might most meaningfully represent samples that indicate outliers

It is suggested you break up you dataset into: 1) Training (55%) 2) Testing (25%)

Calculate the following stats: Mean (mu or μ) and Standard Deviation (σ)

$$\mu_j = \frac{1}{m} \sum_{i=1}^{m} x_j^{(i)}$$

$$\sigma_j^2 = \frac{1}{m} \sum_{i=1}^{m} (x_j^{(i)} - \mu_j)^2$$

Implement our Model, which is simply the probability function Y= p(X)

Note: We (naturally need the values of Mean and Standard Deviation from the previous step)

$$y = \frac{1}{\sqrt{2\pi}} e^{-(x-\mu)^2/2\sigma}$$

μ == Mean
σ == Standard Deviation
$\pi \approx 3.14159$
$e \approx 2.71828$

Generate your predictions Y, after calculating probability (density) values for each testing set datapoint (Transaction or Distance feature)

Compute FPs, FNs, TPs, and TNs, to come up with model performance Evaluation (double) metrics: 1) Precision, 2) Recall, and the 3) F1 measure

Run the algorithm over a range of Error Terms to come up with Best Error Term (Epsilon). Optimize our model with the Best Error Term

Fraud detection flowchart

That said, let's get started. We do so by setting up an implementation infrastructure first.

Getting started

In this section, we will talk about setting up an implementation infrastructure or using the existing infrastructure from previous chapters. The following upgrades to your infrastructure are optional but recommended.

Starting in `Chapter 3`, *Stock Price Predictions*, we set up the **Hortonworks Development Platform** (**HDP**) Sandbox as a virtual machine. That said, three kinds of (isolated) HDP Sandbox deployments are possible. Of the three, we will only talk about two of them and those are:

- **Virtual machine environment (with Hypervisor) for Sandbox deployment:** HDP Sandbox running in an Oracle VirtualBox virtual machine.
- **A cloud-based environment for Sandbox deployment:** This option is attractive for users that have host machine memory limitations. The Sandbox runs in the cloud as opposed to a virtual machine that runs on your host machine.

With that opening point made, you can always run the fraud detection system code on the Spark shell. You have two options here:

- Use **Simple Build Tool** (**SBT**) to build and deploy your application in your Spark environment
- Open a Spark shell, develop interactively, and run it inside the shell

Last, but not least, you need the following software to simply launch the Spark shell and develop locally:

- Spark 2.3
- Scala 2.11.12
- SBT 1.0.4
- IntelliJ IDEA 2018.1.5 Community Edition
- At least 16 GB of RAM; 32 GB is even better.

Please refer back to the *Setting up prerequisite software* section in `Chapter 1`, *Predict the Class of a Flower from the Iris Dataset*. That sets us up with Java, Scala, and Spark, allowing us to use the Spark shell for interactive development.

In the next section, we will explain how to set up the Hortonworks Sandbox deployment on the Microsoft Azure Cloud, thereby proceeding to the implementation part.

Setting up Hortonworks Sandbox in the cloud

You might ask, why Microsoft Azure? Like any popular cloud services provider out there (and Google Compute Cloud is another solid offering), Azure prides itself as a set of robust cloud services that lets individual users and organizations develop and provision their applications on the cloud.

Creating your Azure free account, and signing in

The following are the steps to create an account:

1. To get started, head over to the `https://azure.microsoft.com/en-us/` web address. Click on the **Start free** button. Doing so will take you to the account login screen. If you do not have an account, set one up. This process only gives you a new Microsoft Azure account, not an actual cloud account; at least not yet.

2. Enter a password that you would like to choose with your new Microsoft Azure Cloud account.

3. Next, head over to your email account, and verify your email address by entering the security code.

4. If everything went well, your new Azure account is ready to use.

The next step is accessing the Azure Marketplace. In this marketplace, we will proceed with further steps, such as deployment. For now, let's locate the marketplace.

The Azure Marketplace

The following are the steps involved:

1. Head over to **Azure Marketplace**:

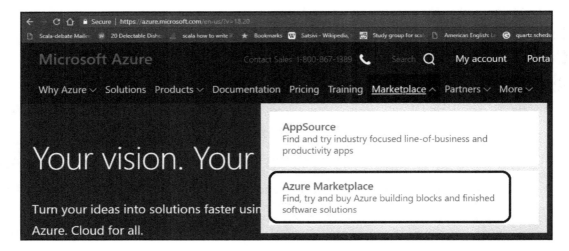

Looking for Azure Marketplace

2. After clicking on **Azure Marketplace**, type in `Hortwonworks` in the search box on the right, as shown in the following screenshot:

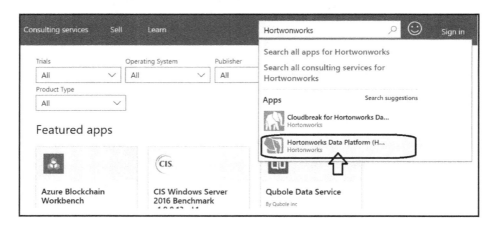

Searching for the Hortonworks Data Platform link

Click on the **Hortonworks Data Platform** link, as shown in the preceding screenshot. This takes you to the HDP Sandbox page.

The HDP Sandbox home page

On the HDP page, here is what you can expect to find:

1. Sign in to the Microsoft Azure Marketplace portal.
2. Kick off the Sandbox creation process, and the follow-through steps.
3. After the Sandbox creation has finished, deployment should follow. All the subsequent steps will be explained as we work through this.

Please perform the following steps to meet the preceding expectations:

1. For now, click on the **GET IT NOW** button, as shown in the following screenshot:

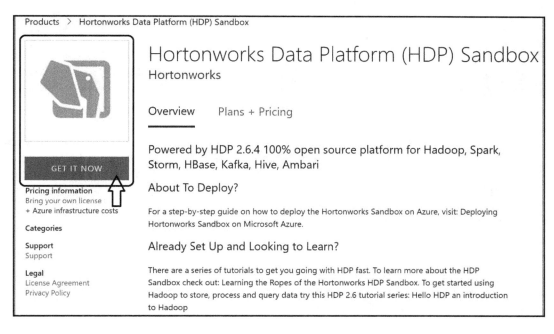

The HDP GET IT NOW page

2. After clicking on the **GET IT NOW** blue button, the next thing likely to happen is a dialog asking you to sign in to Microsoft Azure:

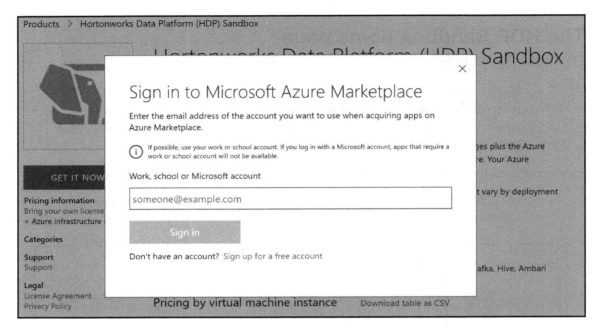

Sign-in page

3. The sign-in process takes you to another page, a page that lists a form where you need to enter details, such as your name, work email, job role, country/region, and phone number. You will be redirected to the Azure portal, as shown in the following screenshot:

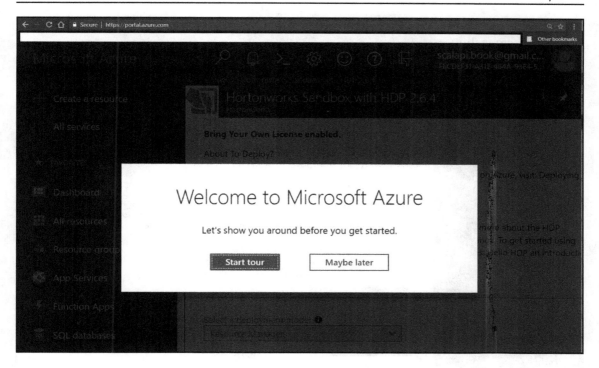

The Welcome to Microsoft Azure portal page

On the welcome screen of your portal, you can take the tour if you like, or simply click **Maybe later** and get down to business. Let's get on with the business of getting the Sandbox deployed on Azure.

4. The next step is to locate the blue **Create** button, as shown in the following screenshot:

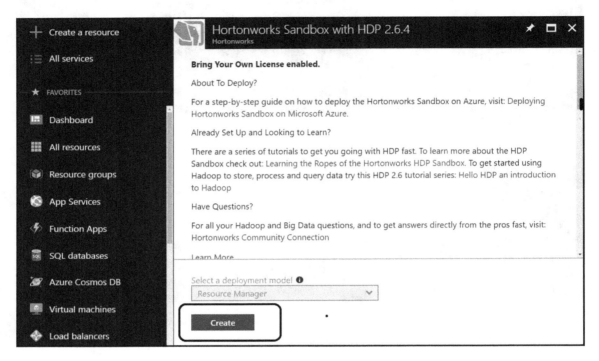

Create button screenshot

5. Now, we will finally get started on the Sandbox deployment process. Note that clicking on the **Create** button does not actually start the deployment process right away. The first order of business is creating a virtual machine:

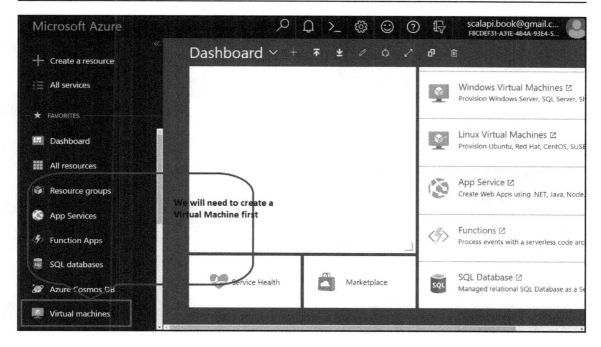

The creation of virtual machines screenshot

Let's get started on a virtual machine now.

Implementation objectives

The following implementation objectives cover the steps required to implement the Gaussian Distribution algorithm. We will perform the preliminary steps, such as **Exploratory Data Analysis** (**EDA**) once, and develop the implementation code. The breakdown is as follows:

1. Get the breast cancer dataset from the **UCI Machine Learning Repository**.
2. Carry out the preliminary EDA in the Sandbox Zeppelin Notebook environment (or Spark shell), and run a statistical analysis.
3. Develop the pipeline incrementally in your local Spark shell, or in a Zeppelin Notebook on your host machine, managed virtual machine, or your virtual machine on the Azure Cloud. Or simply run your Spark fraud detection application as an SBT application and deploy it in Spark by creating an Uber JAR using `spark-submit`.

4. Flesh out your code in IntelliJ. What this means is:
- Do not forget to wire up all the necessary dependencies in the `build.sbt` file.
- Interpret the classification process, because you want to know how well the classifier performed, how close the predicted values are to those in the original dataset, and so on.

Implementation steps

A good way to start is to download the skeleton SBT project archive file from the `ModernScalaProjects_Code` folder.

The step-by-step instructions are as follows:

1. EDA on the testing (cross-validation) dataset.
2. Calculate the probability densities.
3. Generate a fraud detection model.
4. Generate scores that measure the accuracy of the model:
   - Compute the best F1 score
   - Compute the best error term
5. Calculate outliers by repeatedly having the model generate predictions over each value of error term in a range.

We will create a `FraudDetection` trait now.

Create the FraudDetection trait

In an empty `FraudDetectionPipeline.scala` file, add in the following imports. These are imports that we need for `Logging`, `Feature Vector` creation, `DataFrame` and `SparkSession` respectively:

```
import org.apache.log4j.{Level, Logger}
import org.apache.spark.ml.linalg.Vectors
import org.apache.spark.sql.{DataFrame, SparkSession}
```

This is an all-important trait, holding a method for `SparkSession` creation and other code. The code from classes that extend from this trait can share one instance of a `SparkSession`:

```
trait FraudDetectionWrapper {
```

Next, we need the path to the testing dataset, meant for cross-validation, which is crucial to our classification:

```
val trainSetFileName = "training.csv"
```

The entry point to programming Spark with the `Dataset` and `DataFrame` API is the `SparkSession`, which creates `SparkSession` for our fraud detection pipeline, as shown in the following code:

```
lazy val session: SparkSession = {
  SparkSession
  .builder()
  .master("local")
  .appName("fraud-detection-pipeline")
  .getOrCreate()
  }
```

These two statements turn off `INFO` statements. Feel free to turn them on, as follows:

```
Logger.getLogger("org").setLevel(Level.OFF)
Logger.getLogger("akka").setLevel(Level.OFF)
```

The path to the dataset file is as follows:

```
val dataSetPath =
"C:\\Users\\Ilango\\Documents\\Packt\\DevProjects\\Chapter5A\\"
```

Create convenience tuples for holding the name of the `features` vector column and the `label` column names `val fdTrainSet_EDA =` (`"summary"`, `"fdEdaFeaturesVectors"`) are as follows:

```
val fdFeatures_IndexedLabel_Train = ("fd-features-vectors","label")
val fdFeatures_IndexedLabel_CV = ("fd-features-vectors","label")
```

This method allows us to transform our cross-validation dataset into a `DataFrame`. It takes in the training `Dataset` and outputs `DataFrame`:

```
def buildTestVectors(trainPath: String): DataFrame= {
 def analyzeFeatureMeasurements:
Array[(org.apache.spark.ml.linalg.Vector,String)] = {
 val featureVectors = session.sparkContext.textFile(trainPath, 2)
 .flatMap { featureLine => featureLine.split("\n").toList }
 .map(_.split(",")).collect.map(featureLine => ( Vectors.dense(
featureLine(0).toDouble,featureLine(1).toDouble),featureLine(2)))
 featureVectors
 }
```

Create `DataFrame` by transforming an array of a tuple of `Feature Vectors` and `Label`:

```
val fdDataFrame =
session.createDataFrame(analyzeFeatureMeasurements).toDF(fdFeatures_Indexed
Label_CV._1, fdFeatures_IndexedLabel_CV._2)
```

This `package` statement is required. Place this file in a package of your choice:

```
package com.packt.modern.chapter5
```

The following imports are required as we are going to pass around features as serializable vectors; therefore, we need `DenseVector`. The other imports are self-explanatory. For example, we cannot do without `DataFrame`, our fundamental unit of abstraction of data in Spark:

```
import org.apache.spark.ml.linalg.DenseVector
import org.apache.spark.sql.{DataFrame, Dataset, Row}
import org.apache.spark.rdd.RDD
```

The purpose of this program is to develop a data pipeline for detecting outliers, so-called data anomalies representing data points that point to fraud:

```
object FraudDetectionPipeline extends App with FraudDetectionWrapper {
```

The pipeline program entry point is as follows:

```
def main(args: Array[String]): Unit = {
```

Now, convert raw data from a training dataset to `DataFrame`. The test data resides in the `testing.csv` file that is right under the root of our SBT project folder. The training data contains two columns holding double values. The first column contains `Cost Data` and the second column contains `Distance`:

```
val trainSetForEda: DataFrame = session.read
.format("com.databricks.spark.csv") .option("header",
false).option("inferSchema", "true") .load(dataSetPath + trainSetFileName)
```

The raw training set `DataFrame` (`rawTrainsSetForEda`) we just obtained is meant for EDA. For example, we could inspect it for missing values or characters that don't belong. That said, we will inspect all the rows of the dataset by running the `show()` command:

```
cachedTrainSet.show()
```

This builds a `DataFrame` for a testing dataset. Its main purpose is cross-validation, an important ML technique that is explained back in the theory section:

```
val testingSet: DataFrame = buildTestVectors(dataSetPath +
```

```
crossValidFileName)
```

Display the new `DataFrame` test set:

```
trainSetEdaStats.show()
```

Next, the `summary` method is used to display the results of the EDA, including standard deviation, mean, and variances. These are required in our fraud detection classification task:

```
val trainSetEdaStats: DataFrame = cachedTrainSet.summary()
```

Next, persist the training set dataframe with the default storage level (`MEMORY_AND_DISK`).

Now, let's display the summary of that Spark extracted for us:

```
trainSetEdaStats.show()
```

Extract the `summary` row containing `"mean"` for both columns:

```
val meanDf: DataFrame = trainSetEdaStats.where("summary == 'mean'")
```

Display the new `DataFrame`—a one-row `DataFrame`:

```
meanDf.show()
```

Next, convert `DataFrame` to an array of rows. Issuing a `map` function call on this array extracts the `"mean"` row into this array containing a single tuple containing the mean values of both the `Cost` and `Distance` values. The result is a `"Mean Pairs"` array containing a tuple of strings:

```
val meanDfPairs: Array[(String, String)] = meanDf.collect().map(row =>
(row.getString(1), row.getString(2)))
```

Pull out both values of `mean` from the `"Mean Pairs"` tuple:

```
val transactionMean = meanDfPairs(0)._1.toDouble
val distanceMean = meanDfPairs(0)._2.toDouble
```

Now, we want to issue the `where` query to extract just the values of standard deviation from the training dataset EDA statistics `DataFrame`:

```
val trainSetSdDf: DataFrame = trainSetEdaStats.where("summary == 'stddev'
")
```

Display the content of this standard `DataFrame` deviations:

```
trainSetSdDf.show()
```

We have `DataFrame` containing two standard deviation values. Extract these values into an array of tuples. This array contains just one tuple holding two string values of standard deviation:

```
val sdDfPairs: Array[(String, String)] = trainSetSdDf.collect().map(row =>
(row.getString(1), row.getString(2)))
```

Extract the standard deviation values from the enclosing tuple. First, we need the standard deviation value for the transaction feature:

```
val transactionSD = sdDfPairs(0)._1.toDouble
```

Next, we want to extract the standard deviation of the distance feature:

```
val distanceSD = sdDfPairs(0)._2.toDouble
```

Let's build the following tuple pair for making a `broadcast` variable:

```
val meanSdTupleOfTuples = ( (transactionMean,distanceMean),(transactionSD,
distanceSD) )
```

Now, let's wrap the preceding tuple pair in `DenseVector`. Why are we doing this? Simple. We need a vector to send down into the cluster as a `broadcast` variable. Create an array of transaction vectors containing both mean and standard deviation values. What we want inside the transaction vector looks like this [Transaction Mean, Transaction SD]:

```
val meansVector = new DenseVector(Array(meanSdTupleOfTuples._1._1,
meanSdTupleOfTuples._1._2))
```

Let's display the vector. Scala offers an elegant way to display the content of a collection structure:

```
println("Transaction Mean and Distance Mean Vector looks like this: " +
meansVector.toArray.mkString(" "))
```

Create an array of distance vectors containing mean and standard deviation. And since we need a second vector, it looks like this [Distance Mean, Distance SD):

```
val sdVector: DenseVector = new DenseVector(Array
(meanSdTupleOfTuples._2._1, meanSdTupleOfTuples._2._2))
```

Display the standard deviation vector:

```
println("Distance Mean and Distance SD Vector looks like this: " +
sdVector.toArray.mkString(" "))
```

It is now time to broadcast the following into all the nodes in your Spark cluster:

- Mean vectors
- Standard deviation vectors

Broadcasting mean and standard deviation vectors

The `sparkContext` variable provides a `broadcast` method:

```
val broadcastVariable = session.sparkContext.broadcast((meansVector,
sdVector))
```

Everything we did up until now was in preparation to calculate the PDF, a value that denotes the probability of fraud. That said, we will see how to calculate a PDF in the next section.

Calculating PDFs

For each sample in the testing dataset, a PDF value is to be computed. Therefore, we will iterate over the entire dataset, and pass each feature vector into the `probabilityDensity` function. That function should, for each sample, compute the `probabilityDensity` value of type `Double`. Ultimately, we build an entire dataset containing PDF values, all of type `Double`.

The `testingDF` dataframe contains two columns:

- `feature` vector column
- `label`

Therefore, inside `map`, each `labelledFeatureVectorRow.getAs()` returns the feature vector.

Next, extract the features vector out of the testing dataframe. For each sample in the testing dataset, a PDF value is to be computed. Therefore, we will iterate over the entire dataset, and pass each feature vector into the `probabilityDensity` function. That function should, for each sample, compute the `probabilityDensity` value of type `Double`. Ultimately, we build an entire dataset containing probability density function values, all of type `Double`. The following are two datasets that are extracted from the EDA dataset.

The first dataset shows `mean`, while the second one shows standard deviation:

```
+-------+-----------------+-----------------+
|summary|        _c0|        _c1|
+-------+-----------------+-----------------+
|   mean|97.37915046250084|6.127270023033664|
+-------+-----------------+-----------------+
|summary|        _c0|        _c1|
+-------+-----------------+-----------------+
| stddev|10.83679761471887|3.2438494882693900|
+-------+-----------------+-----------------+
```

We need `implicits` here to account for the fact that an implicit encoder is needed to convert `DataFrame` into `Dataset` holding doubles. These `implicits` are provided to us by our `SparkSession` instance `session`, as shown here:

```
import session.implicits._
```

Iterate over the testing dataset, and for each feature vector row inside it. Apply a method to calculate a probability density value. A dataset of doubles is returned that has with in it double values of computed probabilities:

```
val fdProbabilityDensities: DataFrame =
testingDframe.map(labelledFeatureVectorRow => probabilityDensity(
labelledFeatureVectorRow.getAs(0) /* Vector containing 2 Doubles*/ ,
broadcastVariable.value) ).toDF("PDF")
```

Display the dataset of probability values, as shown here:

```
fdProbabilityDensities.show()
```

F1 score

Since our fraudulent class is the important one, we are going to need the following to help us choose a classifier that has the best F1 score as follows

- Labeled data is the test `DataFrame`—`testingDf`

- PDF—a product of probabilities computed in the `probabilityDensity` function

Keeping in mind that we need labeled data (points) to arrive at the best F1 score, the following background information is helpful as follows:

- What is the role of cross-validation? To understand cross-validation, we revisit the validation process, where a subset of the samples from the training set is used to train the model. Cross-validation is an improvement over validation, because of the fact that there are more observations available for the model to be fitted. Cross-validation becomes an attractive option because we are now able to pick from several models.
- What are the prerequisites before calculating the Epsilon and the F1 score? Those prerequisites are:
  - The step size = *the maximum of probability density - the minimum probability density / 500*
  - To arrive at the maximum value of probability, we need calculate the probability density value for each sample in the testing dataset and then derive the maximum
  - Labeled data points and features in the form of vectors:

```
409.7061,27.1669,0
430.4786,28.6422,0
455.6604,30.4306,0
71.3736,3.1384,0
225.8935,14.1124,0
157.3365,9.2435,0
422.0336,28.0424,1
241.3928,15.2132,0
476.2173,31.8905,0
119.105,6.5283,1
159.2634,9.3803,0
101.3141,5.2648,0
96.6736,4.9352,0
```

Labeled data points and features in the form of vectors

For each labeled data point, one PDF value needs to be computed. This requires prior knowledge of the following statistics:

- Mean cost, mean distance
- The standard cost deviation and, the standard deviation of the instance
- The data point itself

Each labeled data point (or feature) has two mean values and two standard deviations value. One labeled data point (feature) has one cost value and one distance value. We will take both mean and standard deviation into account and calculate the PDF for that labeled data point.

It turns out that each feature pair returns a probability density value pair, of course. We take the product of both probabilities in this pair and return a combined probability value as the PDF for that particular feature row.

We have enough information to calculate the combined probability value:

```
def probabilityDensity(labelledFeaturesVector: Vector,
broadcastVariableStatsVectorPair: (Vector / Transactions /, Vector /
Distance / )): Double = {
}
```

The strategy is to convert the labeled feature passed in into an array and then invoke a `map` operation on it. We want the probability density for each data point. Each data point is like this, `{ feature 1, feature 2}`, where `feature 1` has one mean, and one standard deviation, and `feature 2` has the same. To do this, we need to apply the mean and standard deviation of the entire dataset.

Inside the PDF, write the following code. Define an inner function inside called `featureDoubles`:

```
def featureDoubles(features: Array[Double],
                transactionSdMeanStats: Array[Double],
distanceSdMeanStats: Array[Double]): List[(Double, Double, Double)] = {
}
```

Inside the inner function, place the following code. The idea is to assemble a list of tuples that looks like this:

```
(93.47397393,79.98437516250003,18.879)
(6.075334279,5.13..,1.9488924384002693)
```

In the first tuple, `93.47397393` is the transaction feature value of the first row, `79.98437516250003` is the mean of all the transactions, and `18.879` is the standard deviation of all the transactions.

In the second tuple, `6.075334279` is the distance feature value of the first row, `5.13..` is the mean of all the distances, and `1.9488924384002693` is the standard deviation of all the distances.

The goal then is to calculate the PDF of each data point. Since there are two features, there are two PDFs per data point. The combined probability then is the product of the two.

What we first want is a tuple containing our testing `DataFrame features` in the form of an `Array[Double]`, a transaction `DataFrame` containing mean and standard deviation in the form of an `Array[Double]`, and a distance `DataFrame` containing mean and standard deviation in the form of `Array[Double]`:

```
(features, transactionSdMeanStats, distanceSdMeanStats).zipped.toList
```

The inner function, `featureDoubles`, is done. Let's define a variable called `pdF`, representing a list of probability density tuples.

The finished function, `featureDoubles`, looks like this:

```
def featureDoubles(features: ....,
                 transactionSdMeanStats: ...,
                 distanceSdMeanStats: ...): List[(Double, Double, Double)]
= {
  (features, transactionSdMeanStats, distanceSdMeanStats).zipped.toList)

}
```

Next, we need a PDF calculator that we call `pDfCalculator`. `pDfCalculator` is a name that represents a `List` of three tuples per row in the test dataset; each tuple contains three doubles. What we want inside each tuple looks like this: a transaction value, a transaction mean, and a transaction sd. Since there is a second tuple, the second tuple looks like this: (distance value, distance mean, and distance sd). When `map` is invoked, each tuple in turn inside the list (of tuples) is operated upon. Three values inside the tuple are there for a reason. All three are needed to calculate the probability density of one feature, as follows:

```
val pDfCalculator: List[(Double, Double, Double)] = featureDoubles(
  labelledFeaturesVector.toArray,
  broadcastVariableStatsVectorPair._1.toArray,
  broadcastVariableStatsVectorPair._2.toArray)
```

In the next line of code, we will carry out a `map` operation. Inside the `map` operation, we will apply a function that returns `probabilityDensityValue`. To do this, we will fall back on the `NormalDistribution` class in the Apache Commons Math library. The constructor to the `NormalDistribution` class requires mean and standard deviation and the data point itself. There are two features in a single feature row. That feature row contains two columns—`Transaction` and `Distance`. Therefore, `map` will successively calculate the probability density value for both data points, a `Transaction` data point, and a `Distance` data point, respectively:

```
val probabilityDensityValue: Double = pDfCalculator.map(pDf => new
NormalDistribution(pDf._2,pDf._3).density(pDf._1)).product
```

The `probabilityDensity` function in its final form looks something like this:

```
def probabilityDensity2(labelledFeaturesVector: ----,
broadcastVariableStatsVectorPair: (----,----)): Double = {

  def featureDoubles(features: -----,
               transactionSdMeanStats: ----,
               distanceSdMeanStats: -----): List[(Double, Double,
Double)] = {

 A tuple converted to a  List[(Double, Double, Double)]
(Feature Vector, Mean and Standard Deviation of Transaction, Mean and
Standard Deviation of Distance)

}
```

Finally, we want the `probabilityDensity` function to return the probability density value computed by `val probabilityDensityValue`.

With the probability density calculation behind us, we will now shift our attention to calculating the best error term. The error term is denoted by the Greek letter, Epsilon.

Calculating the best error term and best F1 score

In this section, we will write a function to calculate:

- The best error term (also known as the Epsilon)
- The best F1 score

We start by defining a function called `errorTermCalc`. What parameters does it require? It is apparent that we need two parameters:

- Our cross-validation dataset—`DataFrame`
- `DataFrame`, containing probability densities

There you go. We now have a function called `errorTermCalc` that takes two parameters and returns both the best error term and the best F1.

Why are these numbers important? To answer that question, we want to detect the outliers first. These are labeled data points that indicate fraud. Generating a new dataframe that classifies labeled data points as either fraudulent or not is the first step before we get down to calculating the best error term and best F1.

These are:

- Smallest of all the PDFs—`pDfMin`
- Largest of all the PDFs—`pDFMax`

The algorithm inside the code starts by assigning a baseline value, `pdFMin`, to the best error term. It then loops through to `pdfMax` in terms of a carefully selected step size. Remember, we want the best F1 score and the best way to do that is to assign 0, the worst value that any F1 score can potentially take.

The algorithm then works its way through the range of PDF values and arrives at the final values of both the best error term and the best F1 score, respectively. Basically, these final values are obtained starting with the following primary checks:

1. Is an intermediate calculated value of the best F1 score greater than 0?
2. Is the value of any error term less than the probability density value for a certain labeled data point?

 Remember, there is a probability density for every data point; so we are cycling through the entire (cross-) validation dataset.

If the test in primary check 1 passes, the best F1 at that point is updated to that intermediate calculated value of the best F1 score. PDF step-wise values are compared to the predefined error term. If the PDF is less than the predefined Epsilon, that data point becomes a predicted fraudulent value.

The definition for the `errorTermCalc` function looks like this:

```
private def errorTermCalc(testingDframe: DataFrame, probabilityDensities:
DataFrame/*Dataset[Double] */) = { }
```

We will start fleshing out of details inside the curly braces of the new function.

Maximum and minimum values of a probability density

Here is how we extract the smallest and largest values of the probability density:

```
val maxMinArray: Array[Double] = probabilityDensities.collect().map(pbRow
=> pbRow.getDouble(0) )
```

We need a reasonable, carefully selected step size for the error term. That is what we will be doing in the next step.

Step size for best error term calculation

Now, let's define a `step` size to calculate the best Epsilon:

```
val stepsize = (maxMinPair._1 - maxMinPair._2) / 1000.0
```

We need a loop for the algorithm to step through and calculate the `labelAndPredictions` dataframe at each `step` size value of the error term. This will also help us to find the best F1.

A loop to generate the best F1 and the best error term

Let's find the best F1 for different Epsilon values:

```
for (errorTerm <- maxMinPair._2 to maxMinPair._1 by stepsize) {
```

Broadcast the error term into Spark. Create the `broadcast` variable first:

```
val broadCastedErrorTerm:Broadcast[Double] =
session.sparkContext.broadcast(errorTerm)

val broadcastTerm: Double = broadCastedErrorTerm.value
```

Generate predictions here. If the `Double` value in the probability densities dataframe happens to be less than the `broadCastedErrorTerm`, that value is flagged as `fraud`.

It is possible you may run into the following error:

```
Unable to find encoder for type stored in a Dataset. Primitive types
(Int, String, etc) and Product types (case classes) are supported by
importing spark.implicits._ Support for serializing other types will be
added in future releases.
```

To get around this problem, we add the following `import` statement:

```
import session.implicits._
```

For data of a certain datatype to be put away in a new `DataFrame`, Spark wants you to pass in appropriate `Encoders`. With that out of the way, let's get down to generating predictions.

Generating predictions – outliers that represent fraud

We start by transforming the `probabilityDensities` dataframe from before:

```
val finalPreds: DataFrame= probabilityDensities.map { probRow =>
if (probRow.getDouble(0) < broadcastTerm) {
1.0 /* Fraud is flagged here */
} else 0.0
}.toDF("PDF")
```

Now, let's create a new dataframe with two dataframes—the testing dataframe, and the final predictions dataframe. Drop the `"label"` column in the testing dataframe and do a cross-join with the `finalpreds` dataframe. Do not forget to persist the new dataframe with the default storage level (`MEMORY_AND_DISK`):

```
val labelAndPredictions: DataFrame =
testingDframe.drop("label").crossJoin(finalPreds).cache()
println("Label And Predictions: " )
labelAndPredictions.show()
```

Next, we want to generate the best error term and the best F1 measure.

Generating the best error term and best F1 measure

In this section, we want to come up with the number of false positives, the number of true positives, and the number of false negatives. First, we want to know how many false positives there are:

```
val fPs = positivesNegatives(labelAndPredictions, 0.0, 1.0)
println("No of false negatives is: " + fPs)
```

Now, we want to know how many true positives there are:

```
val tPs = positivesNegatives(labelAndPredictions, 1.0, 1.0)
```

We also want to know how many false negatives exist:

```
val fNs = positivesNegatives(labelAndPredictions, 1.0, 0.0)
```

Now that we have fNs, tPs, and fPs, we can calculate the precision and recall metrics.

Preparing to compute precision and recall

Here are the lines of code that implement a simple mathematical equation to come up with the precision and recall scores.

Let's calculate precision now:

```
val precision = tPs / Math.max(1.0, tPs + fPs)
```

Followed by a calculation of recall:

```
val recall = tPs / Math.max(1.0, tPs + fNs)
```

We have both precision and recall. This gives us what we need to calculate the F1 score or the f1Measure, as follows:

```
val f1Measure = 2.0 * precision * recall / (precision + recall)
```

Next, let's determine bestErrorTermValue and bestF1measure:

```
if (f1Measure > bestF1Measure){ bestF1Measure = f1Measure
bestErrorTermValue = errorTerm //println("f1Measure > bestF1Measure")
scores +( (1, bestErrorTermValue), (2, bestF1Measure) ) } }
```

We are almost done with the calculation of the best error term (Epsilon) and the best F1 measure.

In the next step, we will summarize what we just did to generate the best Epsilon and the best error term.

A recap of how we looped through a ranger of Epsilons, the best error term, and the best F1 measure

We implemented a loop just prior to arriving here. Here is a breakdown of those steps in pseudocode:

```
for (errorTerm <- maxMinPair._2 to maxMinPair._1 by stepsize) {

//Step 1: We broadcast the error term (epsilon) into Spark

//Step 2: We generate predictions

//Step 3: We will crossjoin the final predictions dataframe with our
initial Testing Dataframe

//Step 4: We calculate False Negatives, True Negatives, False Negatives and
True Positives

//Step 5: Calculate Precision and Recall

//Step 6: Calculate F1

Step 7: Return Best Error Term and Best F1 Measure

}
```

In the preceding Step 3, we derived thelabelsAndPredictions dataframe. In Step 4, we set out to calculate the following:

- False positives
- False negatives
- True positives

In the next section, we will implement the method called `positivesNegatives` to calculate false positives, false negatives, and true positives. Here is a representation of the `evalScores` method function, where the algorithm does a lot of processing:

```
def evalScores(testingDframe: DataFrame,probabilityDensities: DataFrame):
ListMap[ Int, Double] = {

/*
  Extract the smallest value of probability density and the largest.  */
val maxMinArray: Array[Double] = probabilityDensities.collect().map(pbRow
=> pbRow.getDouble(0) )

/*
  A sensible step size
*/
val stepsize = (maxMinPair._1 - maxMinPair._2) / 750.0

/*
   Write the loop to calculate the best Epsilon and the best F1 at that
Best Epsilon
*/
for (errorTerm <- maxMinPair._2 to maxMinPair._1 by stepsize) {
   //Step 1: We broadcast the error term (epsilon) into Spark
     val broadCastedErrorTerm:Broadcast[Double] = ----
     //Step 2: We generate predictions
   import session.implicits._
   val finalPreds: DataFrame= probabilityDensities.map { ...... }

    //Step 3: We will crossjoin the final predictions dataframe with our
initial Testing Dataframe
     val labelAndPredictions: DataFrame =
testingDframe.drop("label").crossJoin(finalPreds).cache()

    //Step 4: We calculate False Negatives, True Negatives, False Negatives
and True Positives

    //Step 5: Calculate Precision and Recall
    val fPs = <<Invoke the positivesNegatives here >>
    val tPs =  <<Invoke the positivesNegatives here >>
    val tPs =  <<Invoke the positivesNegatives here >>

   //The Precision and recall based on Step 5
    val precision = tPs / Math.max(1.0, tPs + fPs)
    val recall = tPs / Math.max(1.0, tPs + fNs)

   //Step 6: Calculate F1 based on results from Step 5
    val f1Measure = 2.0 * precision * recall / (precision + recall)
    //Step 7: Return Best Error Term and Best F1 Measure
```

```
        /*
        //The logic to get at the Best Error Term (epsilon) and the F1 is
this:
        // At any point of time, in the looping process, if the F1 measure
value from Step 6 is
        // greater than 0,  then that F1 value is assigned to the Scala val
representing the Best F1
        // Both these value are added into a Scala ListMap
        //When the loop is done executing we have an updated ListMap that
contains two values: The Best F1     //and the Best Error Term
```

Up until this point, we talked about wanting to calculate the best error term and the best F1 measure. Both of those metrics need computed values of precision and recall, which, in turn, depend on computed values of fPs, fNs, and tPs. That brings us to the next task of creating a function that calculates these numbers. That is the focus of the next step.

Function to calculate false positives

In this section, we write a `positivesNegatives` function that takes in the `labelsAndPredictions` dataframe from `Step 3` and spits out either false positives, false negatives, or true positives, depending on what we want.

It also takes in two other parameters:

- A target label that can take the following values:
  - A value of `1.0` for true positives
  - A value of `0.0` for false positives
  - A value of `1.0` for false negatives
- A final predicted value that can take the following values:
  - A value of `1.0` for true positives
  - A value of `1.0` for false positives
  - A value of `0.0` for false negatives

Accordingly, here is one method that calculates all three: true positives, false positives, and false negatives:

```
def positivesNegatives(labelAndPredictions: DataFrame /* Dataset[(Double,
Double)] */,
  targetLabel: Double,
  finalPrediction: Double): Double = {

}
```

The body of the method is a single line of code that calculates a `Double` value, of course:

```
labelAndPredictions.filter( labelAndPrediction =>
labelAndPrediction.getAs("PDF") == targetLabel &&
labelAndPrediction.get(1) == finalPrediction ).count().toDouble
```

The finished method looks like this:

```
def positivesNegatives(labelAndPredictions: DataFrame /* Dataset[(Double,
Double)] */, targetLabel: Double, finalPrediction: Double): Double = {

    //We do a filter operation on our labelsAndPredictions DataFrame. The
    filter condition is as follows:
    // if the value under the label column matches the incoming targetLabel
    AND the value in the predictions column matches the finalPrediction value
    then count the number of datapoints that satisfy this condition. This will
    be your count of False Positives, for example.

        labelAndPredictions.filter( <<the filter
condition>>).count().toDouble

}
```

This completes the implementation of the fraud detection system. In the next section, we will summarize what this chapter has accomplished.

Summary

Fraud detection is not a supervised learning problem. We did not use the random forests algorithm, decision trees, or **logistic regression** (**LR**). Instead, we leveraged what is known as a Gaussian Distribution equation to build an algorithm that performed classification, which is really an anomaly detection or identification task. The importance of picking an appropriate Epsilon (error term) to enable the algorithm to find the anomalous samples cannot be overestimated. Otherwise, the algorithm could go off the mark and label non-fraudulent examples as anomalies or outliers that indicate a fraudulent transaction. The point is, tweaking the Epsilon parameter does help with a better fraud detection process.

A good part of the computational power required was devoted to finding the so-called best Epsilon. Computing the best Epsilon was one key part. The other part, of course, was the algorithm itself. This is where Spark helped out a lot. The Spark ecosystem provided us with a powerful environment, letting us write code that parallelizes and orchestrates our data analytics efficiently in a distributed manner.

In the next chapter, we will carry out data analysis tasks on flight performance data.

Questions

The following are questions that will consolidate and deepen your knowledge of fraud detection:

1. What is a Gaussian Distribution?
2. The algorithm in our fraud detection system requires something really important to be fed into it, before generating probabilities? What is that?
3. Why is the selection of an error term (Epsilon) such a big deal in detecting outliers and identifying the correct false positives and false negatives?
4. Why is fraud detection not exactly a classification problem?
5. Fraud detection is essentially an anomaly identification problem. Can you name two properties that define anomaly identification?
6. Can you think of other applications that can leverage anomaly identification or outlier detection?
7. Why is cross-validation so important?

8. Why is our fraud detection problem not a supervised learning problem?
9. Can you name a couple of ways to optimize the Gaussian Distribution algorithm?
10. Sometimes, our results may not be satisfactory because the algorithm failed to identify certain samples as a fraud. What could we do better?

It is time to move to the last section, where we invite readers to further enrich their learning journey by referring to the resources indicated.

Further reading

PayPal's data platforms carry out real-time decision making that prevents fraud. Their systems crunch several petabytes every single day. Check out `https://qcon.ai/` for a recent conference on AI and ML. Study their use cases and learn how companies such as PayPal leverage the latest advances in AI and ML to help combat fraud.

Explore how Kafka can work with Spark to bring near real-time fraud detection to your fraud detection procedures.

We are all familiar with Airbnb (`https://www.airbnb.com/trust`). Find out how Airbnb's trust and safety team is combating fraud, while they protect and grow their business model that is so critically based on trust.

6
Build Flights Performance Prediction Model

Flight delays and cancellations are travel annoyances. Will a Chicago-bound flight arrive late causing a traveler to miss their connecting flight to Denver? Another traveler at Chicago Airport just learned that their connecting flight to Philly was delayed, perhaps even canceled. If both travelers could predict the odds of their respective experiences actually occurring, travel would get so much better.

That said, implementing a flight delay pipeline that can predict outcomes on the lines just described is the overarching learning objective of this chapter. The next section lists all the learning objectives in terms of topics covered in this chapter.

All learning objectives in this chapter depend on the following datasets compiled by the United States Department of Transportation. These are flight data, airline carrier data, and flight performance data, respectively.

Each topic covered in this chapter has specific learning objectives, broken down into two categories:

- Background theory, starting with coverage of the years 2007 and 2008 flights, carrier, and flight performance datasets
- A Spark-Scala implementation of a flight delay prediction model

That said, the immediate learning objective is to gain an understanding of the flight on-time performance dataset for 2007 and 2008. A good place to start is the *Flight dataset at a glance* section:

- Understanding background theory relevant to understanding flight
- Formulating the flights performance problem by applying the background theory

- We learn which dataset to pick from the US Department of Transportation website the dataset we pick belong to the years 2007 and 2008
- We want to learn what we can from the data, by conducing data exploratory steps
- Dividing data into test and training datasets
- Implementation of a model in Scala and Spark to predict flights performance

Overview of flight delay prediction

In this chapter, we will implement a logistic regression-based machine learning model to predict flight delays. This model learns from flight data described in the next section, *Flight dataset at a glance*.

A real-life situation goes like this—travel company T has a new prediction feature in their booking system that is designed to enhance a customer's travel experience. How so? For example, say traveler *X* wants to get on Southwest flight *SW1* from origin *A* (St Louis) to destination *C* (Denver) with a connection at city *B* (Chicago). If T's flight booking system could predict the odds of *X*'s flight arriving late at Chicago, and furthermore the odds of missing the connecting flight as well, *X* has information at their disposal that lets him or her decide the next course of action.

With these opening point made, let's take a look at our flight dataset.

The flight dataset at a glance

Data analysis in this chapter relies on a flight dataset, a dataset consisting of the following individual datasets. Download these datasets from the `ModernScalaProjects` folder:

- `Airports.csv`
- `AirlineCarriers.csv`
- `Flights.csv`
- `OnTime2007Short.xlsx`
- `OnTime2008Short.xlsx`

The following screenshot is an overall view of the airports and airline carrier's datasets:

Type of Data	Dataset Name	Fields
Airports	Airports.csv	IATA – International Airport Code AIRPORT – Name of Airport CITY – City of Airport STATE – State of Airport COUNTRY – Country of Airport LATITUDE – Longitude Reading LONGITUDE – Latitude Reading

View of Data

IATA	AIRPORT	CITY	STATE	COUNTRY	LATITUDE	LONGITUDE
00M	Thigpen	Bay Springs	MS	USA	31.95376472	-89.2345
00R	Livingston Municipal	Livingston	TX	USA	30.68586111	-95.01793
00V	Meadow Lake	Colorado Springs	CO	USA	38.94574889	-104.5699
01G	Perry-Warsaw	Perry	NY	USA	42.74134667	-78.05208

Carrier Codes	AirlineCarriers.csv	CODE – Airline Carrier Code DESCRIPTION – Airline Carrier Name

View of Data:

CODE	DESCRIPTION
02Q	Titan Airways
04Q	Tradewind Aviation
05Q	Comlux Aviation, AG
06Q	Master Top Linhas Aereas Ltd.
07Q	Flair Airlines Ltd.
09Q	Swift Air, LLC

The airport and airline dataset

The following table describes the structure of the on-time dataset
(`OnTime2008Short.xlsx`). It lists all the 28 fields. The table consists of denormalized, semi-structured data:

FlightYear /* 1 */	**FlightMonth** /* 2 */
FlightDayOfmonth /* 3 */	**FlightDayOfweek** /* 4 */
FlightDepTime /* 5 */	**FlightCrsDeptime** /* 6 */
FlightArrtime /* 7 */	**FlightCrsArrTime** /* 8 */
FlightUniqueCarrier /* 9 */	**FlightNumber** /* 10 */
FlightTailNumber /* 11 */	**FlightActualElapsedTime** /* 12 */
FlightCrsElapsedTime /* 13*/	**FlightAirTime** /* 14 */
FlightArrDelay /* 15 */	**FlightDepDelay** /* 16 */
FlightOrigin /* 17 */	**FlightDest** /* 18 */
FlightDistance /* 19 */	**FlightTaxiin** /* 20 */
FlightTaxiout /* 21 */	**FlightCancelled** /* 22 */
FlightCancellationCode /* 23 */	**FlightDiverted** /* 24 */
FlightCarrierDelay /* 25 */	**FlightWeatherDelay** /* 26 */
FlightNasDelay /* 27 */	**FlightSecuritDelay** /* 28 */

FlightLateAircraftDelay /* 29 */

The OnTime2008Short file dataset

The description of the fields are into the following categories:

- **Causes of delay on account of the airline (carrier) (in minutes)**:
  - FlightCarrierDelay: It denotes the delay caused by the carrier
  - FlightWeatherDelay: It denotes the delay caused by weather
  - FlightNASDelay: It denotes the delay caused by the National Air System
  - FlightSecurityDelay: It denotes the delay on account of security checks or other security reasons
  - FlightLateAircraftDelay: It denotes that the aircraft arrives late for reasons other than the preceding causes described

- **Flight aircraft data**:
  - FlightUniqueCarrier: A unique two-letter sequence in uppercase, or a one-number-one-letter sequence (for example, US, DL, 9E)

The section represents a comprehensive overview of the project. To start with, we formulate at a high level the nature of the underlying problem we want to solve. The problem formulation step paves the way for implementation. First, let's formulate the flight delay prediction problem.

Problem formulation of flight delay prediction

A high-level description of the problem of flight delays is summed up in one statement—we want to implement a prediction mode that will make predictions on flight delays. In short, a traveler with an itinerary wants to know whether his/her flight or flights are running late.

Getting started

This section starts by laying out the implementation infrastructure for Chapter 4, *Building a Spam Classification Pipeline*. The goal of this section will be to get started on developing one data pipeline to analyze the flight-on-time dataset. The first step is to set up prerequisites, before implementation. That is the goal of the next subsection.

Setting up prerequisite software

The following prerequisites or prerequisite checks are recommended. A new prerequisite on this list is MongoDB:

- Increase Java memory
- Review JDK version
- Self-contained Scala application based on **Simple Build Tool** (**SBT**), where all dependencies are wired into the `build.sbt` file
- MongoDB

We start by detailing the steps to increase the memory available to the Spark application. Why would we want to do that? This and other points related to Java heap space memory are explored in the following topic.

Increasing Java memory

Flight on-time records, compiled over a period of time, say, month by month, become big or medium data. Processing such volumes of data on a local machine is not trivial. In most cases, a local machine with limited RAM simply won't cut it.

As challenging as this situation can be, we want to make the best use of our local machine. That brings us to why we want to increase Java memory. For example, trying to process a typical one-time dataset file of 27 columns and 509,520 rows, is enough to cause Java to run out of memory (see the following screenshot):

```
18/06/29 00:14:49 ERROR SparkUncaughtExceptionHandler: Uncaught exception in thread Thread[Executor task launch worker f
or task 1,5,run-main-group-0]
java.lang.OutOfMemoryError: GC overhead limit exceeded
        at java.nio.ByteBuffer.wrap(ByteBuffer.java:373)
        at org.apache.hadoop.io.Text.decode(Text.java:389)
        at org.apache.hadoop.io.Text.toString(Text.java:280)
        at org.apache.spark.SparkContext$$anonfun$textFile$1$$anonfun$apply$8.apply(SparkContext.scala:825)
        at org.apache.spark.SparkContext$$anonfun$textFile$1$$anonfun$apply$8.apply(SparkContext.scala:825)
        at scala.collection.Iterator$$anon$11.next(Iterator.scala:410)
        at scala.collection.Iterator$class.foreach(Iterator.scala:891)
        at scala.collection.AbstractIterator.foreach(Iterator.scala:1334)
        at scala.collection.generic.Growable$class.$plus$plus$eq(Growable.scala:59)
        at scala.collection.mutable.ArrayBuffer.$plus$plus$eq(ArrayBuffer.scala:104)
        at scala.collection.mutable.ArrayBuffer.$plus$plus$eq(ArrayBuffer.scala:48)
        at scala.collection.TraversableOnce$class.to(TraversableOnce.scala:310)
        at scala.collection.AbstractIterator.to(Iterator.scala:1334)
        at scala.collection.TraversableOnce$class.toBuffer(TraversableOnce.scala:302)
        at scala.collection.AbstractIterator.toBuffer(Iterator.scala:1334)
        at scala.collection.TraversableOnce$class.toArray(TraversableOnce.scala:289)
        at scala.collection.AbstractIterator.toArray(Iterator.scala:1334)
        at org.apache.spark.rdd.RDD$$anonfun$collect$1$$anonfun$12.apply(RDD.scala:939)
        at org.apache.spark.rdd.RDD$$anonfun$collect$1$$anonfun$12.apply(RDD.scala:939)
        at org.apache.spark.SparkContext$$anonfun$runJob$5.apply(SparkContext.scala:2074)
        at org.apache.spark.SparkContext$$anonfun$runJob$5.apply(SparkContext.scala:2074)
        at org.apache.spark.scheduler.ResultTask.runTask(ResultTask.scala:87)
        at org.apache.spark.scheduler.Task.run(Task.scala:109)
        at org.apache.spark.executor.Executor$TaskRunner.run(Executor.scala:345)
```

GC overhead limit exceeded

Firstly, `java.lang.OutOfMemory` occurs when the Java VM on your machine tries to go over its threshold memory allocation, as set by the `-Xmx` parameter.

The `-Xmx` parameter has to do with memory management. It is used to set the maximum Java heap size. From Java 1.8 onwards, the JVM will allocate heap size proportional to the physical memory on the machine

To address this situation, here are a few different ways to increase Java memory:

- Method 1: On the command line, we pass into SBT the following runtime parameters:
    - Maximum allowable heap size
    - Java thread stack size
    - Initial heap size

- Method 2: Setting maximum Java heap size in the Java control panel.
- Method 3: Globally setting these parameters in the environment variable, `JAVA_OPTS`.

To address the `GC Overhead Limit exceeded` problem illustrated in the preceding screenshot, we can quickly allocate more heap space right on the command line, like this:

```
C:\Users\Ilango\Documents\Packt\DevProjects\Chapter63>set SBT_OPTS="-XX:MaxPermSize=1G -Xmx2G"

C:\Users\Ilango\Documents\Packt\DevProjects\Chapter63>sbt
"C:\Users\Ilango\.sbt\preloaded\org.scala-sbt\sbt\"1.0.4"\jars\sbt.jar"
Java HotSpot(TM) 64-Bit Server VM warning: ignoring option MaxPermSize=1G -Xmx2G; support was removed in 8.0
[info] Loading settings from idea.sbt ...
[info] Loading global plugins from C:\Users\Ilango\.sbt\1.0\plugins
[info] Loading project definition from C:\Users\Ilango\Documents\Packt\DevProjects\Chapter63\project
[info] Loading settings from build.sbt ...
[info] Set current project to Chapter63 (in build file:/C:/Users/Ilango/Documents/Packt/DevProjects/Chapter63/)
[info] sbt server started at 127.0.0.1:5191
sbt:Chapter63>
```

Allocating heap space

Note the `-Xmx2G` setting. We set the `SBT_OPTS` environment variable with the value of `-Xmx2G`, the maximum allocated Java heap space memory. We set that and then run SBT.

Before we move on to the next method, it might be useful to know the following JVM heap allocation statistics:

- Total memory
- Maximum memory
- Free memory

This is useful. Heap memory utilization numbers are revealing. The following screenshot shows how to do this:

```
C:\Users\Ilango\Documents\Packt\DevProjects\Chapter63>scala
Welcome to Scala 2.11.12 (Java HotSpot(TM) 64-Bit Server VM, Java 1.8.0_172).
Type in expressions for evaluation. Or try :help.

scala> import java.lang.Runtime
import java.lang.Runtime

scala> val jvmMemoryStats = Runtime.getRuntime.totalMemory / (1024 * 1024)
jvmMemoryStats: Long = 175

scala> val jvmMemoryStats = Runtime.getRuntime
jvmMemoryStats: Runtime = java.lang.Runtime@251c4280

scala> val totalMemory = jvmMemoryStats.totalMemory/(1024 * 1024)
totalMemory: Long = 177

scala> val maxMemory = jvmMemoryStats.maxMemory/(1024 * 1024)
maxMemory: Long = 1820

scala> val freeMemory = jvmMemoryStats.freeMemory/(1024 * 1024)
freeMemory: Long = 76

scala>
```

Heap memory

Next up, we will talk about method 2, where we go through the steps to set Java runtime parameters globally.

The following steps apply to Windows machines.

1. Navigate to **Start** | **Control Panel**, and under **Category**, choose **Small icons**:

Control Panel

2. The ensuing panel allows you to make changes to your computer's settings. The Java setting is one of those. Locate **Java** in the **Control Panel**:

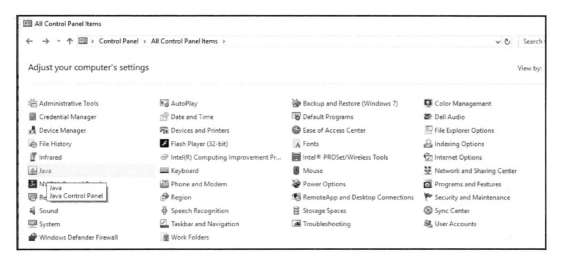

All Control Panel Items

3. Clicking on **Java**, as in the preceding screenshot, will take you to the **Java Control Panel**:

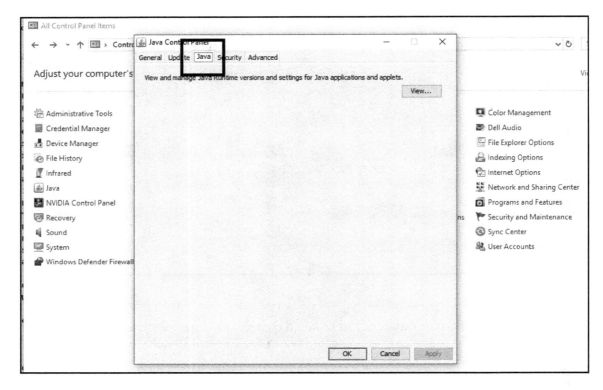

Java Control Panel

4. Select the **Java** tab results in the **Java Runtime Environment Settings** panel, where you may inspect the **Runtime Parameters**, such as the Java heap size:

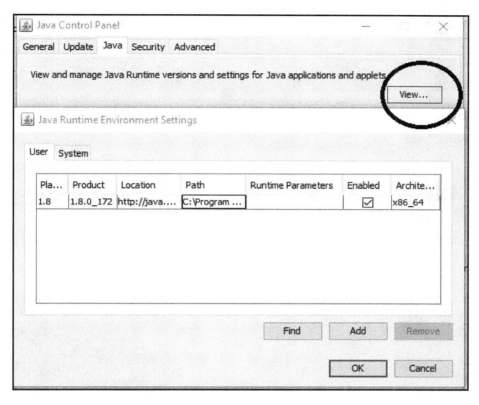

Java Control Panel's User tab

Referring to the **Java Control Panel** representations, we want to set the maximum Java heap size in the **Runtime Parameters** box. Xmx2048m is the new value of the maximum heap space, where m stands for megabytes. It is easy to modify the value of the -Xmx parameter. Click on it, then change the value to 2048 and click **OK**.

There is no space between -Xmx and 2048m or 2 GB.

That's it. Exit the Control Panel:

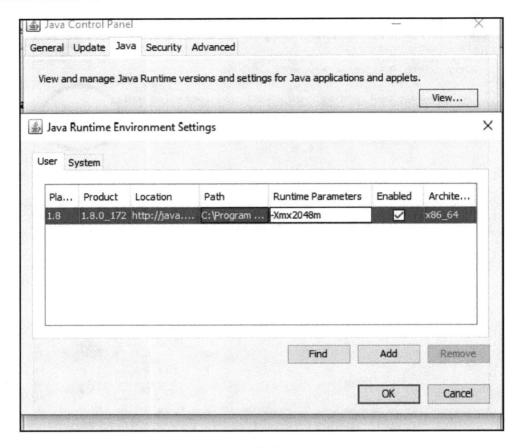

Java Control Panel Runtime Parameters

Speaking of Java memory management and the settings that are available to help us manage Java memory usage in our Spark application, here is a list of command line options available on running the `java -X` command line:

```
C:\Users\Ilango\Documents\Packt\DevProjects\Chapter63>java -X
    -Xmixed           mixed mode execution (default)
    -Xint             interpreted mode execution only
    -Xbootclasspath:<directories and zip/jar files separated by ;>
                      set search path for bootstrap classes and resources
    -Xbootclasspath/a:<directories and zip/jar files separated by ;>
                      append to end of bootstrap class path
    -Xbootclasspath/p:<directories and zip/jar files separated by ;>
                      prepend in front of bootstrap class path
    -Xdiag            show additional diagnostic messages
    -Xnoclassgc       disable class garbage collection
    -Xincgc           enable incremental garbage collection
    -Xloggc:<file>    log GC status to a file with time stamps
    -Xbatch           disable background compilation
    -Xms<size>        set initial Java heap size
    -Xmx<size>        set maximum Java heap size
    -Xss<size>        set java thread stack size
    -Xprof            output cpu profiling data
```

java -X command line

The preceding screenshot illustrates a comprehensive list of command line options. These options let you tweak different Java environment settings related to memory usage of your JVM-based Spark application. We are interested in the Xmx setting.

We just described method 2, where we outlined how to set the Java runtime parameter, – Xmx, in the Java Control Panel.

That leaves us with method 3, where we describe how to set three runtime parameters globally. In reference to the preceding screenshot, these are:

- –Xmx: Sets (or allocates) the size in megabytes that the Java heap space is allowed to grow to. A typical default setting is 64m.
- –Xms: Sets the initial Java heap size. The default is 2 MB.
- –Xss: Sets the Java thread stack size.

We will set these parameters in an environmental variable called JAVA_OPTS.

The following steps illustrate how to do just this:

1. To start with, we right-click on **This PC** and select **Properties**:

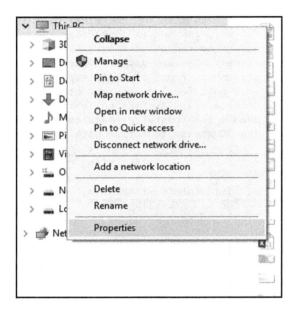

Properties option tab

2. Clicking on **Properties** takes us to the following screen:

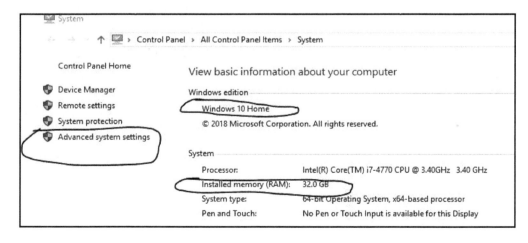

System tab

3. Clicking on **Advanced system settings** takes us to the following screen:

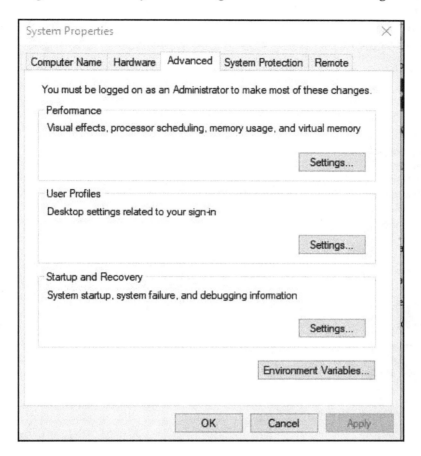

System Properties tab

4. Click on **Environment Variables...** next. In the ensuing screen, we will be able to set JAVA_OPTS. If JAVA_OPTS is not present, create a new one. Click on **New** and enter the appropriate values in the **Variable name** and **Variable value** boxes. Dismiss the box by clicking **OK**:

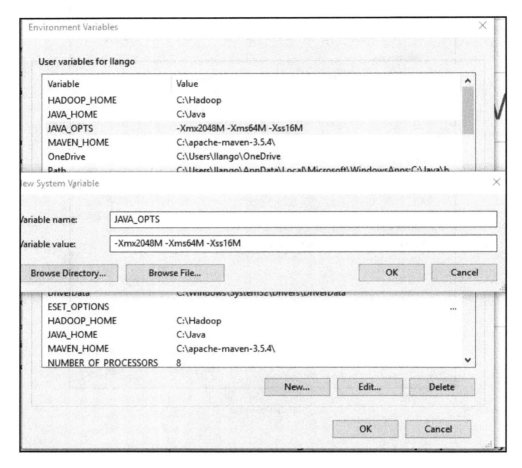

New System Variable

5. Your new `JAVA_OPTS` variable is now ready:

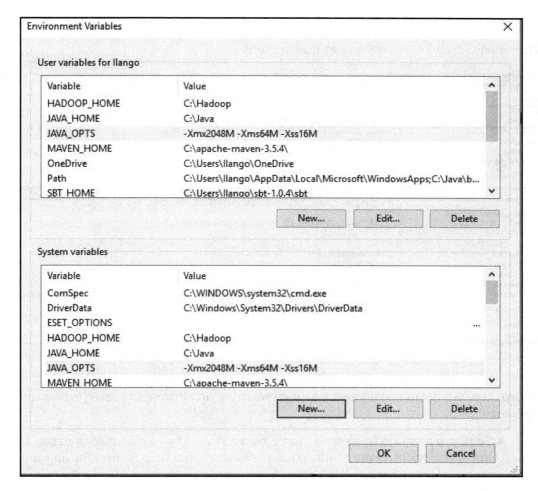

Environment Variables

In the environment setting we just made, set the `JAVA_OPTS` environment variable to the value `JAVA_OPTS = =Xmx2048M -Xms64M -Xss16M`.

Refer back to the preceding screenshot for a quick refresher on what those settings are.

To take stock of all environment variables, launch the Windows PowerShell (there should be a PowerShell app on the desktop). The following is a complete listing of all the environment variables. Note the ones that are relevant:

```
HADOOP_HOME              C:\Hadoop
HOMEDRIVE                C:
HOMEPATH                 \Users\Ilango
JAVA_HOME                C:\Java
JAVA_OPTS                -Xmx2048M -Xms64M -Xss16M
LOCALAPPDATA             C:\Users\Ilango\AppData\Local
LOGONSERVER              \\LIVINGROOM
MAVEN_HOME               C:\apache-maven-3.5.4\
NUMBER_OF_PROCESSORS     8
OneDrive                 C:\Users\Ilango\OneDrive
OS                       Windows_NT
Path                     C:\Program Files (x86)\Common Files\Oracle\Java\javapath;C:\WINDOWS\system32;C:\WINDO.
PATHEXT                  .COM;.EXE;.BAT;.CMD;.VBS;.VBE;.JS;.JSE;.WSF;.WSH;.MSC;.CPL
PROCESSOR_ARCHITECTURE   AMD64
PROCESSOR_IDENTIFIER     Intel64 Family 6 Model 60 Stepping 3, GenuineIntel
PROCESSOR_LEVEL          6
PROCESSOR_REVISION       3c03
ProgramData              C:\ProgramData
ProgramFiles             C:\Program Files
ProgramFiles(x86)        C:\Program Files (x86)
ProgramW6432             C:\Program Files
PSModulePath             C:\Users\Ilango\Documents\WindowsPowerShell\Modules;C:\Program Files\WindowsPowerShel..
PUBLIC                   C:\Users\Public
SBT_HOME                 C:\Users\Ilango\sbt-1.0.4\sbt
SCALA_HOME               C:\Program Files (x86)\scala
SPARK_HOME               C:\spark-2.3.1-bin-hadoop2.7
```

Hadoop Environment settings

To recap, here is a list of considerations when selecting an appropriate Java (maximum Java heap size):

- Setting maximum heap space, in bytes, and initial heap size, also in bytes. These are appropriate memory allocation pool values that help control the amount of memory usage for our JVM-based Spark application.
- The $-Xmx$ option changes the maximum heap space for the VM. Some example settings are $-Xmx2048$, $-Xmx81920k$, and $-Xmx1024m$.

$-Xmx10G$ is the same as $-Xmx1024m$ or $-Xmx1024g$.

The $-Xms$ option allows us to set an initial heap size. The default value is 64 MB or 640 KB, for example, $Xms64m$. Consider the following:

- To determine how much can be a higher heap size setting, we recommend increasing the Java heap space to no more than 50% of the total RAM available. For example, if your machine has 32 GB of available RAM, we recommend setting the maximum heap no higher than 16 GB.
- Setting the maximum heap space to a value above 16 GB in our example would cause problems with performance.

Next, we will review your system JDK.

Reviewing the JDK version

If you have JDK 8, that is all you need to safely skip this section. If you want to install JDK 9, do not. Spark is incompatible with any JDK version greater than 8. Also, please ensure that you did not install the JDK into a path that has spaces in it. This is a minor detail, but we want to make sure.

In the next section, we get into the installation of MongoDB. We will talk about the why and the how.

MongoDB installation

What is MongoDB and why do we even need it? Firstly, MongoDB's document model makes it easy to map objects in application code to equivalent JSON representations in MongoDB. There is more to this. Spark has good integration with MongoDB. One clear advantage is being able to publish our on-time dataframe into MongoDB as a document. Fetching a dataframe document from MongoDB is good from a performance standpoint too.

There are two prerequisites to installing MongoDB (on Windows):

- Only 64-bit machines are able to support MongoDB
- Be sure to get the latest Windows updates

To get started, download the latest stable version of the MongoDB Community Server from the **MongoDB Download Center** page on the `mongodb.com` website. That will be 4.0. Depending on whichever operating system you have, download the appropriate version. The instructions here are for Windows 10, 64-bit users.

 The MongoDB product no longer supports 32-bit x86 operating system platforms.

In the next few steps, we will install MongoDB as a service:

1. Click on the MongoDB installer, an MSI file:

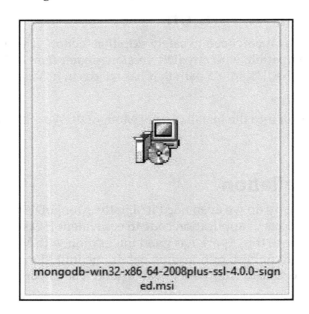

mongodb-win32-x86_64-2008plus-ssl-4.0.0-sign ed.msi

MSI file of MongoDB

2. Click **Install**, as shown in the following screenshot:

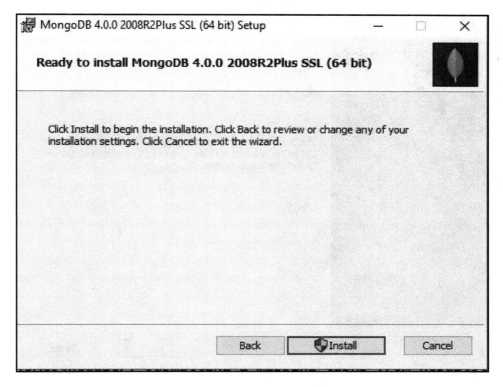

Install screen of MongoDB

3. Click **Next** and proceed with the complete setup type of installation:

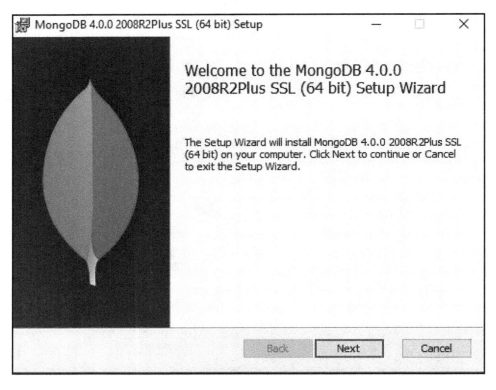

The Next button of MongoDB

4. Click on **Complete** and proceed with the complete setup type of installation:

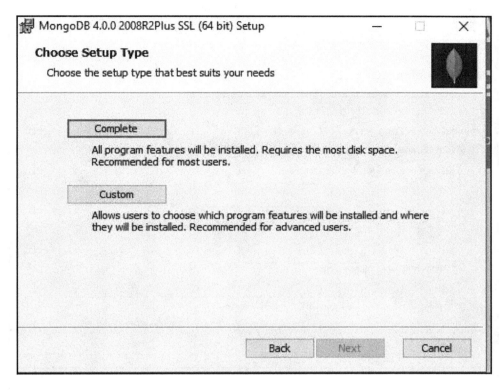

The Complete option of MongoDB

5. As already stated, we will choose not to install MongoDB as a service. Therefore, uncheck the **Install MongoDB as a Service** option:

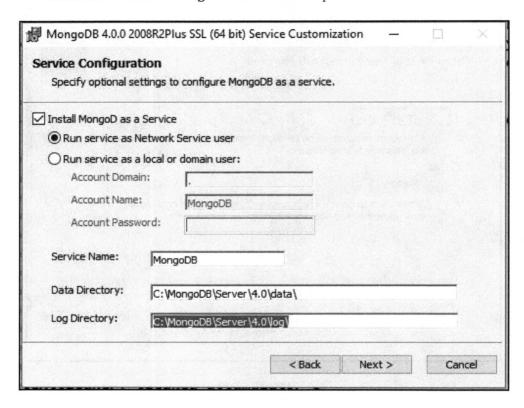

Service Configuration MongoDB

Note where you are installing MongoDB into. The server is installed at `C:\MongoDB\Server\4.0`. The data folder is at `C:\MongoDB\Server\4.0\data`.

6. Next, you will see the screen of the MongoDB Compass:

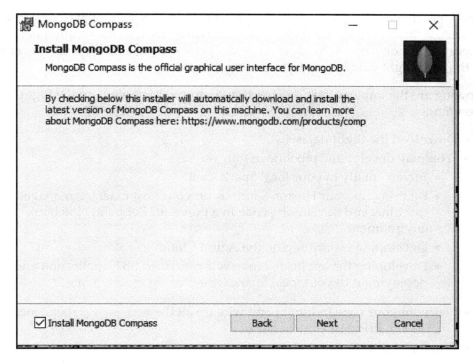

Install MongoDB Compass

In the next section, we will show you how and why we put MongoDB to work. With the prerequisites out of the way and the application building infrastructure in place, we proceed to the *Implementation and deployment* section.

Implementation and deployment

Implementation depends on setting up the big data infrastructure. Please verify that your MongoDB installation is running properly. Now we shall list implementation objectives as follows:

- Splitting data into test, train and validation datasets
- Data ingestion
- Data analysis

Implementation objectives

The overall objective is to perform data analysis on an on-time flight dataset corresponding to the year 2007-2008. Of the 2007 flight data, 80% will be used as the training dataset and the rest as a validation dataset. In so far as model performance evaluation is concerned, 100% of the 2008 flight data becomes the testing dataset.

The following are the implementation objectives required to implement the flight prediction model:

- Download the flight dataset.
- You may develop the pipeline in four ways:
  - Incrementally in your local Spark shell
  - By firing up your Horton Sandbox on your host machine managed virtual machine, and developing code in a powerful Zeppelin Notebook environment
  - Developing everything on the Azure Cloud
  - Developing the application as a self-contained SBT application and deploying it to your local Spark cluster using `spark-submit`
- Flesh out your code in IntelliJ and wire up all the necessary dependencies in the `build.sbt` file.
- Run the application and interpret the results.

In the next subsection, we will document step-by-step instructions for implementing the project. In the succeeding step, we will create a new Scala project in IntelliJ and call it `Chapter6`.

Creating a new Scala project

Let's create a Scala project called `Chapter6`, with the following artifacts:

- `AirlineWrapper.scala`
- `Aircraft.scala`

The following screenshot is representative of what our project looks like:

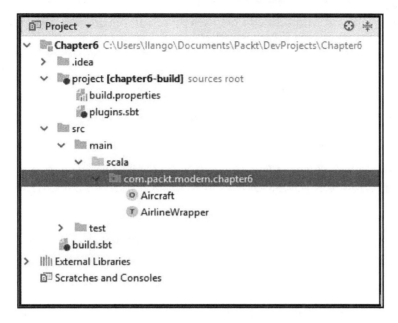

IntelliJ project structure

Let's break down the project structure:

- .idea: These are the generated IntelliJ configuration files.
- project: Contains a build.properties and plugins.sbt. For example, plugins.sbt may be used to specify the SBT assembly plugin.
- src/main/scala: A folder that houses Scala source files in the com.packt.modern.chapter6 package.
- src/main/resources: Any data or configuration files; for example, a log4j configuration file called log4j.xml.
- target: This is where artifacts of the compile process are stored. Any generated assembly JAR files go there.
- build.sbt: This is the main SBT configuration file. Spark and its dependencies are specified here.

At this point, we will start developing. We start with the AirlineWrapper.scala file and end with the deployment of the final application JAR into Spark with spark-submit.

Building the AirlineWrapper Scala trait

The `AirlineWrapper` contains code to create a `SparkSession` instance called `session`. It also declares case classes to represent our flights dataset.

Let's create the `trait` definition first:

```
trait AirlineWrapper {  }
```

The entry point to programming is as follows: The first thing we do in the `trait` is to declare a `lazy val` called `session`. This is where we lazily create an instance of `SparkSession`. Lazily implies that the `val` is only executed when it is encountered the first time around. The session is our entry point to programming Spark with the `DataSet` and `DataFrame` API is `SparkSession`:

```
lazy val session = { SparkSession.builder()..getOrCreate() }
```

In the following code snippet, `CarrierCode` is an identification number assigned by US DoT to identify a unique airline (carrier):

```
case class AirlineCarrier(uniqueCarrierCode: String)
```

In the following code, `originOfFlight` is the origin of the flight (IATA airport code) and `destOfFlight` is the destination of the flight (IATA airport code):

```
case class Flight(monthOfFlight: Int, /* Number between 1 and 12 */
                  dayOfFlight: Int, /*Number between 1 and 31 */
                  uniqueCarrierCode: String,
                  arrDelay: Int, /* Arrival Delay - Field # 15*/
                  depDelay: Int, /* Departure Delay - Field # 16 */
                  originAirportCodeOfFlight: String, /* An identification
number assigned by US DOT to identify a unique airport. */
                  destAirportCodeOfFlight: String, /* An identification
number assigned by US DOT to  identify a unique airport.*/
                  carrierDelay: Int, /* Field # 25*/
                  weatherDelay: Int, /* Field # 26*/
                  lateAircraftDelay: Int /* Field # 29*/
)
```

In the following code snippet, `iataAirportCode` is the international airport abbreviation code:

```
case class Airports(iataAirportCode: String, airportCity: String,
airportCountry: String)
```

Load and create a `File` object out of the airport's dataset:

```
val airportsData: String = loadData("data/airports.csv")
```

Load and create a `File` object out of the airline carrier dataset:

```
val carriersData: String = loadData("data/airlines.csv")
```

Create a `File` object out of the main FAA dataset:

```
val faaFlightsData: String = loadData("data/faa.csv")
```

This method takes in a relative path to the data inside the `resources` folder of your folder:

```
def loadData(dataset: String) = {
                    //Get file from resources folder
                    val classLoader: ClassLoader = getClass.getClassLoader
                    val file: File = new
File(classLoader.getResource(dataset).getFile)
                    val filePath = file.getPath
                    println("File path is: " + filePath)
                    filePath
    }
```

Next, we will write a method called `buildDataFrame`:

```
import org.apache.spark.sql.SparkSession
import org.apache.spark.SparkConf
import org.apache.spark.ml.linalg.{Vector, Vectors}
import org.apache.spark.rdd.RDD
```

Remember to update your import statements. The necessary input statements look like the following code. This is all we need to be able to compile all of the code that we developed up until now:

```
def buildDataFrame(dataSet: String): RDD[Array[String]] = {
//def getRows2: Array[(org.apache.spark.ml.linalg.Vector, String)] = {
def getRows2: RDD[Array[String]] = {session.sparkContext.
textFile(dataSet).flatMap {
                    partitionLine =>
                    partitionLine.split("\n").toList
                    }.map(_.split(","))
```

```
    }
    //Create a dataframe by transforming an Array of a tuple of Feature
    Vectors and the Label
    val dataFrame = session.createDataFrame(getRows2).
    toDF(bcwFeatures_IndexedLabel._1, bcwFeatures_IndexedLabel._2)
    //dataFrame
    //val dataFrame = session.createDataFrame(getRows2)
    getRows2
}
```

Import the MongoDB packages, including the connector package, in particular:

```
/*
Import the MongoDB Connector Package
*/

import com.mongodb.spark._
import com.mongodb.spark.config._
import org.bson.Document
```

Create the `Aircraft` object:

```
object Aircraft extends AirlineWrapper {
```

Create a `main` method inside the `Aircraft` object, like this:

```
def main(args: Array[String]): Unit = {

}
```

The `object` now looks like this:

```
object Aircraft extends AirlineWrapper {
    def main(args: Array[String]): Unit = {

}

}
```

Create a `case` `class` to represent carefully selected features in the dataset that we decide will contribute most to this data analysis:

```
case class FlightsData(flightYear: String, /* 1 */
flightMonth : String, /* 2 */
flightDayOfmonth : String, /* 3 */
flightDayOfweek : String, /* 4 */
flightDepTime : String, /* 5 */
flightCrsDeptime : String, /* 6 */
```

```
flightArrtime : String, /* 7 */
flightCrsArrTime : String, /* 8 */
flightUniqueCarrier : String,/* 9 */
flightNumber : String, /* 10 */
flightTailNumber : String, /* 11 */
flightActualElapsedTime : String, /* 12 */
flightCrsElapsedTime : String, /* 13 */
flightAirTime : String, /* 14 */
flightArrDelay : String, /* 15 */
flightDepDelay : String, /* 16 */
flightOrigin : String, /* 17 */
flightDest : String, /* 18 */
flightDistance : String, /* 19 */
flightTaxiin : String, /* 20 */
flightTaxiout : String, /* 21 */
flightCancelled : String, /* 22 */
flightCancellationCode : String, /* 23 */
flightDiverted : String, /* 24 */
flightCarrierDelay : String, /* 25 */
flightWeatherDelay : String, /* 26 */
flightNasDelay : String, /* 27 */
flightSecuritDelay : String, /* 28 */
flightLateAircraftDelay : String, /* 29 */ record_insertion_time: String,
/* 30 */ uuid : String /* 31 */
                    )
```

Next, create a dataframe to represent the `FlightData`:

```
val airFrame: DataFrame = session.read .format("com.databricks.spark.csv")
.option("header", true).option("inferSchema",
"true").option("treatEmptyValuesAsNulls", true) .load("2008.csv")
```

We just loaded the dataset and created a dataframe. Now, we are able to print the schema:

```
println("The schema of the raw Airline Dataframe is: ")
airFrame.printSchema()
```

The `printschema()` method displays the following schema:

```
        Year: integer (nullable = true)
|-- Quarter: integer (nullable = true)
|-- Month: integer (nullable = true)
|-- DayofMonth: integer (nullable = true)
|-- DayOfWeek: integer (nullable = true)
|-- FlightDate: string (nullable = true)
|-- UniqueCarrier: string (nullable = true)
|-- AirlineID: integer (nullable = true)
|-- Carrier: string (nullable = true)
|-- TailNum: string (nullable = true)
|-- FlightNum: integer (nullable = true)
|-- OriginAirportID: integer (nullable = true)
|-- OriginAirportSeqID: integer (nullable = true)
|-- OriginCityMarketID: integer (nullable = true)
|-- Origin: string (nullable = true)
|-- OriginCityName: string (nullable = true)
|-- OriginState: string (nullable = true)
|-- OriginStateFips: integer (nullable = true)
|-- OriginStateName: string (nullable = true)
|-- OriginWac: integer (nullable = true)
|-- DestAirportID: integer (nullable = true)
|-- DestAirportSeqID: integer (nullable = true)
|-- DestCityMarketID: integer (nullable = true)
|-- Dest: string (nullable = true)
|-- DestCityName: string (nullable = true)
|-- DestState: string (nullable = true)
|-- DestStateFips: integer (nullable = true)
|-- DestStateName: string (nullable = true)
|-- DestWac: integer (nullable = true)
|-- CRSDepTime: integer (nullable = true)
|-- DepTime: integer (nullable = true)
|-- DepDelay: integer (nullable = true)
|-- DepDelayMinutes: integer (nullable = true)
|-- DepDel15: integer (nullable = true)
|-- DepartureDelayGroups: integer (nullable = true)
|-- DepTimeBlk: string (nullable = true)
|-- TaxiOut: integer (nullable = true)
|-- WheelsOff: integer (nullable = true)
|-- WheelsOn: integer (nullable = true)
|-- TaxiIn: integer (nullable = true)
|-- CRSArrTime: integer (nullable = true)
|-- ArrTime: integer (nullable = true)
```

We will need a cast on some fields. To call the `cast` method, we call in the following import:

```
import org.apache.spark.sql.functions._
```

Now, we will create a local temporary view and give it the name `airline_onTime`. This temporary view only exists for as long as the lifespan of the `SparkSession` that we used to create our dataframe:

```
airFrame.createOrReplaceTempView("airline_onTime")
```

Run a `count` on the number of rows in the dataframe:

```
print("size of one-time dataframe is: " + airFrame.count())
```

Create a local temporary view using the given name. The lifetime of this temporary view is tied to the `SparkSession` that was used to create this dataset:

```
airFrame.createOrReplaceTempView("airline_ontime")
print("size of one-time dataframe is: " + airFrame.count())
```

Create a local temporary view using the given name. The lifetime of this temporary view is tied to the `SparkSession` that was used to create this dataset:

```
airFrame.createOrReplaceTempView("airline_ontime")
print("size of one-time dataframe is: " + airFrame.count())
```

Having trimmed and cast our fields and made sure the numeric columns work, we can now save our data as JSON lines and parquet. Call the `toJSON` method to return the content of the dataset as a dataset of JSON strings:

```
val airFrameJSON: Dataset[String] = clippedAirFrameForDisplay.toJSON
```

Display the new dataset in JSON format:

```
println("Airline Dataframe as JSON is: ")
airFrameJSON.show(10)
```

Save our JSON airline dataframe as a `.gzip` JSON file:

```
airFrameJSON.rdd.saveAsTextFile("json/airlineOnTimeDataShort.json.gz",
classOf[org.apache.hadoop.io.compress.GzipCodec])
```

Next, we need to convert our dataframe to `parquet` records. The following code does just that:

```
clippedAirFrameForDisplay.write.format("parquet").save("parquet/airlineOnTi
meDataShort.parquet")
```

Let's read our newly created JSON archive and display the first 20 rows of it:

```
val airlineOnTime_Json_Frame: DataFrame =
session.read.json("json/airlineOnTimeDataShort.json.gz")
println("JSON version of the Airline dataframe is: ")
airlineOnTime_Json_Frame.show()
```

Let's load the `parquet` version as well:

```
val airlineOnTime_Parquet_Frame: DataFrame =
session.read.format("parquet").load("parquet/airlineOnTimeDataShort.parquet
")
```

Print out the `parquet` version of the airline dataframe:

```
println("Parquet version of the Airline dataframe is: ")
airlineOnTime_Parquet_Frame.show(10)
```

Next, write to the MongoDB database, `airlineOnTimeData`. The call to the `save` method produces a `DataFrameWriter` that contains a `.mode` method; `mode` takes in an `"overwrite"` parameter. Thus, if the `collection` already exists in Mongo, the new records will still be written into the MongoDB database:

```
MongoSpark.save( airlineOnTime_Parquet_Frame.write.option("collection",
"airlineOnTimeData").mode("overwrite") )
```

To confirm that the data was written into MongoDB, launch the MongoDB Compass Community app. In the **Connect to Host** opening screen, click on **Connect** and in the resulting screen click on database test. The benefit of writing to MongoDB is that, it gives us a easy way to retrieve our data and import it into Spark if something were to corrupt our data `airlineOnTimeData` collection.

Finally, submit the application into a Spark local cluster using the `spark-submit` command.

Summary

In this chapter, we carried out **machine learning** (**ML**) data analysis tasks on flight performance data. One such task is the implementation of a regression model fitted on a training subset of data. Given a new or unknown flight with delayed departure data, this model was able to predict whether the flight under investigation made up for time lost and arrived at the destination on time. One important takeaway from this ML exercise is this—the origin to destination distance contributed most toward predicting time gained. Carrier delays contributed least toward a prediction. A longer flight, it turns out, is able to gain more time.

This chapter provided the foundation to build more sophisticated models. A model with more predictor variables (for example, taking into account, the weather and security delays) could yield deeper, sharper predictions. That said, this chapter hopefully opens a window for opportunity readers to understand how flight performance insights could help travelers snag an optimal travel experience in terms of money and time spent.

In the next chapter and the last one, we will develop a recommender system. Get inspired by Amazon's recommendation algorithms and Netflix's ratings system for bringing us relevant movies. The recommendation system that we build will take advantage of all our accumulated skills in Spark ML this far.

Questions

Before readers head to the next chapter, we invite readers to attempt an upgrade on the flight performance model. The idea is this—feed in a couple more predictors that enhance the flight delay ML process in a way that makes predictions deeper and more incisive.

Here are a few questions to open further vistas of learning:

1. What is a `parquet` file and what are its advantages, especially when a dataset becomes larger, and data shuffling between nodes becomes necessary?
2. What are the advantages of data compressed in a columnar format?

3. Occasionally, you might run into this error: `"Unable to find encoder stored in Dataset. Primitive types (Int, String, and so on) and Product types (case classes) are supported by importing spark.implicits._"`. How do you get around this error? What is the root cause? Hint—build a simple dataframe with a dataset from the first chapter. Use the `spark.read` approach and attempt a `printSchema` on it. If that produces the aforementioned error, investigate if it could be that an explicit schema is required

4. As an alternative to MongoDB, would you rather submit flight performance data to HDFS?

5. Why did MongoDB prove to be useful in this chapter?

6. What is semi-structured data?

7. Name one big benefit of Spark that sets it apart from Hadoop? For example, think programming paradigms.

8. Can you read in the flight's data from Kafka? If so, how and what might be a reason to do this?

9. What is data enrichment and how is it related to munging if both the terms are related?

10. Create a dataframe with two case classes, each with a small subset from the carriers CSV and airports CSV datasets respectively. How would you write this to MongoDB?

Further reading

The following article on *Introduction to Multivariate Regression Analysis* is about the importance of regression analysis: https://www.ncbi.nlm.nih.gov/pmc/articles/PMC3049417/

Building a Recommendation Engine

7

Millions of people order items from Amazon, where they save money and time. Recommendation algorithms are learned from customers, ordering preferences and bring them tailored you may also like recommendations, which are suggestions that help the customer update their cart or add interesting items to a wishlist for later.

Building our own recommendations engine is a learning journey, where we hit several objectives along the way. At the problem formulation stage, we learn that recommendations are a collaborative filtering machine learning problem. We will take advantage of the Spark ML collaborative filtering algorithm to implement a recommendations engine that will generate ratings-based recommendations.

Netflix is famous for its movies where you might enjoy the recommendation feature. Back in 2006, Netflix announced a prize of $1 million for the best enhancement over their aging **CineMatch** movie recommendation algorithm. This trendsetting competition spawned some of the best advances in machine learning. Working on a treasure trove of Netflix-released movie ratings, several crack teams of coders across the world battled for the top prize. Their goal—to build an algorithm that would predict user ratings (and hence better recommendations) up to 10% better than CineMatch.

Since then, algorithms that make recommendations about **items** to users have come a long way. In this chapter, we set out to build a recommendation system with Scala and Apache Spark. What problem is this recommendation system going to solve? This and other questions are going to be answered shortly.

The overarching learning objective of this chapter is to implement a recommendations engine. The following list is a comprehensive breakdown of individual learning objectives:

- Learning the ropes of recommendations; recommendation systems are also known as **recommender systems**.

- Learning by example—understand (with screenshots) that Amazon's on-site recommendations are double-edged; they enhance customer satisfaction and ramp up sales revenue for Amazon.
- Given the plethora of product choices on offer on an online store, customers need all the help they can get. In this chapter, we will learn that recommendations can help people make these choices better and faster. This is good for customers and good for an online retailer that wants to convert prospects to clients.
- The next tangible learning objective is understanding which types of recommendations are implicit and which ones are not.
- Learning about the different kinds of recommendations and what they can do is good. We want to go further by learning what kinds of data do not need many details. Why? We want to set up datasets to model a recommendation system and match this dataset with a suitable algorithm that only needs a relationship between users and products. Nothing more, nothing less. Such an algorithm that fits the bill is the collaborative filtering algorithm.
- What collaborative filtering can achieve is a work in progress. We will only learn more about the algorithm if we create custom datasets, build a collaborative filtering algorithm trained on the data, and see what the outcome is.

We will learn how to leverage the model-based collaborative filtering algorithm provided by Spark ML to build a recommendation system. We will learn that our implemented recommendation system, like others in its class, helps recommend products based on other customers preferences.

We will start with the *Problem overviews* section.

In this chapter we will cover the following topics:

- Problem overviews
- Detailed overview
- Implementation and deployment

Problem overviews

We will organize this section into overviews on select topics in a sequential order. Here are the topics we are going to cover:

- Recommendations on Amazon
- Recommendation systems, also known as recommender systems or recommendation engines

- Categorizing recommendations, such as:
  - Implicit recommendations
  - Explicit recommendations

- Recommendations for machine learning
- Problem formulation for explicit recommendations—the details
- Weapon sales leads and past sales data—the details

Each topic will be reviewed with an explanation. We will start with the first topic—*Recommendations on Amazon*.

Recommendations on Amazon

This topic is presented in two parts—a *Brief overview* and a *Detailed overview*.

Brief overview

This topic (details are laid out in the *Detailed overview* section) will lay out a roadmap, starting with a generalized understanding of recommendations from a non-machine learning perspective. We will show you what recommendations on Amazon look like with supporting illustrations. Not only that, we will highlight the fact that powerful machine learning algorithms power Amazon's recommendation systems to help users make products choices more easily.

The brief overview of this topic is behind us now. Its detailed overview follows.

Detailed overview

To build a recommendation system, the approach we must take focuses on understanding recommendations at a conceptual level. Examples of questions providing insights into recommendations are as follows:

- What are the recommendations?
- What are two important recommendation types?

Whether you are an online retailer looking to make a recommendation engine work for you in profitable ways, or someone exploring Spark ML's powerful recommendation algorithms from up close, this section will get you started.

We will then zero in on suitable machine learning techniques that we can leverage to build a recommendation system.

Jeff Bezos, multi-billion dollar business, `Amazon.com`, continues to report healthy sales numbers. Recommendation systems have always facilitated increasing streams of revenue for Amazon. These systems are backed by machine learning recommendation algorithms that help deliver customer-specific recommendations in real time. Without question, recommendations are an integral part of the Amazon landscape, playing a part in every aspect of a customer's purchase process.

There are two categories of Amazon recommendations:

- On-site recommendations
- Off-site recommendations

We will only focus on on-site recommendations. Both on-site and off-site recommendations are big revenue earners for Amazon. Off-site recommendations are not covered in this chapter, however, the reader is encouraged to probe this side of Amazon's recommendations landscape. We have a question or two regarding off-site recommendations in the very last section of this chapter.

On-site recommendations

Two main flavors of on-site recommendations are readily available by simply clicking on the link **XYZ's Amazon.com**. These are:

- **Recommended for you, XYZ:**

  The **Recommended for you, XYZ** link looks like this:

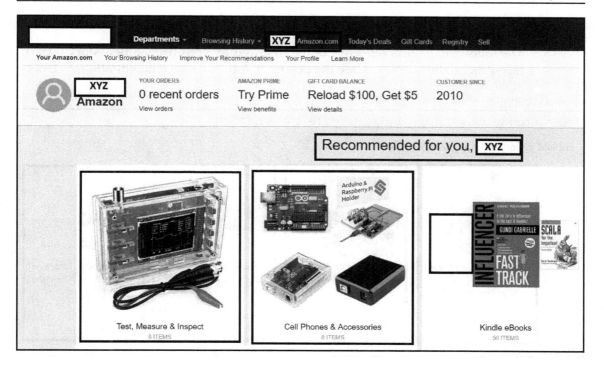

Observe the Recommended for you, XYZ link

It contains Amazon's recommendations of products that it thinks you are likely to click on and buy. How did these recommendations come to you? This question has a two-part answer. First, recommendation algorithms tracked your browsing history. Secondly, this will take you to a page showing a list of products from various categories.

- **Your recently viewed items and featured recommendations**:

Another related example of recommendations is shown as follows. These recommendations, according to Amazon's machine learning recommendations system, are in several categories, such as:

- **Inspired by your browsing history**:

    The following page is reflective of the **Inspired by your browsing history** type of recommendations. We can see the power of Amazon's recommendation systems at work:

Your recently viewed items and featured recommendations

Inspired by your browsing history

Java Precisely (The MIT Press)	Clean Architecture: A Craftsman's Guide to...
› Peter Sestoft	› Robert C. Martin
⭐⭐⭐⭐⭐ 1	⭐⭐⭐⭐☆ 47
Paperback	Paperback
$27.90 ✓prime	$30.82 ✓prime

Design Patterns: Elements of Reusable...	Refactoring: Improving the Design of Existing...
› Erich Gamma	› Martin Fowler
⭐⭐⭐⭐☆ 462	⭐⭐⭐⭐☆ 213
Hardcover	Hardcover
$56.97 ✓prime	$55.11 ✓prime

Observe the items under Inspired by your browsing history link

- **Inspired by your purchases**:

    Once again, the goal is simple—place a palette of products in front of the customer. This makes it easy for the customer to buy a different product, in this case, a book that is closely related to books falling under a category of interest. How did Amazon come up with the palette of books under the **Inspired by your browsing history** category? The recommendation system brings you products that you showed an interest in, at some point in time:

Inspired by your purchases

 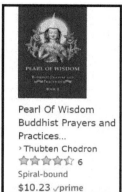  

Zero Trust Networks: Building Secure...	Pearl Of Wisdom Buddhist Prayers and Practices...	Long Walk to Freedom: The Autobiography of...	The Autobiography of Martin Luther King,...
› Evan Gilman	› Thubten Chodron	› Nelson Mandela	› Clayborne Carson
⭐⭐⭐⭐⭐ 4	⭐⭐⭐⭐ 6	⭐⭐⭐⭐ 921	⭐⭐⭐⭐ 219
Paperback	Spiral-bound	Paperback	Paperback
$35.76 ✓prime	$10.23 ✓prime	$11.39 ✓prime	$9.98 ✓prime

Observe the items under Inspired by your purchases link

- **Frequently bought together**:

  This type of recommendation is even more interesting. Say you click on the *Lego Mindstorms* book, the one featured in the following screenshot. We are taken to a new page that has **Frequently bought together** recommendation.

  The following screenshot displays the **Frequently bought together** recommendation:

Frequently bought together

Total price: **$54.77**

Add both to Cart

Add both to List

☑ **This item:** Definitive Guide to LEGO MINDSTORMS, Second Edition by Dave Baum Paperback $29.99

☑ Extreme Mindstorms: an Advanced Guide to Lego Mindstorms by Michael Gasperi Paperback $24.78

Observe the Frequently bought together link

- **Customers who also bought this item**:

  This type of recommendation is Amazon's up-sell and cross-sell recommendation feature at work. The recommendation system is offering products that other customers bought together when they clicked on the *Lego Mindstorm* book you just clicked:

Customers who bought this item also bought

Defensive Security Handbook: Best Practices for Securing Infrastructure	Intelligence-Driven Incident Response: Outwitting the Adversary	Crafting the InfoSec Playbook: Security Monitoring and Incident...
› Lee Brotherston	› Scott J. Roberts	› Jeff Bollinger
⭐⭐⭐⭐☆ 39	⭐⭐⭐⭐⭐ 7	⭐⭐⭐⭐☆ 9
Paperback	Paperback	Paperback
$28.95 ✓prime	$48.47 ✓prime	$41.27 ✓prime

Observe the items under Customer who bought this item also bought link

The next *Problem overviews* section that follows is *Recommendations with machine learning*. Recommendations on Amazon are tied to powerful machine learning-based recommendation systems. The topic that follows is an attempt at describing a recommendation system from a high-level, non-machine learning perspective. Therefore, we want to know what a recommendations system looks like at a high-level and the different types of recommendations that such a system may or may not handle.

Attaining this level of understanding of recommendations, and recommendation systems will pave the way for a further exploration into the realm of recommendations as a problem in some subset of the machine learning space.

All the flavors of recommendation share the following goals:

- Customer satisfaction
- Increasing sales revenue for Amazon

We will take up each recommendation flavor in turn. We will take up the most important on-site recommendation first, which is the **Recommended for you, XYZ** page.

That said, we will step into the next topic, *Recommendation systems*.

Recommendation systems

In the previous overview topic, we explored the salient aspects of recommendation and recommendation systems at Amazon. Let's attempt to bring some of that together and put together a definition of recommendation systems.

Definition

Recommendation systems can be defined as software applications that draw out and learn from data like such as preferences, their actions (clicks, for example), browsing history, and generated recommendations, which are products that the system determines are appealing to the user in the immediate future.

The following diagram is representative of a typical recommendation system:

Users preferred, liked and bought products

Recommendation System

1) Recommendation system draws out user and product information

Users
With similar tastes

2) Users "interact" with products via Interactions or transactions by providing feedback

Products

Recommendation system produces recommendations of products to Users based on similar users

Star Rating
★ ★ ★ ★ ★

Recommendation system

In the preceding diagram, can be thought of as a recommendation ecosystem, where the recommendation system is at the heart of it. This system needs three entities:

- **Users**
- **Products**
- **Transactions between users and products where transactions contain feedback from users about products**

A transaction can be thought of in terms of the following action—a user provides a rating for a product. That is not all, though. The nature of the transaction implies that the user is providing feedback about the product(s). This explains the solid arrow starting from the **Users** box and extending into the **Products** box. As is evident from the diagram, the **Recommendations system** generates a recommendation after collecting all of the user-product interactions, that is, feedback data.

There are different types of transactions, which brings us to look at the different types of recommendations.

Categorizing recommendations

This topic will draw on from the previous topic. In particular, we made more than a mention of user-product interactions or feedback data. Indeed, there can be two types of such interactions. User feedback is a better term.

Based on the types of user feedback, we can identify two types of recommendations, as follows:

- Implicit
- Explicit

Each type of recommendation follows. We will first explain recommendations using feedback of the implicit kind.

Implicit recommendations

A good example of such data is implicit information, such as user preferences, their clicks, browsing history, purchase history, search terms, and so on.

This scenario represents an example of an implicit feedback-based recommendation system at work. The key characteristic of such a system is this—what did the user do? Some examples of implicit user feedback, in reference to a user on Amazon, is—what did the user buy? What book did they click on? What was their search phrase? All of these questions bear answers that reflect on a user's **behavior**. That said, we will get right down to a problem formulation phase, where we will document what is needed to build a recommendation problem with collaborative filtering. Whether this recommendation system is implicit or explicit will be decided when we get to that point.

Explicit recommendations

This is a collaborative filtering problem that requires explicit data to model the relationship between each user (customer) and product (item). A good example of such data is an explicit rating.

Recommendations for machine learning

We discussed the role played by recommendations at Amazon. This gives us a good idea of what recommendations are, and what recommendation systems are, from a layperson's point of view. We provided examples for each flavor of recommendations. Machine learning algorithms generated these Amazon recommendations, and that is the common denominator here.

With that said, this topic is presented with the clear purpose of explaining the role played by machine learning in the context of recommendations. As always, this topic is approached in two parts: a brief overview part giving a summarized view of what to expect from the topic, and a detailed overview part. Here is the brief overview.

Collaborative filtering algorithms

Recommendations are a collaborative filtering problem in the machine learning space. Two underlying principles define how collaborative filtering algorithms work:

- Filtering
- Collaborative

The filtering part is associated with the act of recommending. The algorithm makes recommendations happen by ingesting preferences information from many users. A simple example will go a long way in illustrating how collaborative filtering algorithms work. Imagine that our algorithm is working off of a pool of three users (countries) *U1, U2,* and *U3*. However trivial this case may be, it will explain how collaborative filtering algorithms work. Say, at a recent global air show, countries looking for new fighter aircraft were asked to provide ratings for three front-line fighter aircraft. The **Rafaele** is a French fighter. The **SU-35** is Russian and the **F-35** is American, and arguably the world's foremost air-superiority fighter.

The aircraft-countries tables are listed as follows, which is a recommendation algorithm based on collaborative filtering and a user-product matrix:

Ratings are on a scale of 1 – 10 with 1 being deplorable to 10 being awesome			
Fighter Aircraft	**Rafaele Air Superority Fighter**	**SU-35 Flanker**	**The F-35 Joint Strike Fighter**
Country/Customer	**Product 1**	**Product 2**	**Product 3**
U1 — India	Rating = 7	Rating = 8	Rating = 7
U2 — Turkey	Rating = 6		Rating = 7
U3 — Saudi Arabia	Rating = 7		

User-product matrix

Looking at the preceding table, each country rated a certain aircraft in slightly different ways. India gave all three fighter aircraft reasonably good ratings, with the Flanker receiving the highest rating. The second country, Turkey, assigned good ratings only to the Rafaele and the F-35, and no rating at all for the SU-35. It is assumed that when no rating is provided that that country received a negative rating of –1. Lastly, Saudi Arabia liked the Rafaele and F-35, whereas they did not have anything to say about the SU-35. There are empty squares in the matrix. They are left empty for a reason.

Let's say we have a collaborative algorithm called **CF**. We want CF to work on this matrix with a plan. The first part of the plan is to tell the algorithm to find out which users like the same products. The algorithm will get to work and make the following observations:

- User U1 (India) liked the following:
  - Product 1 (Rafaele)
  - Product 2 (Flanker)
  - Product 3 (F-35)

- User U2 (Turkey) liked the following:
  - Product 1 (Rafaele)
  - Product 3 (F-35)

- User U3 (Saudi Arabia) liked the following:
  - Product 1 (Rafaele)

The algorithm has a greater mandate. It needs to look closer at the matrix and make a recommendation for Saudi Arabia regarding an aircraft.

The collaborative filtering algorithm comes up with a recommendation for Saudi Arabia with the following reasoning:

India likes all three aircraft (the Rafaele, the Flanker, and the F-35) while Turkey like two (the Rafaele and the F-35). Countries that liked the Rafaele **ALSO** liked the F-35. Note the capitalized word ALSO. Based on India and Turkey having similar likes, the algorithm decides that Saudi Arabia will like what India and Turkey liked—in this case, the F-35. To make sense of the final recommendation, we will draw a Venn diagram-like structure:

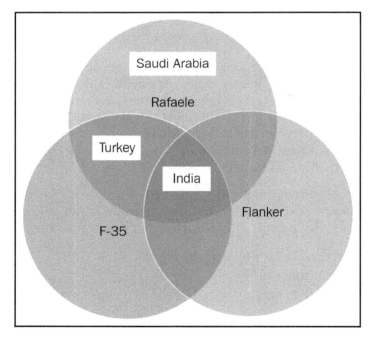

Venn diagram

We just demonstrated what recommendations can do for us. What we have done so far is a step in the right direction regarding implementation.

We have not said yet what kind of data that's available in these datasets would either qualify them as explicit or implicit. Data in these datasets describe interactions between users and products. We have seen evidence of those interactions from the preceding discussion. We also went so far as to make a recommendation for Saudi Arabia. We predicted what weapons system Saudi Arabia is likely to buy in the future. The user-product matrix was our go-to resource for arriving at this recommendation for Saudi Arabia. This matrix boasted of one feature—a user-product interaction. This is a hard number, and a rating, which makes this data explicit.

This is a collaborative filtering problem that requires implicit data to model the relationship between each user (customer) and product (item).

It's time to move on to the next topic, which happens to be a brief overview of the formulation of an explicit recommendations problem.

Recommendations problem formulation

This topic, as its title suggests, will provide a (recommendation) problem formulation. In other words, it would build the contours of a recommendation system based on explicit (user) feedback.

The problem formulation topic represents a critical stage in the implementation of one type of recommendation system. Coming up next is a topic that deals with weapons sales lead data and past weapons sales data, respectively.

Understanding datasets

Taking off from where the previous topic left us, this important talk proposes two datasets, a weapon sales leads dataset and a past sales data dataset, respectively.

At this point, we are done with the brief overview of topics we want to cover, which we decided are relevant toward the implementation of a recommendation system.

Thus far, we have given overviews of topics that are essential to the implementation of a recommendations system. These topics were as follows:

- Recommendations
- Implicit recommendations
- Explicit recommendations
- Recommendation problem formulation
- Weapon sales leads and past sales data
- Recommendations and ML

Detailed overview

The detailed overview section for this topic is the most important section of this chapter.

Recommendations regarding problem formulation

In the detailed version of this topic, we will build a narrative (or story), in which the following features dominate:

- Users
- Products
- Understanding of sales leads and past sales
- Backing up data that's been built with an understanding of sales leads and past sales

Where data is concerned, we will compile custom sales leads data and past sales data that is related to weapons systems. In this phase, we will take up the formal formulation and support descriptions of a recommendation system based on explicit feedback from users. Such a formulation is broken down into two tasks:

- Defining what explicit feedback is
- Building a narrative (a story) around the recommendation problem involving explicit feedback

What kinds of data constitutes explicit feedback? We set out to answer this question right away.

Defining explicit feedback

Explicit feedback, like its implicit counterpart, depends on user preferences. The machine learning model we will be building later is based on such explicit feedback. The datasets we are about to describe contains explicit feedback. Such explicit feedback data is a compilation of user/customer/client preferences concerning their choice of some weapon system (the product/item). It turns out that we are building a recommendation system that will predict what ratings users might leave for products they loved (or not). Indeed, ratings are a great example of feedback. We are all familiar with what star ratings look like. We generated the following start rating graphic using a little CSS and HTML. This is similar to a **Star Rating** seen on restaurant portal `yelp.com`:

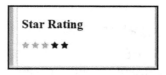

Restaurant ratings

We will not actually generate a star rating graphic for the impending explicit feedback-based recommendation system. However, the point here is that ratings have a central place in this chapter.

Building a narrative

Weapons maker X is a weapons manufacturer that caters to the defense needs of client nations across the globe. To us, this weapons maker is simply **WMX**. Government customer IEX is a typical WMX customer, identified simply as IEX. IEX wants to phase out its aging fighter aircraft with modern fifth-generation replacements. IEX figures are prominently on WMX's past sales data records. Therefore, WMX views IEX as more than just a prospective client. In this scenario, two kinds of actors are evident:

- WMX—supplier of weapons systems products
- Customers like IEX—these are countries that buy X's weapons systems and allocate ratings to them

We now have the contours of an interesting use case. Actors 1 and 2 are useless without data. We plan on making two datasets available:

- Weapon sales leads—data from a leads campaign
- Past weapon sales data—data from the past describing which customer purchased what weapons system (the item or product)

Before proceeding further with a deeper discussion on the later use case, we will take a necessary detour. We want to explain the sales leads part in weapon sales leads. What are leads, anyway? What is the role of past sales data? Both questions are answered in the next phase.

Sales leads and past sales

A business needs a product or products (or services) to sell and make money, of course. A familiar business strategy is a practice of generating sales leads. What is a sales lead? A **lead** is like a clue or a break that investigators stumble upon in a criminal investigation case. This lead is identifying the helpful information that may lead investigators to pursue a certain line of investigation. Such a lead, in the hands of a skilled, seasoned investigator might help potentially crack the case, nailing the culprit, or getting a fix on a potential suspect.

Applying the criminal investigation analogy back to our sales use case, a sales lead is a sort of identifier in the sense that it represents identifying data early on in the sales process. Naturally, a lead generates the anticipation that a certain person or company will be a potential client down the road. A sales lead does not necessarily have to nail down a potential customer. However, a well-planned sales lead generation campaign can take advantage of "past sales data" to help the business identify a person or other business as a near or long-term prospect. A paying customer that shows up in past sales data may point to a future prospective client, which may be a repeat paying customer. Therefore, the business is not shooting in the dark, as it can use this information to figure out which customer to reach out to.

Our detour ends here. Moving into the next phase, we will apply our recently acquired knowledge of sales leads and past sales data to actual weapon sales leads and past sales data datasets.

Weapon sales leads and past sales data

To get started, download the following files from the `ModernScalaProjects` folder.

- `PastWeaponSalesOrders.csv`, compiled from scratch, requiring no citation
- `WeaponSalesLeads.csv`, compiled from scratch, requiring no citation

`PastWeaponSalesOrders.csv` is representative of WMX's past weapons sales data, while `WeaponSalesLeads.csv` of WMX weapons sales leads data. Both datasets are designed to build a recommendation engine.

Let's assume that our weapons corporation WMX stores its past sales data records in `PastWeaponSalesOrders.csv`. This dataset's records are depicted as follows:

CustomerId	CustomerName	ItemId	ItemName	ItemUnitPrice	OrderSize	AmountPaid
1	Australia	217	WeaponsSystem217	2	25	50
1	Australia	183	WeaponsSystem183	6	9	64
2	Seychelles	355	WeaponsSystem355	3	20	60
3	Fiji	99	WeaponsSystem99	5	3	15
3	Fiji	217	WeaponsSystem217	2	10	20
4	Turkey	160	WeaponsSystem160	5	20	100
4	Turkey	45	WeaponsSystem45	3	10	40
5	Jordan	100	WeaponsSystem100	2	4	8
5	Jordan	57	WeaponsSystem57	3	5	15
6	SKorea	81	WeaponsSystem81	5	8	40
6	SKorea	217	WeaponsSystem217	2	26	52
7	Djibouti	107	WeaponsSystem107	3	15	45
7	Djibouti	30	WeaponsSystem30	4	4	16
7	Djibouti	355	WeaponsSystem355	3	5	15
8	India	217	WeaponsSystem217	2	36	72
8	India	99	WeaponsSystem99	5	120	600
8	India	45	WeaponsSystem45	3	20	60

Past sales data records

Before we get into a description of data in the fields, we need a schema that is representative of the fields in this dataset:

```
root
 |-- sCustomerId: integer (nullable = true)
 |-- sCustomerName: string (nullable = true)
 |-- sItemId: integer (nullable = true)
 |-- sItemName: string (nullable = true)
 |-- sItemUnitPrice: double (nullable = true)
 |-- sOrderSize: double (nullable = true)
 |-- sAmountPaid: double (nullable = true)
```

Representation of the field in dataset

Seven columns exist, of which the first two columns represent customer data. Eight customers are listed in alphabetical order, as follows:

1. **Australia**—Customer #1
2. **Seychelles**—Customer #2
3. **Fiji**—Customer #3
4. **Turkey**—Customer #4
5. **Jordan**—Customer #5
6. **South Korea**—Customer #6
7. **Djibouti**—Customer #7
8. **India**—Customer #8

The next two columns, **ItemId**, followed by **ItemName**, represent a weapons system. The fifth column stores the price in millions of dollars per weapons system unit. Each cell of data in the sixth **OrderSize** column represents the number of units of a certain weapons system ordered by a certain customer. For example, Australia had, sometime in the past, ordered 25 units of **WeaponsSystem217** at a price of 2 million dollars per unit.

While both datasets are by no means comprehensive, they are a representative sampling, which is enough to create our recommendation system.

In our case, we are building a sample sales lead prediction model based on past sales orders.

Here are few sample records from both datasets:

CustomerId	CustomerName	ItemId	ItemName
1	Australia	99	WeaponsSystem99
1	Australia	101	WeaponsSystem101
2	Seychelles	89	WeaponsSystem89
2	Seychelles	217	WeaponsSystem217
3	Fiji	160	WeaponsSystem160
3	Fiji	217	WeaponsSystem217
4	Turkey	183	WeaponsSystem183
4	Turkey	100	WeaponsSystem100
4	Turkey	160	WeaponsSystem160
8	India	217	WeaponSystem217
5	Jordan	99	WeaponsSystem99
5	Jordan	355	WeaponsSystem355
6	SKorea	107	WeaponsSystem107
6	SKorea	217	WeaponsSystem217
7	Djibouti	57	WeaponsSystem57
7	Djibouti	355	WeaponsSystem355
7	Djibouti	183	WeaponsSystem183
8	India	45	WeaponsSystem45
8	India	81	WeaponsSystem81
8	India	160	WeaponsSystem160
8	India	355	WeaponsSystem355

Sample datasets

Both datasets are ready. We want to know what to make of this data and where to go from here. We set about putting together the data with one immediate goal—creating a model that would somehow help us make predictions. That goal wasn't so clear-cut then. Now that we have two datasets, we want a clear goal. The key lies in the weapons sales leads dataset. What if we want to build a weapons sales lead model drawing on data from purchase history? Our past weapons sales dataset represents that purchase history. That then brings us to a sharper goal implementing a weapons sales prediction rating model. In other words, we want our model to do the following:

- Predict what recommendation to make for each customer. There are 8 customers, ranging from Australia to India. We want our model to only recommend a weapons system that is right for a certain customer. The right weapons system for a customer is based on what they ordered in the past.
- In making a recommendation to each customer, the model is also producing a rating that it believes the customer would give a certain product he/she did not purchase before a new product or products.

Let's reiterate what both datasets have in common. The first is simple—there's a customer, which in this case is a nation. Then, there is a product an (item), which in this case is a weapons system. The first dataset has this much to say:

- There is a nation that ordered a certain number of weapons systems, each such system costing a certain unit price in millions of dollars.
- The second dataset doesn't reveal much beyond its stated brief, which is to provide a listing of potential prospects. The company manufacturing these systems decides that some of these prospects are more than prospects.

The point we are trying to make here is that even though it is not that apparent, it is clear now that the data did not have to reveal many details. The customer is a nation that purchased a certain weapons system at a certain price. That's it, but that's enough. On the other hand, the weapons sales lead data tells a different kind of story, a likely scenario of a future scenario, where a certain company, in the company's estimates, is said to be likely to show interest in a certain type of weapons system.

We have data about users and products. Not detailed information, but apparently enough. This kind of data requires an algorithm that only needs to extract the relationship between users and products. It simply needs to see evidence of an interaction between the two. Both datasets at hand appear to be a fit for a collaborative filtering algorithm. That is why we can, in the next section, initiate a discussion on the basic mechanism driving the workings of a collaborative filtering algorithm.

Implementation and deployment

The following are implementation objectives that are required to implement the recommendations system:

1. Download the past weapons sales order and weapon lead sales datasets from the `ModernScalaProjects` data folder.
2. You may develop the pipeline in three ways:
   - Incrementally in your local Spark Shell.
   - Recommended: Flesh out your code in IntelliJ and wire up all necessary dependencies in the `build.sbt` file. Set SBT up to generate a fat JAR by wiring in an assembly plugin. The resultant self-contained SBT application is then deployed to your local spark cluster using `spark-submit`.
   - Run the application and interpret the results.

3. In the next section, *Implementation*, we will document step-by-step instructions for implementing the project.

Implementation

Implementation is documented in the following subsections. All code is developed in an Intellij code editor. The very first step is to create an empty Scala project called `Chapter7`.

Step 1 – creating the Scala project

Let's create a Scala project called `Chapter7` with the following artifacts:

- `RecommendationSystem.scala`
- `RecommendationWrapper.scala`

Let's break down the project's structure:

- `.idea`: Generated IntelliJ configuration files.
- `project`: Contains `build.properties` and `plugins.sbt`.
- `project/assembly.sbt`: This file specifies the `sbt-assembly` plugin needed to build a fat JAR for deployment.
- `src/main/scala`: This is a folder that houses Scala source files in the `com.packt.modern.chapter7` package.
- `target`: This is where artifacts of the compile process are stored. The generated assembly JAR file goes here.
- `build.sbt`: This is the main SBT configuration file. Spark and its dependencies are specified here.

At this point, we will start developing code in the IntelliJ code editor. We will start with the `AirlineWrapper` Scala file and end with the deployment of the final application JAR into Spark with `spark-submit`.

Step 2 – creating the AirlineWrapper definition

Let's create the `trait` definition. The trait will hold the `SparkSession` variable, schema definitions for the datasets, and methods to build a dataframe:

```
trait RecWrapper {  }
```

Next, let's create a schema for past weapon sales orders.

Step 3 – creating a weapon sales orders schema

Let's create a schema for the past sales order dataset:

```
val salesOrderSchema: StructType = StructType(Array(
  StructField("sCustomerId", IntegerType,false),
  StructField("sCustomerName", StringType,false),
  StructField("sItemId", IntegerType,true),
  StructField("sItemName",  StringType,true),
  StructField("sItemUnitPrice",DoubleType,true),
  StructField("sOrderSize", DoubleType,true),
  StructField("sAmountPaid",  DoubleType,true)
))
```

Next, let's create a schema for weapon sales leads.

Step 4 – creating a weapon sales leads schema

Here is a schema definition for the weapon sales lead dataset:

```
val salesLeadSchema: StructType = StructType(Array(
  StructField("sCustomerId", IntegerType,false),
  StructField("sCustomerName", StringType,false),
  StructField("sItemId", IntegerType,true),
  StructField("sItemName",  StringType,true)
))
```

Next, let's build a weapon sales order dataframe.

Step 5 – building a weapon sales order dataframe

Let's invoke the `read` method on our `SparkSession` instance and `cache` it. We will call this method later from the `RecSystem` object:

```
def buildSalesOrders(dataSet: String): DataFrame = {
  session.read
    .format("com.databricks.spark.csv")
    .option("header", true).schema(salesOrderSchema).option("nullValue",
"")
    .option("treatEmptyValuesAsNulls", "true")
    .load(dataSet).cache()
}
```

Next up, let's build a sales leads dataframe:

```
def buildSalesLeads(dataSet: String): DataFrame = {
  session.read
    .format("com.databricks.spark.csv")
    .option("header", true).schema(salesLeadSchema).option("nullValue", "")
    .option("treatEmptyValuesAsNulls", "true")
    .load(dataSet).cache()
}
```

This completes the `trait`. Overall, it looks like this:

```
trait RecWrapper {

  1) Create a lazy SparkSession instance and call it session.
  2) Create a schema for the past sales orders dataset
  3) Create a schema for sales lead dataset
  4) Write a method to create a dataframe that holds past sales order
     data. This method takes in sales order dataset and
     returns a dataframe
  5) Write a method to create a dataframe that holds lead sales data

}
```

Bring in the following imports:

```
import org.apache.spark.mllib.recommendation.{ALS, Rating}
import org.apache.spark.rdd.RDD
import org.apache.spark.sql.{DataFrame, Dataset, SparkSession}
```

Create a Scala object called `RecSystem`:

```
object RecSystem extends App with RecWrapper {     }
```

Before going any further, bring in the following imports:

```
import org.apache.spark.rdd.RDD
import org.apache.spark.sql.DataFrame
```

Inside this object, start by loading the past sales order data. This will be our training data. Load the sales order dataset, as follows:

```
val salesOrdersDf = buildSalesOrders("sales\\PastWeaponSalesOrders.csv")
```

Verify the schema. This is what the schema looks like:

```
salesOrdersDf.printSchema()
root
 |-- sCustomerId: integer (nullable = true)
 |-- sCustomerName: string (nullable = true)
 |-- sItemId: integer (nullable = true)
 |-- sItemName: string (nullable = true)
 |-- sItemUnitPrice: double (nullable = true)
 |-- sOrderSize: double (nullable = true)
 |-- sAmountPaid: double (nullable = true)
```

Here is a partial view of a dataframe displaying past weapon sales order data:

```
+-----------+-------------+-------+------------------+--------------+----------+-----------+
|sCustomerId|sCustomerName|sItemId|         sItemName|sItemUnitPrice|sOrderSize|sAmountPaid|
+-----------+-------------+-------+------------------+--------------+----------+-----------+
|          1|    Australia|    217|WeaponsSystem217  |           2.0|      25.0|       50.0|
|          1|    Australia|    183|WeaponsSystem183  |           6.0|       9.0|       64.0|
|          2|   Seychelles|    355|WeaponsSystem355  |           3.0|      20.0|       60.0|
|          3|         Fiji|     99| WeaponsSystem99  |           5.0|       3.0|       15.0|
|          3|         Fiji|    217|WeaponsSystem217  |           2.0|      10.0|       20.0|
|          4|       Turkey|    160|WeaponsSystem160  |           5.0|      20.0|      100.0|
|          4|       Turkey|     45| WeaponsSystem45  |           3.0|      10.0|       40.0|
|          5|       Jordan|    100|WeaponsSystem100  |           2.0|       4.0|        8.0|
+-----------+-------------+-------+------------------+--------------+----------+-----------+
```

Partial view of dataframe displaying past weapon sales order data

Now, we have what we need to create a dataframe of ratings:

```
val ratingsDf: DataFrame = salesOrdersDf.map( salesOrder =>
Rating( salesOrder.getInt(0),
salesOrder.getInt(2),
salesOrder.getDouble(6)
) ).toDF("user", "item", "rating")
```

Save all and compile the project at the command line:

```
C:\Path\To\Your\Project\Chapter7>sbt compile
```

You are likely to run into the following error:

```
[error]
C:\Path\To\Your\Project\Chapter7\src\main\scala\com\packt\modern\chapter7\R
ecSystem.scala:50:50: Unable to find encoder for type stored in a Dataset.
Primitive types (Int, String, etc) and Product types (case classes) are
supported by importing spark.implicits._ Support for serializing other
types will be added in future releases.
[error] val ratingsDf: DataFrame = salesOrdersDf.map( salesOrder =>
[error]                                                  ^
[error] two errors found
[error] (compile:compileIncremental) Compilation failed
```

To fix this, place the following statement at the top of the declarations of the rating dataframe. It should look like this:

```
import session.implicits._
  val ratingsDf: DataFrame = salesOrdersDf.map( salesOrder => UserRating(
salesOrder.getInt(0), salesOrder.getInt(2), salesOrder.getDouble(6) )
).toDF("user", "item", "rating")
```

Save and recompile the project. This time, it compiles just fine. Next, import the `Rating` class from the `org.apache.spark.mllib.recommendation` package. This transforms the rating dataframe that we obtained previously to its RDD equivalent:

```
val ratings: RDD[Rating] = ratingsDf.rdd.map( row => Rating( row.getInt(0),
row.getInt(1), row.getDouble(2) ) )
  println("Ratings RDD is: " + ratings.take(10).mkString(" ") )
```

The following few lines of code are very important. We will be using the ALS algorithm from Spark MLlib to create and train a `MatrixFactorizationModel`, which takes an `RDD[Rating]` object as input. The ALS train method may require a combination of the following training hyperparameters:

- `numBlocks`: Preset to −1 in an auto-configuration setting. This parameter is meant to parallelize computation.
- `custRank`: The number of features, otherwise known as latent factors.
- `iterations`: This parameter represents the number of iterations for ALS to execute. For a reasonable solution to converge on, this algorithm needs roughly 20 iterations or less.
- `regParam`: The regularization parameter.

- `implicitPrefs`: This hyperparameter is a specifier. It lets us use either of the following:
  - Explicit feedback
  - Implicit feedback
- `alpha`: This is a hyperparameter connected to an implicit feedback variant of the ALS algorithm. Its role is to govern the baseline confidence in preference observations.

We just explained the role played by each parameter needed by the ALS algorithm's train method.

Let's get started by bringing in the following imports:

```
import org.apache.spark.mllib.recommendation.MatrixFactorizationModel
```

Now, let's get down to training the matrix factorization model using the ALS algorithm. Let's train a matrix factorization model given an RDD of ratings by customers (users) for certain items (products). Our train method on the ALS algorithm will take the following four parameters:

- Ratings.
- A rank.
- A number of iterations.
- A Lambda value or regularization parameter:

```
val ratingsModel: MatrixFactorizationModel = ALS.train(ratings,
   6, /* THE RANK */
  10, /* Number of iterations */
  15.0 /* Lambda, or regularization parameter */
  )
```

Next, we load the sales lead file and convert it into a tuple format:

```
val weaponSalesLeadDf = buildSalesLeads("sales\\ItemSalesLeads.csv")
```

In the next section, we will display the new weapon sales lead dataframe.

Step 6 – displaying the weapons sales dataframe

First, we must invoke the `show` method:

```
println("Weapons Sales Lead dataframe is: ")
weaponSalesLeadDf.show
```

Here is a view of the weapon sales lead dataframe:

```
+-----------+-------------+-------+----------------+
|sCustomerId|sCustomerName|sItemId|       sItemName|
+-----------+-------------+-------+----------------+
|          1|    Australia|     99| WeaponsSystem99|
|          1|    Australia|    101|WeaponsSystem101|
|          2|    Seychelles|    89| WeaponsSystem89|
|          2|    Seychelles|   217|WeaponsSystem217|
|          3|         Fiji|    160|WeaponsSystem160|
|          3|         Fiji|    217|WeaponsSystem217|
|          4|       Turkey|    183|WeaponsSystem183|
|          4|       Turkey|    100|WeaponsSystem100|
|          4|       Turkey|    160|WeaponsSystem160|
|          8|        India|    217| WeaponSystem217|
|          5|       Jordan|     99| WeaponsSystem99|
|          5|       Jordan|    355|WeaponsSystem355|
|          6|       SKorea|    107|WeaponsSystem107|
|          6|       SKorea|    217|WeaponsSystem217|
|          7|     Djibouti|     57| WeaponsSystem57|
|          7|     Djibouti|    355|WeaponsSystem355|
|          7|     Djibouti|    183|WeaponsSystem183|
|          8|        India|     45| WeaponsSystem45|
|          8|        India|     81| WeaponsSystem81|
|          8|        India|    160|WeaponsSystem160|
+-----------+-------------+-------+----------------+
only showing top 20 rows
```

View of weapon sales lead dataframe

Next, create a version of the sales lead dataframe structured as (customer, item) tuples:

```
val customerWeaponsSystemPairDf: DataFrame =
weaponSalesLeadDf.map(salesLead => ( salesLead.getInt(0),
salesLead.getInt(2) )).toDF("user","item")
```

In the next section, let's display the dataframe that we just created.

Step 7 – displaying the customer-weapons-system dataframe

Let's the show method, as follows:

```
println("The Customer-Weapons System dataframe as tuple pairs looks like:
")
customerWeaponsSystemPairDf.show
```

Here is a screenshot of the new customer-weapons-system dataframe as tuple pairs:

```
The Customer-Weapons System dataframe as tuple pairs looks like:
+----+----+
|user|item|
+----+----+
|   1|  99|
|   1| 101|
|   2|  89|
|   2| 217|
|   3| 160|
|   3| 217|
|   4| 183|
|   4| 100|
|   4| 160|
|   8| 217|
|   5|  99|
|   5| 355|
|   6| 107|
|   6| 217|
|   7|  57|
|   7| 355|
|   7| 183|
|   8|  45|
|   8|  81|
|   8| 160|
+----+----+
only showing top 20 rows
```

New customer-weapons-system dataframe as tuple pairs

Next, we will convert the preceding dataframe into an RDD:

```
val customerWeaponsSystemPairRDD: RDD[(Int, Int)] =
customerWeaponsSystemDf.rdd.map(row =>
(row.getInt(0),
row.getInt(1))
                                                            )
/*
Notes: As far as the algorithm is concerned, customer corresponds to "user"
and "product" or item corresponds to a "weapons system"
*/
```

We previously created a `MatrixFactorization` model that we trained with the weapons system sales orders dataset. We are in a position to predict how each customer country may rate a weapon system in the future. In the next section, we will generate predictions.

Step 8 – generating predictions

Here is how we will generate predictions. The `predict` method of our model is designed to do just that. It will generate a predictions RDD that we call `weaponRecs`. It represents the ratings of weapons systems that were not rated by customer nations (listed in the past sales order data) previously:

```
val weaponRecs: RDD[Rating] =
ratingsModel.predict(customerWeaponsSystemPairRDD).distinct()
```

Next up, we will display the final predictions.

Step 9 – displaying predictions

Here is how to display the predictions, lined up in tabular format:

```
println("Future ratings are: " + weaponRecs.foreach(rating => { println(
"Customer: " + rating.user + " Product:  " + rating.product + " Rating: " +
rating.rating ) } ) )
```

The following table displays how each nation is expected to rate a certain system in the future, that is, a weapon system that they did not rate earlier:

```
Customer Nation: 1 Weapons System:  99 Rating: 110.64294367754968
Customer Nation: 2 Weapons System:  217 Rating: -14.59353061514684
Customer Nation: 8 Weapons System:  45 Rating: 58.8411030583238
Customer Nation: 6 Weapons System:  217 Rating: 27.983562575277176
Customer Nation: 7 Weapons System:  183 Rating: -4.752616315700221
Customer Nation: 5 Weapons System:  355 Rating: -0.0226995391627649730
Customer Nation: 6 Weapons System:  107 Rating: -6.146977037630051
Customer Nation: 8 Weapons System:  217 Rating: 70.75430361741672
Customer Nation: 3 Weapons System:  160 Rating: -2.7402710706968243
Customer Nation: 3 Weapons System:  217 Rating: 7.4330505088971295
Customer Nation: 4 Weapons System:  100 Rating: 0.018719075478031554
Customer Nation: 8 Weapons System:  160 Rating: 149.8431054419417
Customer Nation: 4 Weapons System:  160 Rating: 80.745570797776903
Customer Nation: 7 Weapons System:  355 Rating: 14.726831549178502
Customer Nation: 8 Weapons System:  81 Rating: 68.79163228044008
Customer Nation: 8 Weapons System:  355 Rating: -33.267337863617
Customer Nation: 5 Weapons System:  99 Rating: 0.13603012624246374
Customer Nation: 7 Weapons System:  57 Rating: -0.025637651994121942
Customer Nation: 4 Weapons System:  183 Rating: 5.413882517433166
```

System rating by each nation

Our recommendation system proved itself capable of generating future predictions.

Up until now, we did not say how all of the preceding code is compiled and deployed. We will look at this in the next section.

Compilation and deployment

The steps regarding compilation and deployment are as follows:

1. Compile
2. Build an assembly JAR file of the recommendation system application
3. Use the `spark-submit` command to deploy the recommendation system application

We will compile the project first.

Compiling the project

Invoke the `sbt compile` project at the root folder of your `Chapter7` project. You should get the following output:

```
C:\Users\Ilango\Documents\Packt\DevProjects\Chapter7A>sbt compile
"C:\Users\Ilango\.sbt\preloaded\org.scala-sbt\sbt\"1.0.4"\jars\sbt.jar"
[info] Loading settings from idea.sbt ...
[info] Loading global plugins from C:\Users\Ilango\.sbt\1.0\plugins
[info] Loading settings from assembly.sbt,plugins.sbt ...
[info] Loading project definition from C:\Users\Ilango\Documents\Packt\DevProjects\Chapter7A\project
[info] Loading settings from build.sbt .
[info] Set current project to Chapter7A (in build file:/C:/Users/Ilango/Documents/Packt/DevProjects/Chapter7A/)
[info] Executing in batch mode. For better performance use sbt's shell
[success] Total time: 1 s, completed Jul 16, 2018 6:54:25 PM
```

Output on compiling the project

Besides loading `build.sbt`, the compile task is also loading settings from `assembly.sbt`, a file we have not talked about yet, but which we will create soon.

What is an assembly.sbt file?

We have not yet talked about the `assembly.sbt` file. Our scala-based Spark application is a Spark job that will be submitted to a (local) Spark cluster as a JAR file. This file, apart from Spark libraries, also needs other dependencies in it for our recommendation system job to successfully complete. The name fat JAR is from all dependencies bundled in one JAR. To build such a fat JAR, we need an `sbt-assembly` plugin. This explains the need for creating a new `assembly.sbt` and the assembly plugin.

Creating assembly.sbt

Create a new `assembly.sbt` in your IntelliJ project view and save it under your `project` folder, as follows:

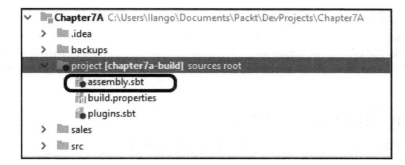

Creating assembly.sbt

What will `assembly.sbt` contain? We will explore this next.

Contents of assembly.sbt

Paste the following contents into the newly created `assembly.sbt` (under the project folder). The output should look like this:

```
addSbtPlugin( dependency = "com.eed3si9n" % "sbt-assembly" % "0.14.7")
```

Output on placing contents of assembly.sbt

The `sbt-assembly` plugin, version 0.14.7, gives us the ability to run an `sbt-assembly` task. With that, we are one step closer to building a fat or Uber JAR. This action is documented in the next step.

Running the sbt assembly task

Issue the `sbt assembly` command, as follows:

```
C:\Users\Ilango\Documents\Packt\DevProjects\Chapter7A>sbt assembly
"C:\Users\Ilango\.sbt\preloaded\org.scala-sbt\sbt\"1.0.4"\jars\sbt.jar"
[info] Loading settings from idea.sbt ...
[info] Loading global plugins from C:\Users\Ilango\.sbt\1.0\plugins
[info] Loading settings from assembly.sbt,plugins.sbt ...
[info] Loading project definition from C:\Users\Ilango\Documents\Packt\DevProjects\Chapter7A\project
[info] Loading settings from build.sbt ...
[info] Set current project to Chapter7A (in build file:/C:/Users/Ilango/Documents/Packt/DevProjects/Chapter7A/)
[error] 112 errors were encountered during merge
[error] java.lang.RuntimeException: deduplicate: different file contents found in the following:
[error] C:\Users\Ilango\.ivy2\cache\org.apache.arrow\arrow-vector\jars\arrow-vector-0.8.0.jar:git.properties
[error] C:\Users\Ilango\.ivy2\cache\org.apache.arrow\arrow-format\jars\arrow-format-0.8.0.jar:git.properties
[error] C:\Users\Ilango\.ivy2\cache\org.apache.arrow\arrow-memory\jars\arrow-memory-0.8.0.jar:git.properties
[error] deduplicate: different file contents found in the following:
```

Running the sbt assembly command

This time, the assembly task loads the assembly-plugin in `assembly.sbt`. However, further assembly halts because of a common duplicate error. This error arises due to several duplicates, multiple copies of dependency files that need removal before the assembly task can successfully complete. To address this situation, `build.sbt` needs an upgrade.

Upgrading the build.sbt file

The following lines of code need to be added in, as follows:

```
mainClass in (Compile, run) := Some("com.packt.modern.chapter7.RecSystem")

libraryDependencies ++= Seq(
  "org.apache.spark" %% "spark-core" % "2.3.1",
  "org.apache.spark" %% "spark-mllib" % "2.3.1",
  "org.apache.spark" %% "spark-sql" % "2.3.1"
)


resolvers += "Sonatype Releases" at "https://oss.sonatype.org/content/repositories/releases/"
resolvers += "Sonatype Snapshots" at "http://oss.sonatype.org/content/repositories/snapshots"
fork in run := true
fork in test := true


assemblyMergeStrategy in assembly := {
  case PathList("META-INF", xs @ _*) => MergeStrategy.discard
  case x => MergeStrategy.first
}
```

Code lines for upgrading the build.sbt file

To test the effect of your changes, save this and go to the command line to reissue the `sbt` `assembly` task.

Rerunning the assembly command

Run the assembly task, as follows:

```
C:\Users\Ilango\Documents\Packt\DevProjects\Chapter7A>sbt assembly
"C:\Users\Ilango\.sbt\preloaded\org.scala-sbt\sbt\"1.0.4"\jars\sbt.jar"
[info] Loading settings from idea.sbt ...
[info] Loading global plugins from C:\Users\Ilango\.sbt\1.0\plugins
[info] Loading settings from assembly.sbt,plugins.sbt ...
[info] Loading project definition from C:\Users\Ilango\Documents\Packt\DevProjects\Chapter7A\project
[info] Loading settings from build.sbt ...
[info] Set current project to Chapter7A (in build file:/C:/Users/Ilango/Documents/Packt/DevProjects/Chapter7A/)
[info] Strategy 'discard' was applied to 520 files (Run the task at debug level to see details)
[info] Strategy 'first' was applied to 438 files (Run the task at debug level to see details)
[info] Packaging C:\Users\Ilango\Documents\Packt\DevProjects\Chapter7A\target\scala-2.11\Chapter7A-assembly-0.1.jar
[info] Done packaging.
[success] Total time: 121 s, completed Jul 16, 2018 6:56:40 PM
```

Rerunning the assembly task

This time, the settings in the `assembly.sbt` file are loaded. The task completes successfully. To verify, drill down to the `target` folder. If everything went well, you should see a fat JAR, as follows:

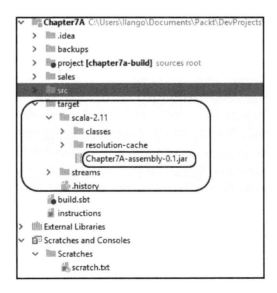

Output as a JAR file

Our JAR file under the `target` folder is the recommendation system application's JAR file that needs to be deployed into Spark. This is documented in the next step.

Deploying the recommendation application

The `spark-submit` command is how we will deploy the application into Spark. Here are two formats for the `spark-submit` command. The first one is a long one which sets more parameters than the second one:

```
spark-submit --class "com.packt.modern.chapter7.RecSystem" --master
local[2] --deploy-mode client --driver-memory 16g -num-executors 2 --
executor-memory 2g --executor-cores 2  <path-to-jar>
```

Leaning on the preceding format, let's submit our Spark job, supplying various parameters to it:

```
C:\Users\Ilango\Documents\Packt\DevProjects\Chapter7A>spark-submit --class "com.packt.modern.chapter7.RecSys
tem" --master local[2] --deploy-mode client --driver-memory 16g --num-executors 2 --executor-memory 2g --exe
cutor-cores 2 "target\\scala-2.11\\Chapter7A-assembly-0.1.jar"
```

Parameters for Spark

The different parameters are explained as follows:

Command-Line Parameter	Value	Explanation
--class	com.packt.modern.chapter7.RecSystem	The entry point to the application
--master	The default value: Local[2]	The Master URL, which defaults to local[*]
--deploy-mode	The default value client	Either deploy on worker-nodes in a cluster or locally
--driver-memory	4g or 8g or 16g	This value at any rate cannot exceed the total RAM on your machine
--num-executors	2	The number of executors to be created
--executor-memory	2g	Memory allocated to each executor
--executor-cores	2	The number of concurrent threads available for every executor

Tabular explanation of parameters for Spark Job

Summary

We learned how to build an explicit feedback type recommendation system. We implemented a predictions model with the Spark MLlib collaborative filtering algorithm that learns from past sales data and makes ratings-based recommendations about products to customers. The algorithm, as we have come to know, made its tailored product predictions on unknown customer-product interactions.

We used Spark's support for recommendations to build a prediction model that generated recommendations for unknown customer-product interactions in terms of sales leads and past weapons sales data. We leveraged Spark's alternating least squares algorithm to implement our collaborative filtering recommendation system.

Other Books You May Enjoy

If you enjoyed this book, you may be interested in these other books by Packt:

Scala Design Patterns - Second Edition
Ivan Nikolov

ISBN: 978-1-78847-130-5

- Immerse yourself in industry-standard design patterns—structural, creational, and behavioral—to create extraordinary applications
- See the power of traits and their application in Scala
- Implement abstract and self types and build clean design patterns
- Build complex entity relationships using structural design patterns
- Create applications faster by applying functional design patterns

Scala Microservices

Jatin Puri, Selvam Palanimalai

ISBN: 978-1-78646-934-2

- Learn the essentials behind Microservices, the advantages and perils associated with them
- Build low latency, high throughput applications using Play and Lagom
- Dive deeper with being asynchronous and understand the superiority it provides
- Model your complex domain data for scale and simplicity with CQRS and Event Sourcing
- Be resilient to failures by using message passing
- Look at best practices of version control workflow, testing, continuous integration and deployments
- Understand operating system level virtualization using Linux Containers. Docker is used to explain how containers work
- Automate your infrastructure with kubernetes

Leave a review - let other readers know what you think

Please share your thoughts on this book with others by leaving a review on the site that you bought it from. If you purchased the book from Amazon, please leave us an honest review on this book's Amazon page. This is vital so that other potential readers can see and use your unbiased opinion to make purchasing decisions, we can understand what our customers think about our products, and our authors can see your feedback on the title that they have worked with Packt to create. It will only take a few minutes of your time, but is valuable to other potential customers, our authors, and Packt. Thank you!

Index

www.ingramcontent.com/pod-product-compliance
Lightning Source LLC
Chambersburg PA
CBHW080622060326
40690CB00021B/4780